NET / JRF / SLET / PET OBJECTIVE QUESTIONS IN LIBRARY & INFORMATION SCIENCE PAPER II AND PAPER III

(With Latest Solved Question Papers)

NET / JRF / SLET / PET OBJECTIVE QUESTIONS

LIBRARY & INFORMATION SCIENCE
PAPER II AND PAPER III
(With Latest Solved Question Papers)

Anil Changdeo Bansode

M.A. M. Lib. & I. Sc. MH- SET, UGC-NET

Librarian, College Of Arts, Bhigwan, Dist. Pune

Ess Ess Publications

New Delhi

NET / JRF / SLET / PET OBJECTIVE QUESTIONS IN LIBRARY & INFORMATION SCIENCE PAPER II AND PAPER III
(With Latest Solved Question Papers)

ISBN: 978-81-7000-811-8

First Published 2016

Published by:
Ess Ess Publications
4831/24, Ansari Road,
Darya Ganj,
New Delhi-110 002.
INDIA
Phones: 23260807, 41563444
Fax: 41563334
E-mail: info@essessreference.com
www.essessreference.com

Cover Design by *Patch Creative Unit*

Printed and bound in India at Salasar Imaging Systems.

Dedicated to
My Parents
&
Library Professionals

Contents

Preface

Library & Information Science is a dynamic fiel of study. It is being taught in India and abroad on various levels leading up to Masters' Degree. More than 124 universities in India impart teaching up to Masters' Degree besides the provision of doctoral programmes. It has also been popular and useful as a professional subject.

To succeed in any examination it is essential that the basics of the subject be very clear. This book has been written keeping this fact in mind. This is not a text book but a consolidated text for quick review of basic facts written within the framework of the JRF/UGC-NET/ SLET/ PET syllabus for the second & third paper of library & information science. At the end of each chapter, answers have been given for helping the readers test their knowledge. All these questions are framed as per the pattern of the exam and have been taken from various standard question banks. All efforts have been made to provide as much matter as possible in condensed from perfect in all regards.

I would like to express thanks to the publisher Ess Ess Publications, New Delhi for having faith in my abilities and giving me this assignment.

Finally I dedicated this book to my parents,

friends & my wife who are the constant source of my motivation.

— Anil Changdeo Bansode

1

Data Interpretation

I. Read the passage given below, and answer the questions based on your understanding of the passage. (Question Nos. 1-5)

The primary concern with the longevity of digital documents is the "viewing problem"(Besser, 2000). Unlike analog or physical information, which tends to exist independent of human involvement, digital information needs constant intervention to survive. History has shown that digital documents are problematic by default. Whereas we can actually look at the Sistine Chapel ceiling, painted 500 years ago, it is difficult if not impossible to simply view

Documents on 8-in. Floppy disks created in the last 20 years, even if there has been an immediate, proactive role in preserving them. Without concerted effort on the part of archivists and preservationists, digital objects quickly become obsolete or inaccessible due to unforeseen, although anticipated, advances in information technology. The variable media art community currently utilizes four digital preservation strategies, all focused on the end product. The first three methods have technical origins and are based on general digital preservation practices. Related to "the viewing problem", they are : *refreshing,* the upgrade of storage mechanisms; *migration,* the premeditated upgrade of file formats; and *emulation,* which focuses on development of operating systems able to run obsolete media. The fourth option, developed by and for the new media art community, is *reinterpretation* (Depocas et al., 2003),where the curators attempt to recreate a work given comprehensive documentation of the

Original artefact. *Migration* and *emulation* are the two primary methods in managing the problem of obsolete file formats (Waters & Garrett,1996). Migration focuses on the files themselves, periodically updating files in new software formats. The second method of preservation is emulation, which can be either at the system or the software level. System emulation focuses on developing systems that mimic the hardware used to create or run the original artefact.

1. Why digital objects become inaccessible quickly ?
   (A) Because of unforeseen advancement of technology
   (B) It is independent of human intervention
   (C) It is independent of any technological advancement
   (D) None of the above
2. Reinterpretation is a digital preservation strategy where curator Intends to
   (A) Upgrade file formats
   (B) Upgrade storage mechanism
   (C) Recreate a work
   (D) Upgrade operating system

3. What is the focus of system Emulation ?
   (A) Developing systems that mimic hardware
   (B) Developing systems that mimic software
   (C) Developing systems that mimic file formats
   (D) None of the above
4. Which of the following is true about migration preservation strategy ?
   (A) Migration is not related to the viewing problem
   (B) Migration is related to the viewing problem
   (C) Migration requires comprehensive documentation
   (D) Migration does not have technical origin
5. Refreshing preservation strategy focuses on
   (A) Comprehensive documentation of original artefact
   (B) Development of operating system
   (C) Not on viewing problem
   (D) Up gradation of storage

II. Read the passage given below, and answer the questions based on your Understanding of the passage. (Question Nos. 6-10)

With the realization across the world that the global economy is going to be increasingly knowledge-based, science and technology have become the subject of discussion not just in classical ministries but also in ministries as diverse as commerce, industry and finance, and in case of United States, even in the State Department. In India, the Prime Minister has made frequent statements about the need to step up scientific research in the country. Several large companies, including multinationals are outsourcing R & D programmes to India. This is partly because scientists are cheaper in India dollar for dollar, but also because India has a large pool of trained scientists. Industry data shows that R & D is now the third-largest segment in India's export of Information Technology (IT) services. Foreign companies have invested over $ 1 billion in research operations in India from 1998 to 2003 and another estimated $ 5 billion are in the pipeline. The United States is the biggest investor followed by Germany, France, Denmark and UK. Japan and China have also begun to invest in research programmes in India. Most foreign investment is being directed to research in computer sciences, pharmaceuticals, molecular chemistry, drug discovery, engineering and automotive design and biotechnology, including plant breeding. Whereas, flow of foreign investments has enthused research institutions that are targeted for collaboration, there is also cause for concern. Although, India now attracts considerable foreign investment in R & D, it has no system in place for assessing how this investment is affecting the country's technological development. Nor is there any mechanism to monitor the impact of such investment on aspects such as skill development, sectoral capacity building etc. Do such foreign – funded research programmes benefit only the scientists and technicians in the form of better salaries and perks or do they also produce benefits for the country as a whole ?

6. Focus on science and technology has increased because
   (A) Indian commerce and Finance Ministries are giving great importance to it.
   (B) World economy has become knowledge based.
   (C) US State Department gives priority on S & T
   (D) Knowledge Commission has identified it as one of the potential area of development

7. The following group of countries are the biggest investors in research :
   (A) U.S., Germany, India, Russia
   (B) Britain, France, U.S., India
   (C) France, Denmark, U.S.A., U.K.
   (D) Japan, China, India, Denmark
8. What is the cause of concern regarding foreign investment in research ?
   (A) Scientists and technicians involved in research are not paid well.
   (B) There are insufficient institutions that can be targeted for research collaboration.
   (C) The benefit of such investments doesn't get transferred to India.
   (D) Sufficient methods to assess and evaluate the impact of such investment are not available.
9. Most foreign investment is being made in the area of
   (A) Microbiology and life sciences.
   (B) Computer science and automotive design.
   (C) Physical sciences and planting.
   (D) Grafting and biology.
10. Foreign companies are outsourcing R & D programmes to India because
   (A) Quality of research is quite high in India.
   (B) Outsourcing is cost effective for foreign companies.
   (C) There is scarcity of skilled manpower in those countries.
   (D) None of the above.

III. Read the following passage and answer the questions 11 - 15 :

While Boyd allows that some people consider email or discussion lists to be Social Software, he makes an important distinction between traditional communication software and Social Software. He explains that traditional software places people into groups with a top-down approach; in other words, it assigns membership. However, Social Software takes a bottom-up approach, which enables people to organize themselves into a network based on their preferences. Therefore, with a bottom-up approach, people can sign up for a system and build communities using their personal preferences (Marenzi *et al.,* 2008). In contrast, traditional communication software uses a top-down approach where people are assigned into a specific organization or groups. Social Software is based on supporting individuals who interact socially with people who have similar interests (Marenzi *et al.,* 2008). In addition, users typically enjoy Social Software itself and work with various Social Software applications voluntarily. For example, the authors of social media enjoy content that they have created themselves, content that is copied from other media, and mash-ups that contain admix of content that could possibly be from several authors (Ahonen and Lietsala,2007). The popularity of social technologies is attributed to the increase in low-cost tools and the critical mass of millions of people who are now connected to the Internet and to the people's need to feel like part of a community (Avram, 2006). These users tend to rely more on their own personal social networks than untraditional business structures. (Vinson2005) describes additional features of Social Software tools: they allow people to easily participate (by both contributing and reading) in the activities; they provide the opportunity for networking and allow forth self-forming of networks since people are usually both consumers and producers; and each individual can be a member on several networks simultaneously (Avram, 2006).

11. People are assigned into specific organization or groups in _______ approach.
    (A) Top-down approach
    (B) Down-top approach
    (C) Top-bottom system approach
    (D) Down-top system approach
12. The basic feature(s) of social software is/are :
    (A) Social interaction
    (B) Personal interaction
    (C) Enjoying social software
    (D) (A) and (C) are correct.
13. Authors of social media enjoy_______ of contents.
    (A) Self created contents
    (B) Contents from magazines
    (C) Contents from many formats
    (D) Contents from many languages
14. The reason/s attributed to the popularity of social networking is/are :
    (A) Masses have started using internet.
    (B) All have free access to internet.
    (C) All are technology literates.
    (D) Stimulation of on-line communities over the traditional communities.
15. The social software tools allow.
    (A) Easy participation
    (B) Quick networking

(C) Consumer networking

(D) Both (A) & (B)

IV. Read the following passage and answer the questions 16-20:

Computing is in nature a problem-driven science and therefore PBL approaches have been applied to teach various subjects. Kayetal. (2000) describe PBL in foundation courses in computer science. The course is driven by specific problems related to programming skills and the instructors have set specific criteria to measure the success of their approach at the end of each problem. Having applied the approach for three years the authors of the study conclude that the PBL approach promoted the collaboration among students and their problem solving abilities. A problem-based approach is used in a software development project (O'Kelly and Gibson, 2006). The authors claim that, with this approach, students are provided with the freedom to think for themselves, activate their prior knowledge and acquire new knowledge in an explorative and creative way. Another study supports that lecture based approaches are not stimulating and the computer skills learnt are not transferable to other situations (Lai, 2005). The author applied PBL in teaching pre-school teachers popular computer applications such as Microsoft Office. Based on their evaluation of the activities, the author concludes that the course was motivational and also promotes higher order thinking skills. Ellis et al. (1998) refer to the full problem-based learning and the guided problem-based learning approaches. In full problem-based learning, the nature of the problem guides and drives the entire learning experience. There are no formal expositions of knowledge from the "expert", and the students develop resources based on requirements they determine. In guided problem-based learning, students have a problem to solve as a group.

16. What was the result of problem based learning approach ?
    (A) Improved peer coordination
    (B) Promoted collaboration among students
    (C) Applied to teach subjects
    (D) Applied to teach only computer science
17. What are the advantages of PBL application in teaching ?
    (A) Self study
    (B) Exploration of literature
    (C) Acquire soft skills
    (D) Freedom to think
18. What are the limitations of lecture based approach?
    (A) Stimulating
    (B) Not stimulating
    (C) Not repetitive
    (D) Transferable to others
19. Which types of approaches are described by Ellis ?
    (A) Group based
    (B) Expert based
    (C) Lecture based
    (D) Guided problem based
20. Which approach has no formal exposition of knowledge from experts ?
    (A) Full problem based
    (B) Guided problem based
    (C) Expert based
    (D) Both (A) and (B)

V. Read the passage given below and answer the questions based on your understanding of the passage (Question Nos. 21-25) :

According to Wikipedia 'social media' is media designed to be disseminated through social interaction, created using highly accessible and scalable publishing techniques. According to search engine partner, the term social media describes media that is posed by the user and can take many different forms. Some type of social media are forums, message boards, blogs, wikis and podcarts. Social media applications include Google, Face book and You tube. In social media, communication takes place through messages, status updates, voice chats etc. or through photos/videos sharing, games, virtual goods etc. Antony Mayfield in his-book titled 'What is Social Media' ? has defined social media as online media, which encourages contributions and feedback from everyone who is interested, is open to feedback and participation, is a two way conversation, allows communities to form quickly and communicate effectively to share common interests and thrive on their connectedness. The growth of social media is phenomenal. It is being used by all netizens all over the world to a great extent in all areas including business, government, fashion etc. A research conducted by the Institute for Prospective Technological Studies (IPTS) indicates that high take up of social media application outside formal educational settings provides new opportunities for innovation and modernisation. With this growing trend, political leaders have also realized its importance as ineffective tool to spread awareness and to reach out their voters. Democratic presidential candidate Barack Obama used it during the Presidential elections. Since then, social media is being highly used by number of politicians all over the world. MySpace has more than 7400 discussion groups related to politics.

According to a survey by manpower, 29% of the companies in America and 20% of companies worldwide have a social mediapolicy. People even update themselves through micro-blogging on every aspect of human life including the natural and human disasters. In China, Twitter became the first media in the world to break the news of the Wenzhou earthquake. Social media is being used in fashion industry as well to generate interest in a brand through publicity across online communities and websites.

India is one of the most culturally, linguistically and genetically diverse regions having more than one billion people. It is ranked third in Asia in terms of the internet users and quite a number of them are using social media. In fact, approximately 60 million to 65 million netizens in India open most of their time on social media/networking sites.

21. Who defined social media as 'online media' which encourages contributions and feedback from everyone who is interested ?
    (A) Wikipedia
    (B) Institute for Prospective Technological Studies (IPTS)
    (C) MySpace
    (D) Antony Mayfield
22. Who used the social media for conversing during recent Presidential Election in U.S.A. ?
    (A) Jimmy Carter
    (B) Barack Obama
    (C) George Bush
    (D) John F. Kennedy
23. In China, which social media became the first media to break the news of earthquake ?

(A) Face book (B) YouTube

(C) Twitter (D) Myzamana

24. In Asia, which country is ranked third in terms of using social media by the people ?

(A) China (B) Pakistan

(C) Japan (D) India

25. Which social website has more than 7400 discussion groups relate to politics ?

(A) Orkut (B) MySpace

(C) Face book (D) Twitter

VI. Read the following passage carefully and answer. the questions that follows : (Question Nos.26 -30)

According to Peter Walsh (2003), knowledge production has historically been based on the expert paradigm in which bodies of knowledge are controlled by groups of experts. The differentiation between interior and exterior, expert and layperson, producer and consumer, creates what Walsh (2003) called "knowledge hegemony" in which control over the creation and distribution of knowledge and information is monopolized in the hands of the few. However, advances in information technology – from the printing press to the World Wide Web – have led to the steady erosion of this hegemony in so far as they have allowed greater numbers of people to participate in knowledge production. The printing press, for example, undermined one of the key elements of the medieval Church's knowledge hegemony: the control of book production and libraries. Mass publishing and the spread of literacy formed the basis the Reformation, the Age of Enlightenment, and the Scientific Revolution.

Today, the web is undermining the knowledge hegemony of a number of fields such as journalism, publishing, education, and museums. Echoing sentiments similar to those expressed by Benjamin in his essay "The Work of Art in the Age of Mechanical Reproduction" (1936/1968), Walsh (2003) argued that loss of physical control over art, owing to new technological means of mass production and distribution, undermines the ability of museums to control what types of art are made accessible to the public, the context in which they are seen, and the types of discourses about them that are considered "appropriate". The availability of easy to use digital technologies for reproducing, creating, and distributing content – artistic, literary, informational, or otherwise – has effectively weakened existing knowledge hegemonies by lowering the barriers to participation in knowledge production. Participatory cultures therefore produce a counter-hegemonic effect in so far as they "erode monopolistic positions held by professions, educational institutions, and experts, and they increase the diversity of perspectives on the way the world is and the way it could be".

26. According to Walsh, knowledge production has been historically based on
    (A) Participatory culture
    (B) Application of technology
    (C) Expert paradigm
    (D) Collective intelligence
27. In knowledge hegemony control over creation of knowledge and information is
    (A) in the printing press
    (B) in the world wide web
    (C) in the libraries
    (D) in the hands of a few
28. The main reason for the erosion of the knowledge hegemony of the medieval church was

(A) the printing press (B) world wide web
(C) the libraries (D) action of a few

29. One of the important factors that helped to usher in the age of enlightenment was
    (A) world wide web
    (B) monopoly of information
    (C) spread of literacy
    (D) control of libraries
30. The diversity of perspective is increased by
    (A) knowledge hegemony
    (B) digital technology
    (C) control of book production
    (D) participatory culture

VII. Read the passage given below and answer the questions based on your understanding of the passage (Question Nos. 31 - 35) :

As the global information landscape increasingly facilitate the sharing, repurposing and dissemination of information, the ways in which students are accustomed to interacting with information resources are also changing. For some new students to universities, their understanding of referencing is based solely on fear (McGowan, 2005) and many are familiar with the basic concept of plagiarism. Some students bring with them the academic process that served them well at school – however, these are not suitable at Universities (Chanock, 2008). Students understand they should not copy words without referencing, but fail to grasp the reasons why; the reasons are not explicit and often cloaked in unfamiliar and impenetrable academic language. Pak's (2003) review of literature proved as a handy summation of the investigations, research, and thinking about plagiarism prior to the implementation of various plagiarism detection software products. There are three main schools of thought in referencing and plagiarism discourse. A punitive approach which focuses on the idea that students often deliberately engage in plagiarism and that the appropriate response is one of punishment (Blum, 2009; Sutherland – Smith, 2010; Bilic – Zulle, et. al. 2008). A Restorative Justice approach, however, suggests that plagiarism is in fact an act against a community (in this case, a community of students), and that steps need to be taken to restore a level of balance (Wenzel; et. al. 2010; Karp and Conrad, 2005; Karp, 2009; Dickson, etc. al. 2009). An educational approach that espouses that the best method of reducing plagiarism is to educate and support students. Marking criteria and assessment tasks should be linked to building referencing skills (especially in the first year) and ensure that the students learn these skills in a discipline related context (Jaschik; 2008). The approach of both the University of Southern Queensland (USQ) and Swinburne University of Technology is clearly aligned with the third school of thought. Students lack proper understanding of the purposes of referencing. For them, referencing and citing is linked to just words, not ideas (Jackson, 2006), so referencing is regarded as separate to the writing process, instead of an integral part. To help students develop good writing and referencing practices, it is useful if universities help them understand the research culture of tertiary study. Faculties need to make their referencing rules explicit and lectures should provide useful exemplars within courses.

31. Understanding of new students on Referencing is based on

    (A) Plagiarism

    (B) Fear

    (C) Ability to write

    (D) Insatiable desire to learn

32. An appropriate response to deliberate act of plagiarism according to punitive school of thought is
    (A) to debar the student from library use
    (B) to orient the student about plagiarism
    (C) to award punishment
    (D) to make him learn about referencing
33. To restore a 'level of balance' is advocated/reflected in
    (A) Deterrent Approach
    (B) Reformative Approach
    (C) Punitive Approach
    (D) Restorative Approach
34. 'Educational approach' which aim sat reducing plagiarism should be linked with
    (A) Building referencing skills of the students
    (B) inculcating reading habits of the students
    (C) building students as information literate
    (D) ignorance of the students on methods of social research
35. Lack of understanding of students about referencing is linked to their
    (A) Ideas (B) Words
    (C) Experience (D) Intuition

ANSWERS

1. A	2. C	3. A	4. B	5. D	6. B
7. C	8. D	9. B	10. B	11. A	12. D
13. A	14. A	15. D	16. B	17. D	18. B
19. D	20. D	21. D	22. B	23. C	24. D
25. B	26. C	27. D	28. A	29. C	30. D
31. B	32. C	33. D	34. A	35. B	

2

Library And Society

1. 'RRRLF' falls under the :
   (A) Ministry of Human Resource Development
   (B) Ministry of Information & Broadcasting
   (C) Ministry of Culture
   (D) Ministry of Science &Technology
2. What are the major driving forces behind an 'Information society' ?
   (i) R T I (ii) I. C. T.
   (iii) Internet (iv) I. T. ACT
   Codes :
   (A) (ii) & (i) are correct (B) (ii) & (iv) are correct
   (C) (i) & (iv) are correct (D) (ii) & (iii) are correct
3. Which libraries are functioning as depository libraries ?
   (i) Delhi Public Library
   (ii) Connemara Public Library
   (iii) British Council Library
   (iv) Central Reference Library

Codes :

(A) (i), (iii), (iv) are correct

(B) (i) & (iii) are correct

(C) (i) & (ii) are correct

(D) (ii) & (iii) are correct

4. Arrange the following according to their year of establishment :

(i) NIC	(ii) DESIDOC
(iii) NISCAIR	(iv) NASSDOC

Codes :

(A) (i), (iii), (ii), (iv)	(B) (iii), (i), (iv), (ii)
(C) (iv), (i), (iii), (ii)	(D) (ii), (iv), (i), (iii)

5. Arrange the following Public Library Acts according to their year of enactment :

(i) Uttar Pradesh PL Act

(ii) Arunachal Pradesh PL Act

(iii) Orissa PL Act

(iv) Gujarat PL Act

Codes :

(A) (iv), (iii), (i), (ii)	(B) (ii), (iii), (i), (iv)
(C) (ii), (i), (iv), (iii)	(D) (iii), (ii), (i), (iv)

6. Match the following :

List - I	**List - II**
(a) Obligation of the State	(i) First Law
(b) Shelf Arrangement & Catalogue	(ii) Second Law
(c) Open Access & Shelf Arrangement	(iii) Third Law
(d) Library location/hours	(iv) Fourth Law

Codes :	**(a)**	**(b)**	**(c)**	**(d)**
(A)	(ii)	(iv)	(iii)	(i)
(B)	(iv)	(iii)	(ii)	(i)
(C)	(i)	(iii)	(iv)	(ii)
(D)	(iii)	(ii)	(i)	(iv)

7. Match the following :

List - I	**List - II**
(a) Law of Parsimony	(i) Classification
(b) Principle of Osmosis	(ii) F. W.Lancaster
(c) Paperless Society	(iii) Overall economy
(d) APUPA pattern	(iv) Reclassification

Codes :	**(a)**	**(b)**	**(c)**	**(d)**
(A)	(ii)	(i)	(iv)	(iii)
(B)	(iv)	(ii)	(i)	(iii)
(C)	(iii)	(iv)	(ii)	(i)
(D)	(i)	(iii)	(ii)	(iv)

8. Match the following :

List - I	**List - II**
(a) RRRLF	(i) Delhi
(b) Connemara Public Library	(ii) Patna
(c) NISCAIR	(iii) Kolkata
(d) Khuda Baksh Oriental Public Library	(iv) Chennai

Codes :	**(a)**	**(b)**	**(c)**	**(d)**
(A)	(iv)	(iii)	(ii)	(i)
(B)	(ii)	(iii)	(iv)	(i)
(C)	(iii)	(iv)	(i)	(ii)
(D)	(iv)	(i)	(ii)	(iii)

9. Match the following :

List - I	List - II
(a) Right man at right library	(i) Annual financial statement
(b) Budget	(ii) Deployment
(c) Journal	(iii) TQM
(d) Identifying user's views and Expectations	(iv) ISSN

Codes :	**(a)**	**(b)**	**(c)**	**(d)**
(A)	(iii)	(i)	(ii)	(iv)
(B)	(ii)	(i)	(iv)	(iii)
(C)	(iv)	(ii)	(iii)	(i)
(D)	(i)	(iii)	(iv)	(ii)

10. Corollary for Second Law of Library Science is
    (A) Books for all (B) Free Books Service
    (C) Free Library Service (D) Books every where
11. Which of the following is not the prerequisite for a National Information Policy ?
    (A) Legislative Frame work
    (B) Production of National Bibliography
    (C) Advisory and Administrative body
    (D) ICT infrastructure facilities
12. World Intellectual Property Organization is related to
    (A) UNESCO
    (B) United Nations
    (C) U.S. Organization
    (D) International Law Organization

13. Match the following :

	List-I	List-II
(a)	Konnemara Public Library	(i) Patna
(b)	Khudabaksha Oriental Public Library	(ii) Kolkata
(c)	Asiatic Society Library	(iii) Chennai
(d)	National Library(India)	(iv) Mumbai

Codes :	**(a)**	**(b)**	**(c)**	**(d)**
(A)	(iv)	(ii)	(i)	(iii)
(B)	(iv)	(i)	(ii)	(iii)
(C)	(iii)	(ii)	(i)	(iv)
(D)	(iii)	(i)	(iv)	(ii)

14. 'Parry Committee' (UK) was set up to advise

(A) School Libraries (B) Public Libraries

(C) Special Libraries (D) University Libraries

15. FRBR is developed by

(A) LC (B) UNESCO

(C) IFLA (D) FID

16. Who were involved in Public Library Movement in India ?

(i) Sayaji Rao Gaikwad II

(ii) C.D. Deshmukh

(iii) S. Radhakrishnan

(iv) S.R. Ranganathan

Codes :

(A) (i) & (iii) are correct

(B) (ii) & (iv) are correct

(C) (i) & (iv) are correct

(D) (ii) & (iii) are correct

17. **Assertion (A) :** Library & Information centres are knowledge/management centres.

    Reason (R) : Libraries handle tacit knowledge.

    Codes :

    (A) Both (A) and (R) are true.

    (B) (A) is partially true, but (R) is false.

    (C) (A) is false, but (R) is true.

    (D) Both (A) and (R) are false.

18. **Assertion (A) :** Information Literacy is a basic skill essential for work environment in 21stcentury.

    Reason (R) : Information Literacy helps to train the users to make use of ICT.

    Codes :

    (A) Both (A) and (R) are true.

    (B) Both (A) and (R) are false.

    (C) (A) is true, but (R) is false.

    (D) (A) is false, but (R) is true.

19. Arrange the following according to their year of first publication :

    (i) Bliss Classification

    (ii) Dewey Decimal Classification

    (iii) Library of Congress Classification

    (iv) Universal Decimal Classification.

    Codes :

    (A) (i), (ii), (iii), (iv) (B) (i), (iii), (ii), (iv)

    (C) (iii), (i), (iv), (ii) (D) (ii), (iv), (i), (iii)

20. Arrange the following IFLA programmes according to their year of commencement :

    (i) UBC (ii) UAP

    (iii) ISBD (iv) International MARC Office

Codes :

(A) (i), (iv), (iii), (ii) (B) (ii), (iv), (i), (iii)

(C) (iv), (i), (ii), (iii) (D) (iii), (i), (ii), (iv)

21. Arrange the following according to their year of origin :

(i) Indian National Bibliography

(ii) British National Bibliography

(iii) Cumulative Book Index

(iv) Books in Print

Codes :

(A) (i), (iii), (iv), (ii) (B) (ii), (i), (iii), (iv)

(C) (iv), (iii), (ii), (i) (D) (iii), (iv), (ii), (i)

22. Arrange the following in a chronological order according to their year of establishment :

(i) Library of Congress

(ii) NISCAIR

(iii) Delivery of Books Act

(iv) National Library of India

Codes :

(A) (iii), (iv), (ii), (i) (B) (ii), (iii), (i), (iv)

(C) (i), (iv), (iii), (ii) (D) (iv), (i), (iii), (ii)

23. Arrange the following according to their year of enactment :

(i) Tamil Nadu Public Library Act

(ii) Kerala Public Library Act

(iii) Maharashtra Public Library Act

(iv) Orissa Public Library Act

Codes :

(A) (i), (iii), (ii), (iv) (B) (ii), (iii), (iv), (i)

(C) (ii), (iii), (i), (iv) (D) (iv), (iii), (ii), (i)

24. In 1974, Zurkowski used for the first time, which of the following term ?
 (A) Digital Literacy (B) Media Literacy
 (C) Computer Literacy (D) Information Literacy

25. Who defined "to be information literate, a person must be able to recognize when information is needed and have the ability to locate, evaluate and use effectively the needed information."?
 (A) SLA (B) ALA
 (C) IFLA (D) CILIP

26. Raja Rammohan Roy Library Foundation (RRRLF) was established by
 (A) Indian Library Association
 (B) Department of Culture, Govt.of India
 (C) Govt. of West Bengal
 (D) Ministry of Home Affairs,Govt. of India

27. Association of College and Research Libraries (ACRL) (USA) is a
 (A) Division of American Library Association
 (B) Independent Association for Academic & Research Libraries
 (C) Division of Special Libraries Association (USA)
 (D) Division of IFLA

28. Which of the following is not an implication of Fourth Law of Library Science ?
 (A) Classified arrangement
 (B) Stack-room-guides
 (C) Issue Methods
 (D) Rural Library Services

29. Which one of the following is not a recommendation of National Knowledge Commission (India) ?

(A) Preparation of a National Census of Library

(B) Encourage greater community participation in library management

(C) Raja Rammohan Roy library foundation to act as the National co-ordination agency

(D) Facilitate donation and maintenance of private collection

30. Which of the following are the scientists' approach according to Melvin J. Voigt (1961) ?

(i) Current Approach

(ii) Everyday Approach

(iii) Exhaustive Approach

(iv) 'Catching up' or 'brushing up' approach.

Codes :

(A) (ii), (iii) and (iv) (B) (i), (iii) and (iv)

(C) (i), (ii) and (iv) (D) (i), (ii) and (iii)

31. **Assertion (A) :** Dr. S.R. Ranganathan has been called 'Father of Library and Information Science' in India.

Reason (R) : Library Science education in India was started by Dr. S.R. Ranganathan.

Codes :

(A) (A) is false but (R) is true.

(B) (A) is true but (R) is false.

(C) Both (A) and (R) are true.

(D) Both (A) and (R) are false.

32. **Assertion (A) :** The exclusive rights conferred by Intellectual property rights can generally be transferred / licensed to third parties.

Reason (R) : The creators want to make monetary benefits out of their intellectual product.

Codes :

(A) (A) is true but (R) is false.

(B) (A) is false but (R) is true.

(C) Both (A) & (R) are true.

(D) Both (A) & (R) are false.

33. Which is the correct sequence of the national libraries in the order of their year of establishment?

(i) British Library (formerly British Museum Library)

(ii) Library of Congress(Washington D.C.)

(iii) Lenin Library (Moscow)

(iv) Bibliotheque Nationale (Paris)

Codes :

(A) (i), (ii), (iii), (iv) (B) (ii), (iii), (i), (iv)

(C) (iii), (ii), (iv), (i) (D) (iv), (iii), (ii), (i)

34. Identify the correct order of the LIS Associations as per their year of establishment

(A) CLA, ALA, SLA, IASLIC

(B) ALA, SLA, CLA, IASLIC

(C) SLA, IASLIC, ALA, CLA

(D) CLA, SLA, IASLIC, ALA

35. Arrange the following State Library Acts in chronological order :

(i) Karnataka Public Library Act

(ii) Uttar Pradesh Public Library Act

(iii) Goa Public Library Act

(iv) Bihar Public Library Act

Codes :

(A) (i), (iii), (ii), (iv) (B) (i), (ii), (iii), (iv)

(C) (ii), (iii), (iv), (i) (D) (iii), (i), (iv), (ii)

36. Information about Government of India's stand on 'FDI' can be found in

(A) Gazetteer of India

(B) Britanniea Book of the Year

(C) Statesman's Yearbook

(D) Asian Recorder

37. "Anomalous State of Knowledge (ASK) Model", one of the users centred models of information retrieval was proposed by

(A) P. Ingwersen (B) T. Saracevic

(C) J.N. Belkin (D) D. Ellis

38. The 'Crane field Test', associated with evaluation of information retrieval system was carried under the direction of ______.

(A) C.W. Clever don

(B) G. Salton

(C) D.C. Blair & M.E. Maron

(D) E. Voorhees

39. Which Law of Library Science, restated with emphasis on information as a dynamic, continuum and never ending phenomenon ?

(A) Fifth Law (B) Fourth Law

(C) Third Law (D) Second Law

40. Andrew Carnegie donated two million pounds for development of ______.

(A) Library Collection (B) Library Building

(C) Library Furniture (D) Library Staff

41. Which Committee/Commission recommended that Imperial Library be designated as Copyright Library?

(A) Fayzee Commission, 1939
(B) Riche Committee, 1926
(C) Statham Committee, 1932
(D) Sadler Committee, 1916

42. Match the following :

List - I	List - II
a. Trade Publisher	i. UNESCO
b. Subject book publisher	ii. American Psychological Society
c. Government Press	iii. Harper Collins
d. Scholarly Publisher	iv. W.B. Saunders

Codes :	(a)	(b)	(c)	(d)
(A)	ii	iv	iii	i
(B)	iv	iii	i	ii
(C)	i	iv	iii	ii
(D)	iii	iv	i	ii

43. Match the following :

List - I	List - II
a. Sinha Committee	i. Library staff strength
b. Dr. S.R. Ranganathan Committee	ii. Central Medical Library
c. Report of Dr. Shaw & Dr. D.B. Krishna Rao	iii. Libraries at Panchayat, Block, District and State level
d. Dr. J. Bhore Committee	iv. National Agricultural System of Agriculture Libraries

Codes :	(a)	(b)	(c)	(d)
(A)	iii	i	ii	iv
(B)	iv	iii	ii	i
(C)	iii	i	iv	ii
(D)	i	iii	ii	iv

44. 'Who's who in India', an irregular publication is published by
    (A) Business Press, Bombay
    (B) Sterling, New Delhi
    (C) Tradesman & Men Asia, Delhi
    (D) Sahitya Samsad, Calcutta

45. Which department of the Government of India deals with Public Libraries ?
    (A) Department of Archaeology
    (B) Department of Culture
    (C) Department of Primary Education
    (D) Department of Science and Technology

46. Information on Prime Minister of Bangladesh can be found in
    (A) International Who's Who
    (B) Who's Who in Bangladesh
    (C) Current Biography
    (D) Statesman's Yearbook

47. 'Eradication of Malaria in India 1990-1999' – a report can be categorised under
    (A) Trend Report
    (B) Review Report
    (C) State of the Art Report
    (D) Research Report

48. WIPO is located at
    (A) New York (B) London
    (C) Geneva (D) Paris
49. The National Mission on Libraries, India was established in which year ?
    (A) 2009 (B) 2010
    (C) 2011 (D) 2012
50. The production of mental reflection and imagination is known as
    (A) Information (B) Idea
    (C) Data (D) Knowledge
51. Which organisation was joined with 'Library Association' to form CILIP in 2007 ?
    (A) Institute of Bibliography
    (B) Institute of Information Scientists
    (C) Institute of Documentation
    (D) Institute of Librarianship
52. Dictionary of National Biography (DNB) contains biography of prominent people of
    (A) All nations (B) Europeans
    (C) Americans (D) Britishers
53. The concept of 'Ask Library Anything' was originally initiated by
    (A) Indian Library Association
    (B) ASLIB
    (C) Special Library Association
    (D) American Library Association
54. Arrange the following State Library Acts according to their year of establishment :

(i) Goa (ii) West Bengal

(iii) Orissa (iv) Karnataka

Codes :

(A) iv ii iii i (B) iv ii i iii

(C) ii i iii iv (D) iii ii i iv

55. Who said, "Public Library is the responsibility of Local and National Authorities. It must be supported by specific legislation and financed by National and Local Governments" ?

(A) S.R. Ranganathan (B) Gopala Rao Ekbote

(C) Sinha Committee (D) UNESCO Manifesto

56. 'Library Technology Project (LTP) Reports' are published by _______.

(A) ILA (B) ALA

(C) CILIP (D) SLA

57. Which Education Commission observed "Nothing can be more damaging to a growing department than to neglect its library or give it a low priority" ?

(A) Kothari Education Commission

(B) Radhakrishnan Education Commission

(C) Calcutta University Commission

(D) Mudaliar Commission on Secondary Education

58. International Advisory Committee on Documentation, Libraries and Archives (UNESCO) was established in

(A) 1966 (B) 1967

(C) 1968 (D) 1969

59. Which law of Library Science states that information is basic input to human growth and development ?

(A) Fourth Law (B) Third Law

(C) Second Law (D) Fifth Law

60. Match the following :

	List - I	List - II
a.	National Library of the World	i. Wilfred Ashworth
b.	Special Libraries	ii. L.J. Strauss
c.	Scientific and Technical Libraries	iii. A. Esdaile
d.	Handbook of Special Libraries	iv. C.M. Lewis

Codes :	**(a)**	**(b)**	**(c)**	**(d)**
(A)	i	iv	iii	ii
(B)	ii	iii	iv	i
(C)	iii	iv	ii	i
(D)	iv	ii	iii	i

61. **Assertion (A) :** Library Associations in India striving hard for the enactment of Library Acts.

Reason (R) : Library Acts help in systematic development of libraries.

Codes :

(A) Both (A) and (R) are true.

(B) Both (A) and (R) are false.

(C) (A) is true, (R) is false.

(D) (A) is false, (R) is true.

62. **Assertion (A) :** It is a time to separate the copyright issues for scholarly works from entertainment works.

Reason (R) : The scholarly works are public funded fact based, collaborative and intellectual heritage of the institution.

Codes :

(A) (A) is false and (R) is true.

(B) Both (A) and (R) are true but (R) is not the correct explanation of (A).

(C) Both (A) and (R) are false.

(D) (A) is true but (R) is false.

63. In which year Janet (U.K.) was established ?

(A) 1957 (B) 1983

(C) 1987 (D) 1989

64. Who developed Repertory Grid Technique for assessing how the users view the world from their own perspective ?

(A) A. Delphi (B) Calvin Mooer

(C) J. Belkin (D) George Kelley

65. IFLA's programme for capacity building of library associations is named as

(A) BSLA (B) ALP

(C) CLM (D) PAC

66. Which of the following organizations are associated with the concept of '1000 crore plan to link 9000 libraries in India' ?

(i) National Library of India

(ii) National Mission on Libraries

(iii) INFLIBNET

(iv) RRRLF

Codes :

(A) (ii) and (iii) are correct.

(B) (iii) and (iv) are correct.

(C) (i) and (iv) are correct.

(D) (ii) and (iv) are correct.

67. Who are associated with the digitization of the collection of Rabindra Bhavan, Vishav Bharati ?

(i) RRRLF (ii) C-DAC

(iii) NIC (iv) National Library of India

Codes :

(A) (i) and (iii) are correct

(B) (i) and (ii) are correct

(C) (ii) and (iv) are correct

(D) (iii) and (iv) are correct

68. Arrange the following according to their year of origin :

i. Indian National Bibliography

ii. British National Bibliography

iii. Cumulative Book Index

iv. Books in Print

Codes :

(A) i ii iv iii (B) iii iv ii i

(C) ii iii iv i (D) iv i ii iii

69. Arrange the following according to their levels :

i. Canons of Cataloguing

ii. Laws of Library Science

iii. General Normative Principles

iv. Principles of Cataloguing

Codes :

(A) ii iv i iii (B) i iii ii iv

(C) iv i iii ii (D) iii ii i iv

70. Arrange in sequence the following Model Public Library Acts/Bills in India:

i. Model Public Library Bill byM.D. Sen Committee

ii. Model Public Library Act byS.R. Ranganathan

iii. Model Public Library Act ofILA

iv. Model Public Library Bill byworking group of PlanningCommission

Codes :

(A) i ii iii iv (B) ii i iv iii

(C) iii iv i ii (D) iv iii ii i

71. Match the following :

List - I	**List - II**
a. Digital Library	i. Collections are stored in electronic media formats and accessible via computers
b. Hybrid Library	ii. Access to electronic information in a variety of remote locations through a local online catalogue or other gateway
c. Virtual Library	iii. Provides services in a mixed mode electronic and paper environment
d. Electronic Library	iv. Collection of electronic resources that provides direct/indirect access to a systematically organised collection of digital objects

Codes :	**(a)**	**(b)**	**(c)**	**(d)**
(A)	iv	iii	ii	i
(B)	i	iii	iv	ii
(C)	iii	i	ii	iv
(D)	i	iii	iv	ii

72. Match the following :

List - I	**List - II**
a. XML	i. Joe Becker
b. METS	ii. Defence Organizations
c. UNICODE	iii. W3C
d. Cryptography	iv. Library ofCongress

Codes :	**(a)**	**(b)**	**(c)**	**(d)**
(A)	i	ii	iii	iv
(B)	iii	iv	i	ii
(C)	ii	iii	iv	i
(D)	iv	i	ii	iii

73. Match the following :

List - I	**Li. II**
a. FRBR	i. Paul Otlet
b. POPSI	ii. IFLA
c. UDC	iii. G. Bhattacharya
d. www	iv. Tem Berners-Lee

Codes :	**(a)**	**(b)**	**(c)**	**(d)**
(A)	ii	i	iii	iv
(B)	ii	iii	i	iv
(C)	ii	iv	i	iii
(D)	iv	ii	iii	i

74. Match the following :

List - I	**List - II**
a. Index Translationum	i. NISCAIR
b. Translation Register Index (TR-I)	ii. NTC, Chicago
c. World Trans Index	iii. UNESCO
d. Common-wealth Index of Unpublished Transtations	iv. ITC, Delft, Netherlands
	v. ASLIB

Codes :	(a)	(b)	(c)	(d)
(A)	ii	iii	i	iv
(B)	iii	ii	iv	v
(C)	v	iii	i	ii
(D)	iv	ii	v	iii

75. Match the following :

List - I	List - II
a. Saraswati Mahal Library, Tanjavur (1535)	i. Lord Curzon
b. Khuda Baksh Oriental Public Library, Patna (1876)	ii. Telugu Nayakas
c. Library of Asiatic Society of Bengal (1784)	iii. Maulana M. B. Khan
d. Imperial Library, Calcutta (1901)	iv. Sir G.William Jones

Codes :	(a)	(b)	(c)	(d)
(A)	iii	ii	iv	i
(B)	ii	iii	i	iv
(C)	ii	iii	iv	i
(D)	iii	ii	i	iv

76. Which committee recommended that imperial library be designated as copyright library ?
(A) Fayzee Committee, 1939
(B) Richey Committee, 1926
(C) Statham Committee, 1932
(D) Sadler Committee, 1916

77. Who was the first Librarian of Imperial Library, Calcutta ?
(A) John MacFarlane (B) Harinath De
(C) B.S. Kesavan (D) S.R. Ranganathan

78. Who coined the phrase 'Information Retrieval' ?

(A) Calvin Mooers (B) S.R. Ranganathan

(C) J.D. Brown (D) H.P. Luhan

79. Name the Indian Librarian who was honoured with the title of "Khan Bahadur" in 1935 by the British Government.

(A) S.R. Ranganathan (B) B.S. Kesavan

(C) K.M. Asadullah (D) D.R. Kalia

80. Arrange the following University Libraries according to the year of their establishment :

(i) Madras University Library

(ii) Delhi University Library

(iii) Calcutta University Library

(iv) Bombay University Library

Codes :

(A) (iv) (ii) (iii) (i) (B) (ii) (i) (iv) (iii)

(C) (i) (iii) (ii) (iv) (D) (iii) (iv) (i) (ii)

81. Arrange the following library associations according to their year of emergence :

(i) CILIP (ii) ALA

(iii) SLA (iv) ASLIB

Codes :

(A) (iii) (iv) (i) (ii) (B) (iii) (iv) (ii) (i)

(C) (ii) (iii) (iv) (i) (D) (ii) (iv) (i) (iii)

82. Match the following :

List - I		**List - II**
i.	1962	a. Library Advisory Committee
ii.	1963	b. Review Committee
iii.	1957	c. DRTC
iv.	1961	d. Sarada Ranganathan Endowned

Codes :	(a)	(b)	(c)	(d)
(A)	iv	iii	ii	i
(B)	iii	iv	i	ii
(C)	ii	i	iii	iv
(D)	i	iv	iii	ii

83. Match the following :

List - I	List - II
a. Curriculum Development Committee (P. N. Kaula)	i. 2001
b. Curriculum Development Committee (C. R. Karrisidappa)	ii. 1992
c. Working Group on Libraries	iii. 1910
d. Library Movement in Baroda	iv. 1964

Codes :	(a)	(b)	(c)	(d)
(A)	ii	i	iv	iii
(B)	i	ii	iv	iii
(C)	iv	ii	iii	i
(D)	iii	iv	ii	i

84. Match the following :

List - I	List - II
a. Current Biography	i. Russia
b. Index Translationum	ii. University ofIllinois
c. VINITI	iii. U.S.A.
d. Library Trends	iv. UNESCO

Codes :	(a)	(b)	(c)	(d)
(A)	iii	iv	i	ii
(B)	iv	i	ii	iii
(C)	i	ii	iii	iv
(D)	ii	iii	iv	i

85. Who introduced the concept of 'knowledge industry'?

    (A) Peter Drucker (B) Fritz Machlup

    (C) Marc Porat (D) William Saffady

86. When the last print version of Encyclopaedia Britannica was published ?

    (A) 2009 (B) 2010

    (C) 2011 (D) 2012

87. Identify the place where IFLA was first found.

    (A) The Hague, Netherlands

    (B) Edinburgh, Scotland

    (C) Helsinki, Finland

    (D) London

88. Information For All Programme (IFAP) was launched by

    (A) IFLA (B) Library of Congress

    (C) OCLC (D) UNESCO

89. Skill Development Programme (SDP) for public librarians in India is initiated by

    (A) Ministry of Human Resource Development, Govt. of India

    (B) Directorate of Library Services, Govt. of West Bengal

    (C) Raja Ram Mohan Roy Library Foundation

    (D) Indian Library Association

90. Arrange the following in chronological order :

    (i) Right to Information Act (India)

    (ii) Information Technology Act (India)

    (iii) Indian Copyright Act

    (iv) Digital Millennium Copyright Act (US)

Codes :

(A) (i) (ii) (iii) (iv) (B) (iv) (i) (ii) (iii)

(C) (ii) (iii) (iv) (i) (D) (iii) (iv) (ii) (i)

91. Match the following electronic applications of information society with relevant service :

List - I	**List - II**
a. E-Commerce	i. Saakshat
b. E-Governance	ii. Living progress
c. E-Education	iii. G2C initiatives
d. E-Health	iv. Snap Deal

Codes :	**(a)**	**(b)**	**(c)**	**(d)**
(A)	iii	iv	i	ii
(B)	ii	iii	iv	i
(C)	iv	iii	i	ii
(D)	iv	ii	i	iii

92. Match the following :

List - I	**List - II**
a. Books are for use.	i. Adopting to future needs
b. Every reader his/ her book.	ii. Long operating hours
c. Every book its reader.	iii. Freedom of access to information & knowledge
d. Library is a growing organism.	iv. Reference Desk

Codes :	**(a)**	**(b)**	**(c)**	**(d)**
(A)	ii	iii	iv	i
(B)	iv	i	ii	iii
(C)	i	ii	iii	iv
(D)	iii	iv	i	ii

93. Match the following :

List - I	**List - II**
a. ETC	i. UK
b. NTC	ii. India
c. BLLD	iii. USA
d. NISCAIR	iv. Netherland

Codes :	**(a)**	**(b)**	**(c)**	**(d)**
(A)	iv	iii	i	ii
(B)	ii	i	iii	iv
(C)	iii	iv	ii	i
(D)	i	ii	iv	iii

94. Who introduced the concept of 'knowledge industry'?

(A) Peter Drucker (B) Fritz Machlup
(C) Marc Porat (D) William Saffady

95. When the last print version of Encyclopaedia Britannica was published ?

(A) 2009 (B) 2010
(C) 2011 (D) 2012

96. Identify the place where IFLA was first found.

(A) The Hague, Netherlands
(B) Edinburgh, Scotland
(C) Helsinki, Finland
(D) London

97. Information For All Programme (IFAP) was launched by

(A) IFLA (B) Library of Congress
(C) OCLC (D) UNESCO

98. Arrange the following in chronological order :

(i) Right to Information Act (India)
(ii) Information Technology Act (India)
(iii) Indian Copyright Act
(iv) Digital Millennium Copyright Act (US)

Codes :

(A) (i) (ii) (iii) (iv) (B) (iv) (i) (ii) (iii)
(C) (ii) (iii) (iv) (i) (D) (iii) (iv) (ii) (i)

99. Match the following electronic applications of information society with relevant service :

List - I	List - II
a. E-Commerce	i. Saakshat
b. E-Governance	ii. Living progress
c. E-Education	iii. G2C initiatives
d. E-Health	iv. SnapDeal

Codes :	(a)	(b)	(c)	(d)
(A)	iii	iv	i	ii
(B)	ii	iii	iv	i
(C)	iv	iii	i	ii
(D)	iv	ii	i	iii

100. Match the following :

List - I	List - II
a. Books are for use.	i. Adopting to future needs
b. Every reader his/ her book.	ii. Long operating hours
c. Every book its reader.	iii. Freedom of access to information & knowledge
d. Library is a growing organism.	iv. Reference Desk

Codes :	**(a)**	**(b)**	**(c)**	**(d)**
(A)	ii	iii	iv	i
(B)	iv	i	ii	iii
(C)	i	ii	iii	iv
(D)	iii	iv	i	ii

101. Match the following :

List - I	**List - II**
a. Biographical source	i. Full text sources online
b. Encyclopaedia	ii. ODLIS
c. Directory	iii. Linkedin
d. Dictionary	iv. Liswiki

Codes :	**(a)**	**(b)**	**(c)**	**(d)**
(A)	i	ii	iii	iv
(B)	ii	iii	i	iv
(C)	iv	ii	iii	i
(D)	iii	iv	i	ii

102. Match the following :

List - I	**List - II**
a. ETC	i. UK
b. NTC	ii. India
c. BLLD	iii. USA
d. NISCAIR	iv. Netherland

Codes :	**(a)**	**(b)**	**(c)**	**(d)**
(A)	iv	iii	i	ii
(B)	ii	i	iii	iv
(C)	iii	iv	ii	i
(D)	i	ii	iv	iii

103. What was the earlier name of National Library of India?

(A) Asiatic Society Library
(B) The Royal Library
(C) Calcutta Public Library
(D) Imperial Library of Calcutta

104. First state-aided Public Library inIndia was established by :
(A) William Jones
(B) W.A. Borden
(C) Maharaja Sayajirao Gaikwad
(D) Raja Ram Mohan Roy

105. In a virtual library :
(A) There is no corresponding physical collection
(B) Collection is available online as well as offline
(C) Collection is available online as well as print form
(D) Collection is available on CD as well as print form

106. Name the author of 'Grammar of Classification' :
(A) S.R. Ranganathan (B) H.E. Bliss
(C) W.C.B. Sayers (D) J. Mills

107. 'OCLC' was founded in the year :
(A) 2001 (B) 2000
(C) 1967 (D) 1978

108. Who is responsible for registration of Indian Publishers ?
(A) INFLIBNET (B) DELNET
(C) RRRLF (D) R.R. BOWKER

109. National Library (Kolkata) receives books on deposit under :
(A) Registration of Books Act, 1867

(B) The Delivery of Books Act,1956

(C) The Copyright Act, 1985

(D) Right to Information Act, 2003

110. Who was the first Librarian of Imperial Library ?

(A) John Macfarlane

(B) J.A. Chapman

(C) Khan Bahadur MA Asadullah

(D) B.S. Kesavan

111. Bodleian Library is in the University of :

(A) Cambridge (B) Oxford

(C) Harvard (D) Stanford

112. Damodaran Committee was appointed in 1971 to review working of

(A) Medical College Libraries

(B) National Science Libraries

(C) Agriculture Libraries

(D) Polytechnic Libraries

113. WIPO Academy deals with

(A) Patent Cooperation Treaty

(B) Courses on Intellectual Property

(C) Trademarks Gateway

(D) All of the above

114. Public Library Association (PLA) is a division of

(A) ALA (B) ILA

(C) IFLA (D) IASLIC

115. Who are associated with the development of OSI Model ?

i. Charles Buchman ii. ISO

iii. MIT, USA iv. UCLA, California

Codes :

(A) i and iv are correct.

(B) i and iii are correct.

(C) i and ii are correct.

(D) ii and iii are correct.

116. Which of the following organizations are involved in providing translation services in India ?

i. NISCAIR

ii. National Library of India

iii. IASLIC

iv. IATLIS

Codes :

(A) ii and iv are correct.

(B) ii and iii are correct.

(C) i and iv are correct.

(D) i and iii are correct.

117. Which of the following are International Referral Centres for Scholarly Information ?

i. DARE

ii. INFOTERRA

iii. International Referral Network

iv. Information Referral

Codes :

(A) ii & iv are correct. (B) i & iv are correct.

(C) i & ii are correct. (D) ii & iii are correct.

118. Which of the following are the works related to IFLA's Committee on Freedom of Access to Information and Freedom of Expression (FAIFE) ?

i. Publish reports, participate innational and international conferences and organize workshops.

ii. Monitor the state of intellectualfreedom within the library community world-wide and publish newsletters and online news.

iii. Respond to violations of freeaccess to information and freedom of expression and make press releases.

iv. Cross-association activities, to bring participants together.

Codes :

(A) i, iii and iv are correct.

(B) ii, iii and iv are correct.

(C) i, ii and iv are correct.

(D) i, ii and iii are correct.

119. Arrange the following Library Acts according to their year of enactment :

i. Uttarakhand ii. Orissa

iii. Manipur iv. Goa

Codes :

(A) iv, i, ii, iii (B) i, ii, iii, iv

(C) iii, iv, ii, i (D) ii, iii, i, iv

120. Arrange the following according to their year of emergence :

i. ERNET ii. NICNET

iii. C-DOT iv. C-DAC

Codes :

(A) ii, iii, i, iv (B) iii, ii, iv, i

(C) iv, ii, iii, i (D) i, iv, iii, ii

121. Arrange the following libraries according to their year of origin :

i. Asiatic Society Library, Bombay

ii. Connemara Public Library, Madras

iii. Delhi Public Library, Delhi

iv. National Library of India,Calcutta

Codes :

(A) i, ii, iv, iii (B) i, iii, iv, ii

(C) ii, iv, iii, i (D) iv, iii, ii, i

122. Arrange the following according to their year of origin :

i. Bowker Annual

ii. Europa World Yearbook

iii. India; a reference annual

iv. Stateman's yearbook

Codes :

(A) iv, i, ii, iii (B) i, ii, iv, iii

(C) iv, iii, i, ii (D) ii, i, iv, iii

123. The term 'Literary warrant' for book classification was introduced by

(A) W.C.B. Sayers (B) Wyndham Hulme

(C) J.D. Brown (D) H.E. Bliss

124. Under which approach of Wersig-Neveling's information theory, information is seen as static relations between physical objects which may be perceived or not ?

(A) The meaning approach

(B) The structural approach

(C) The process approach

(D) The knowledge approach

125. In which scheme of classification, special auxiliaries denote locally recurrent characteristics ?

(A) Deuey Decimal Classification

(B) Universal Decimal Classification

(C) Bibliographic Classification

(D) Colon Classification

126. FRBR Model consist of which of the following four entities ?

(A) Personality, Matter, Energy, Space

(B) Work, Expression, Manifestation, Item

(C) Book, Form, Availability, Type

(D) Action, Place, Impact, Category

127. The primary distinction betweenRDA and AACR is

(A) Structural (B) Relational

(C) Non-structural (D) Combinational

128. Arrange the following Library Acts according to the year of their enactment :

(i) Arunachal Pradesh (ii) Eihar

(iii) Lakshadweep (iv) Rajasthan

Codes :

(A) (ii), (iv), (iii), (i) (B) (iv), (i), (ii), (iii)

(C) (ii), (iii), (i), (iv) (D) (iv), (iii), (ii), (i)

129. Match the following :

List - I		List - II	
a.	CILIP	i.	1972
b.	ASLIB	ii.	2002
c.	ALA	iii.	1876
d.	COMLA	iv.	1924

Codes :	(a)	(b)	(c)	(d)
(A)	ii	iv	iii	i
(B)	iv	iii	ii	i
(C)	iii	iv	i	ii
(D)	ii	iii	iv	i

130. Who has recommended the establishment of district, taluka, town and village libraries ?
   (A) S.R. Ranganathan
   (B) Velaga Venkatappayya
   (C) Fyzee Report
   (D) Library Advisory Committee

131. 'Indian Citation Index' (ICI) is developed by
   (A) Informatics India
   (B) Veeru's technologies
   (C) DELNET
   (D) Knowledge Foundation

132. The CIP (India) Project is an initiation of :
   (A) RRRLF (B) Delhi Public Library
   (C) NISCAIR (D) National Library of India

133. Identify the founders of Wikipedia from the following :
   i. Michael E Davis ii. Jimmy Wales
   iii. Richard Stallman iv. Larry Sanger

   Codes :
   (A) ii and iii are correct.
   (B) i and ii are correct.
   (C) i and iii are correct.
   (D) ii and iv are correct.

134. Match the following :

List - I	List - II
a. ALA	i. 1909
b. CILIP	ii. 1933
c. SLA	iii. 1876
d. ILA	iv. 2002

Codes :	**(a)**	**(b)**	**(c)**	**(d)**
(A)	iv	ii	iii	i
(B)	iii	iv	i	ii
(C)	i	ii	iv	iii
(D)	iii	iv	ii	i

135. Match the following :

List - I	**List - II**
a. Sayaji Rao Gayakwad	i. Revision of salary scale
b. D.P. Chattopadyay	ii. Library building
c. K.D. Metcalf	iii. Public libraries
d. B.S. Kesavan	iv. Librarian of national library

Codes :	**(a)**	**(b)**	**(c)**	**(d)**
(A)	ii	i	iii	iv
(B)	i	ii	iii	iv
(C)	iii	i	ii	iv
(D)	iv	iii	i	ii

136. Match the following national organizations with their relevant mission :

List - I	**List - II**
a. National Mission on Libraries	i. Digitization of AYUSH literature
b. National Mission for Manuscripts	ii. Nurturing of talent
c. T.K.D.L.	iii. Capacity building
d. NME-ICT	iv. Connects India's past with present

Codes :	(a)	(b)	(c)	(d)
(A)	i	ii	iii	iv
(B)	iii	iv	i	ii
(C)	iv	iii	ii	i
(D)	ii	i	iii	iv

137. First state-aided Public Library inIndia was established by :
    (A) William Jones
    (B) W.A. Borden
    (C) Maharaja Sayajirao Gaikwad
    (D) Raja Ram Mohan Roy
138. In a virtual library :
    (A) There is no corresponding physical collection
    (B) Collection is available online as well as offline
    (C) Collection is available online as well as print form
    (D) Collection is available on CD as well as print form
139. Abstracts in LISA (Library and Information Science Abstracts) arearranged according to :
    (A) DDC
    (B) Colon classification
    (C) A special scheme ofclassification
    (D) UDC
140. According to Dr. S.R. Ranganathanthe proportion of expenditure of University Library budget on book sand other reading materials should be :
    (A) 60% (B) 50%
    (C) 40% (D) 30%
141. A Standard TQM tool would be :

(A) Questionnaire (B) Interview
(C) Diary (D) Flow chart

142. Which management school regardsmanagement as a Universalprocess ?
(A) The Human Relations School
(B) The Classical School
(C) The System School
(D) The Social Systems School

143. Likert's name is associated with :
(A) Theory of Motivation
(B) Evolving organizationalstructure
(C) Style of leadership
(D) Decision-making theory

144. Management of the Library by Library Committee is an example of ....
(A) MBO
(B) Participative Management
(C) Decentralisation
(D) Consultative Management

145. Delegation of authority involves :
(A) Responsibility only
(B) Authority and Accountability only
(C) Accountability and Responsibility only
(D) Responsibility, Authority and Accountability

146. 'OCLC' was founded in the year :
(A) 2001 (B) 2000
(C) 1967 (D) 1978

147. Who is responsible for registration of Indian Publishers ?

(A) INFLIBNET (B) DELNET

(C) RRRLF (D) R.R. BOWKER

148. National Library (Kolkata) receives books on deposit under :

(A) Registration of Books Act, 1867

(B) The Delivery of Books Act, 1956

(C) The Copyright Act, 1985

(D) Right to Information Act, 2003

149. Who was the first Librarian of Imperial Library ?

(A) John Macfarlane

(B) J.A. Chapman

(C) Khan Bahadur MA Asadullah

(D) B.S. Kesavan

150. Bodleian Library is in the University of :

(A) Cambridge (B) Oxford

(C) Harvard (D) Stanford

151. Who wrote the book titled "An Introduction to Library Classification" ?

(A) J.D. Brown

(B) S.R. Ranganathan

(C) W.C. Berwick Sayers

(D) Howard Phillips

152. Who is the author of the book "Organization of Knowledge in Libraries" ?

(A) S.R. Ranganathan (B) W.C.B. Sayers

(C) J. Mills (D) H.E. Bliss

153. Name the two states of India, inwhich the Public Libraries Act waspassed in 1989 ?

(A) Kerala and Haryana

(B) Haryana and Goa

(C) Manipur and Mizoram

(D) Kerala and Goa

154. The first Library Association formed in India is :

(A) Andhra Pradesh Library Association

(B) Bengal Library Association

(C) Indian Library Association

(D) Madras Library Association

155. Who has introduced Advancement of Librarianship Programme ?

(A) IFLA (B) UNESCO

(C) FID (D) ICSU

156. Prof. D.P. Chattopadhyaya was Chairman of the committeerelated to :

(A) National Policy on Library and Information System

(B) Development of Libraries and their Organization

(C) Curriculum Development in Library and Information Science

(D) Public Libraries in India

157. Match the following List I and List II and choose the correct answer by using the codes given below:

List-I	List-II
(i) RTI	(a) 1972
(ii) Delivery of Book	(b) 2005 Act
(iii) Press and	(c) 1867 Registration of Book Act
(iv) RRRLF	(d) 1954

Codes :	**(i)**	**(ii)**	**(iii)**	**(iv)**
(A)	(b)	(d)	(c)	(a)
(B)	(d)	(b)	(a)	(c)
(C)	(a)	(d)	(b)	(c)
(D)	(c)	(a)	(d)	(b)

158. Arrange the following Associations as per their establishment year :

(a) ALA (b) LA

(c) IFLA (d) SLA

Select the correct answer :

Codes :

(A) (a) (b) (d) (c) (B) (b) (a) (c) (d)

(C) (d) (a) (b) (c) (D) (c) (a) (b) (d)

159. Match List-I and List-II and choose the correct answer by using the codes given below :

List-I	**List-II**
(i) Baroda Library Association	(a) 1927
(ii) Uttar Pradesh Library Association	(b) 1914
(iii) Madras Library Association	(c) 1910
(iv) Andhra Pradesh Library Association	(d) 1956

Codes :	**(i)**	**(ii)**	**(iii)**	**(iv)**
(A)	(d)	(c)	(b)	(a)
(B)	(c)	(d)	(a)	(b)
(C)	(c)	(d)	(b)	(a)
(D)	(a)	(b)	(d)	(c)

160. **Assertion (A) :** Cataloguing in Publication (CIP) is initiated by IFLA.

Reason (R) : It helps individual libraries in copying down the data.

Select the correct answer from the codes given below :

Codes :

(A) (A) is false but (R) is true

(B) (A) is true but (R) is false

(C) Both (A) and (R) are false

(D) Both (A) and (R) are true

161. Match List-I and List-II and choose the correct answer by using the codes given below :

	List-I	List-II
(i)	Radhakrishnan Commission	(a) 1979
(ii)	Mudaliar Commission	(b) 1964
(iii)	Kothari Commission	(c) 1952
(iv)	Karnataka State University Review Committee	(d) 1948

Codes :	**(i)**	**(ii)**	**(iii)**	**(iv)**
(A)	(d)	(c)	(b)	(a)
(B)	(a)	(c)	(d)	(b)
(C)	(b)	(a)	(c)	(d)
(D)	(d)	(c)	(a)	(b)

162. Which of the following can be identified with Ranganathan's fifth law of Library Science ?

(A) Providing SDI Service

(B) Providing Open Access

(C) Providing analytical entries

(D) Opening Branch Libraries

163. The term 'Canon' was introduced by :

(A) S.R. Ranganathan (B) H.E. Bliss

(C) W.C.B. Sayers (D) E.C. Richardson

164. According to CCC which one of the following entry does not give Class Number ?

(A) BIE (B) CIE

(C) Main Entry (D) CRIE

165. **Statement (1) :** RRRLF which is an agency that supports public library services and systems is not an autonomous organization.

Statement (2) : RRRLF is fully financed by the Ministry of Culture, Government of India.

In the above statement :

(A) Both (1) and (2) are true

(B) (1) is true but (2) is false

(C) (1) is false but (2) is true

(D) Both (1) and (2) are false

166. **Statement (1) :** The British library is very young as it was set up under the British Library Act that was passed in 1972.

Statement (2) : The Library of the British Museum which was set up in 1753 is part of the British Library today.

In the above statements :

(A) Both (1) and (2) are true

(B) (1) is true but (2) is false

(C) (1) is false but (2) is true

(D) Both (1) and (2) are false

167. Match List-I and List-II and choose the correct answer by using the codes given below :

List-I	List-II
(i) John Macfarlane	(a) Library of Congress
(ii) B.S. Kesavan	(b) British Museum Library
(iii) John J. Beckley	(c) Imperial Library
(iv) Anthony Panizzi	(d) National Library of India

Codes :	**(i)**	**(ii)**	**(iii)**	**(iv)**
(A)	(d)	(c)	(a)	(b)
(B)	(c)	(d)	(a)	(b)
(C)	(d)	(c)	(a)	(b)
(D)	(a)	(c)	(b)	(d)

168. The new name of Standing Conference of National and University Libraries (SCONUL) is :
   (A) Standing college, National and University Libraries
   (B) Society of college, National and University Libraries
   (C) Standing Council on National and University Libraries
   (D) Standing Committee on National and University Libraries

169. Match List-I and List-II and choose the correct answer by using the codes given below :

	List-I		**List-II**
(i)	American Library Association	(a)	1946
(ii)	Canadian Library Association	(b)	1932
(iii)	Special Library Association	(c)	1909
(iv)	The Association of Research Libraries	(d)	1876

Codes :	**(i)**	**(ii)**	**(iii)**	**(iv)**
(A)	(a)	(c)	(d)	(b)
(B)	(c)	(a)	(b)	(d)
(C)	(d)	(a)	(b)	(c)
(D)	(d)	(a)	(c)	(b)

170. 'World of Learning' is published from :
   (A) Oxford (B) London
   (C) Cambridge (D) Yorkshire

171. Double Colons (: :) are used in :
   (A) Library of Congress Classification Scheme
   (B) Colon Classification 7th Edition
   (C) Universal Decimal Classification
   (D) Bibliographic Classification

172. Match List-I and List-II and choose the correct answer by using the codes given below :

	List-I		List-II
(i)	National Medical Library	(a)	Mumbai
(ii)	Saraswati Mahal Library	(b)	Tanjore
(iii)	Bhandarkar Oriental Research Institute's Library	(c)	Delhi
(iv)	Asiatic Society's Library	(d)	Pune

Codes :	**(i)**	**(ii)**	**(iii)**	**(iv)**
(A)	(c)	(b)	(d)	(a)
(B)	(a)	(b)	(c)	(d)
(C)	(b)	(c)	(a)	(d)
(D)	(d)	(a)	(b)	(c)

173. Match List-I and List-II and choose the correct answer by using the codes given below :

	List-I		List-II
(i)	NISCAIR	(a)	Union Catalogue of Social Science Periodicals and Serials in India
(ii)	INFLIBNET	(b)	Technology focus
(iii)	NASSDOC	(c)	TKDL
(iv)	DESIDOC	(d)	CALIBER

Codes :	**(i)**	**(ii)**	**(iii)**	**(iv)**
(A)	(d)	(a)	(c)	(b)
(B)	(c)	(d)	(a)	(b)

(C)	(c)	(a)	(b)	(d)
(D)	(b)	(c)	(d)	(a)

174. Arrange the following in chronological sequence of their year of establishment :

(i) IASLIC (ii) IATLIS

(iii) SIS (iv) ILA

Codes :

(A) (iv) (i) (ii) (iii) (B) (i) (ii) (iv) (iii)

(C) (ii) (i) (iv) (iii) (D) (i) (iii) (iv) (ii)

ANSWERS

1. C	2. D	3. C	4. D	5. A	6. A
7. C	8. C	9. B	10. A	11. B	12. B
13. D	14. D	15. C	16. C	17. B	18. C
19. A	20. D	21. D	22. C	2 3. A	24. D
25. B	26. B	27. A	28. D	29. C	30. D
31. B	32. C	33. A	34. B	35. A	36. D
37. C	38. A	39. A	40 . B	41. B	42. D
43. C	44. A	45. B	46. D	47. A	48. C
49. D	50. B	51. B	52. D	53. D	54. B
55. D	56. B	57. A	58. B	59. B	60. C
61. D	62. B	63. B	64. D	65. A	66. D
67. B	68. B	69. D	70. B	71. A	72. B
73. B	74. B	75. C	7 6. B	77. A	78. A
79. C	80. D	81. C	82. B	83. A	84. A
85. B	86. B	87. B	88. D	89. C	90. D
91. C	92. A	93. A	94. B	95. B	96. B
97. D	98. D	99. C	100. A	101. D	102. A
103. D	104. C	105. A	106. C	107. C	108. C
109. B	110. A	111. B	112. D	113. B	114. A
115. C	116. D	117. C	118. D	119. C	120. A
121. A	122. A	123. B	124. B	125. B	126. B
127. A	128. D	129. A	130. C	131. D	132. A

133. D	134. B	135. C	136. B	137. C	138. A
139. C	140. C	141. D	142. B	143. C	144. B
145. D	146. C	147. C	148. B	149. A	150. B
151. C	152. D	153. A	154. A	155. A	156. A
157. A	158. A	159. B	160. D	161. A	162. D
163. C	164. D	165. C	166. A	167. B	168. B
169. D	170. B	171. C	172. A	173. B	174. A

3

Information & Communication

1. Who was the Chairman of 'National Policy on Library & Information Systems' (1986) ?
   (A) D. N. Banerjee
   (B) D. P. Chattopadhyay
   (C) Sam Pitroda
   (D) Kalpana Dasgupta
2. The significance of the year 2011 for LIS education in India is
   (A) Golden Jubilee year
   (B) Platinum Jubilee year
   (C) Diamond Jubilee year
   (D) Centenary year
3. "Shodhganga" is a repository of
   (A) E – Resources (B) E – Thesis
   (C) E – Journals (D) E – Books
4. "Internet Public Library" is being maintained by

(A) MIT, Massachusettes
(B) University of Michigan
(C) University of Arizona
(D) Drexal University

5. Which of the following are 'Inclusive geographical sources'

(i) Maps (ii) Atlases
(iii) Encyclopaedias (iv) Yearbooks

Codes :

(A) (i) & (ii) are correct
(B) (iii) & (iv) are correct
(C) (ii) & (iii) are correct
(D) (ii) & (iv) are correct

6. The factors that influence computer file organisation are

(i) Speed of access (ii) Storage space
(iii) Fixed length fields (iv) File volatility

Codes :

(A) (i), (ii) and (iii) are correct
(B) (i), (ii) and (iv) are correct
(C) (ii), (iii) and (iv) are correct
(D) (i), (iii) and (iv) are correct

7. Major problems of 'Information Communication Technology' are

(i) Information overload
(ii) Information insecurity
(iii) Lack of innovative technologies
(iv) Lack of control overcommunication

Codes :

(A) (ii) and (iv) are correct

(B) (i) and (iv) are correct

(C) (i), (ii) and (iv) are correct

(D) (i), (ii) and (iii) are correct

8. **Assertion (A) :** Users can have access to large number of e-journals.

Reason (R) : Users are not aware of using e-journals.

Codes :

(A) (A) is true, but (R) is false

(B) Both (A) and (R) are true, but (R) is not the correct explanationof (A)

(C) (A) is false, (R) is true

(D) Both (A) and (R) are true and (R) isthe correct explanation of (A)

9. **Assertion (A) :** Book selection must be done judiciously.

Reason (R) : Resource sharing is the need of the hour.

Codes :

(A) Both (A) and (R) are true, but (R) is not the correct statement of (A)

(B) (A) is false, but (R) is true

(C) (A) is true, but (R) is false

(D) Both (A) and (R) are false

10. **Assertion (A) :** Primary sources provide most authentic information for research.

Reason (R) : Primary sources are highly unorganised.

Codes :

(A) (A) is false, but (R) is true

(B) (A) is true, but (R) is false

(C) Both (A) and (R) are correct and (R) is the correct explanation of (A)

(D) Both (A) and (R) are correct, but (R) is not the correct explanationof (A)

11. **Assertion (A) :** Classification plays a significant role in online retrieval.

Reason (R) : Classification played an important role in manual system.

Codes :

(A) (A) is true, but (R) is false

(B) Both (A) and (R) are false

(C) Both (A) and (R) are true

(D) (A) is false, but (R) is true

12. Arrange the following according to their year of first publication :

(i) Encyclopaedia Britannica

(ii) Encyclopaedia Americana

(iii) Encyclopaedia of Library and Information Science

(iv) McGraw-Hill Encyclopaedia of Science and Technology

Codes :

(A) (iv), (iii), (i), (ii)

(B) (i), (ii), (iv), (iii)

(C) (iii), (i), (iv), (ii)

(D) (ii), (iv), (i), (iii)

13. Match the following :

	List - I		List - II
(a)	Asian Recorder	(i)	Location of specific volume of journal
(b)	Union Catalogue of Scientific Serials	(ii)	Articles on Green Revolution
(c)	Books-in-Print	(iii)	Obituary of Dev -Anand
(d)	Social Science Index	(iv)	Availability of books

Codes :	(a)	(b)	(c)	(d)
(A)	(iv)	(iii)	(i)	(ii)
(B)	(i)	(iv)	(ii)	(iii)
(C)	(iii)	(i)	(iv)	(ii)
(D)	(ii)	(iv)	(iii)	(i)

14. Match the following :

	List - I	List - II
(a)	Textualre presentation	(i) Pascal
(b)	Computer language	(ii) Gopher
(c)	Network tool	(iii) Boolean operators
(d)	Searching technique	(iv) ASCI

Codes :	(a)	(b)	(c)	(d)
(A)	(iv)	(i)	(ii)	(iii)
(B)	(i)	(iv)	(iii)	(ii)
(C)	(iii)	(ii)	(iv)	(i)
(D)	(ii)	(iv)	(iii)	(i)

15. The initiation, selection, exploration,formulation, collection and presentation are two stages of which model of information seeking behaviour

(A) Ellis Model (B) Krikelas Model
(C) Kuhlthou Model (D) Wilson Model

16. The publisher of "Information Power : Building Partnership for Learning" is
    (A) AASL (B) AECT
    (C) ALA (D) ILA
17. In 1974, Zurkowski used for the first time which of the following term ?
    (A) Digital Literacy (B) Media Literacy
    (C) Computer Literacy (D) Information Literacy
18. Blair and Maron evaluation study on retrieval effectiveness of full text search is called
    (A) SMART Retrieval Experiment
    (B) MEDLARS evaluation study
    (C) STAIRS project
    (D) Cranefield – II Project
19. In cataloguing, the square brackets[ ] are used
    (A) to enclose information takenfrom outside
    (B) to enclose the details of printed / manufacturer
    (C) to enclose series statements
    (D) to enclose statement ofaccompanying material
20. Which Section of AACR – II (R) dealswith serial publications ?
    (A) Part – A, Section – 3
    (B) Part – B, Section – 3
    (C) Part – A, Section – 12
    (D) Part – B, Section – 12
21. Who propounded "Minimum, Middling and Maximum Theories" of reference service ?
    (A) C.M. Winchell (B) James I. Wyer
    (C) Samuel Rothstein (D) D.W. Lewis
22. Roget's International Thesaurus is a

(A) Classified List of Words
(B) Book of Synonyms
(C) List of Standard Terms
(D) List of Scientific Terms

23. Information about scale and projection can be found in
(A) Encyclopaedias
(B) Hand books of Manuals
(C) Geographical sources
(D) Directories

24. Who of the following is not the author of any reference book ?
(A) C.M. Winchell (B) William A Katz
(C) Louis Shores (D) Maurice B. Line

25. Where the first M. Phil programme in Library and Information Science was started in India ?
(A) University of Madras
(B) University of Delhi
(C) University of Mysore
(D) University of Bombay

26. Redundancy of information is
(A) Unnecessary and should beeliminated
(B) Unnecessary but cannot beavoided
(C) Necessary and some times useful
(D) Necessary and always desirable

27. Science Citation Index is published by
(A) Thomson Reuters (B) H.W. Wilson
(C) Whitaker (D) R.R. Bowker

28. In the information transfer cycles, internet is acting as

(i) Primary Publisher
(ii) Secondary Publisher
(iii) Tertiary Publisher
(iv) Primary Distributor

Codes :

(A) (i), (iii) and (iv) are correct.
(B) (i), (ii) and (iv) are correct.
(C) (ii), (iii) and (iv) are correct.
(D) (i), (ii) and (iii) are correct.

29. Methods and Techniques of Human Resource Planning includes

(i) Selection and Recruitment
(ii) Induction and Placement
(iii) Quality Management
(iv) Performance Evaluation

Codes :

(A) (i), (iv) & (ii) are correct.
(B) (iv), (iii) & (i) are correct.
(C) (i), (ii) & (iv) are correct.
(D) (iii) and (i) are correct.

30. **Assertion (A) :** Many libraries have no written collection development policy and yet have sound collection.

Reason (R) : Demand driven collection plays a strong role inhaving a sound collection.

Codes :

(A) (A) is true, but (R) is false.
(B) (A) is false, but (R) is true.
(C) Both (A) and (R) are true.
(D) Both (A) and (R) are false.

31. **Assertion (A) :** Colan classification is an enumerative classification scheme.

    Reason (R) : Colan classificationhas adopted analytico-synthetic approach for the construction of class number

    Codes :

    (A) (A) is false, but (R) is true.

    (B) (A) is true, but (R) is false.

    (C) Both (A) and (R) are true.

    (D) Both (A) and (R) are false.

32. **Assertion (A) :** LIS Education in India achieved a landmark of 100 years but quality is compromised.

    Reason (R) : Unplanned proliferation of LIS schools and open learning programmes.

    Codes :

    (A) Both (A) and (R) are true.

    (B) Both (A) are (R) are false.

    (C) (A) is false (R) is true.

    (D) (A) is true (R) is false.

33. **Assertion (A) :** LIS education is notuniform throughout India.

    Reason (R) : Adoption of UGC model syllabus is not mandatory, Local LIS requirements varies.

    Codes :

    (A) (A) is true, but (R) is false.

    (B) (A) is false, but (R) is true.

    (C) Both (A) and (R) are true.

    (D) Both (A) and (R) are false.

34. **Assertion (A) :** There is need for Library Legislation in all States of India.

Reason (R) : To make Public Library System independent and without political influence.

Codes :

(A) Both (A) and (R) are true.

(B) (A) is true, but (R) is false.

(C) Both (A) and (R) are false.

(D) (A) is false, but (R) is true.

35. **Assertion (A) :** Though information is considered as a commodity, Libraries are not sound infinances.

Reason (R) : All types of Libraries have failed in promoting information as a commodity.

Codes :

(A) (A) is true, but (R) is false.

(B) (A) is false, but (R) is true.

(C) Both (A) and (R) are true.

(D) Both (A) and (R) are false.

36. Match the following :

List-I	**List-II**
(a) Cole and Eales	(i) Statistical Bibliography
(b) Hume	(ii) Scientometrics
(c) Pritchard	(iii) Statistical Analysis
(d) T. Braun	(iv) Bibliometrics

Codes :	**(a)**	**(b)**	**(c)**	**(d)**
(A)	(iv)	(iii)	(ii)	(i)
(B)	(iii)	(i)	(iv)	(ii)
(C)	(ii)	(iii)	(i)	(iv)
(D)	(i)	(iii)	(iv)	(ii)

37. Match the following :

List-I	**List-II**
(a) Classical School	(i) John cotton Danna
(b) X & Y Theory	(ii) Henry Fayol
(c) Newark Charging System	(iii) Peter Drucker
(d) MBO	(iv) Douglas McGregor

Codes :	**(a)**	**(b)**	**(c)**	**(d)**
(A)	(i)	(iii)	(iv)	(ii)
(B)	(iii)	(iv)	(i)	(ii)
(C)	(ii)	(iv)	(i)	(iii)
(D)	(iii)	(ii)	(iv)	(i)

38. Match the following :

List-I	**List-II**
(a) C.A. Catter	(i) Selective Listing
(b) Kaiser	(ii) Thing-partmaterial-action
(c) J.R. Sharp	(iii) Concrete and process
(d) D.J. Coates	(iv) Syndetic cataloguing

Codes :	**(a)**	**(b)**	**(c)**	**(d)**
(A)	(iv)	(i)	(ii)	(iii)
(B)	(iv)	(iii)	(i)	(ii)
(C)	(iii)	(iv)	(ii)	(i)
(D)	(ii)	(iii)	(iv)	(i)

39. Match the following :

List-I	**List-II**
(a) Guidance touse RTI Act	(i) Documentation service
(b) Orientationin use of multimedia	(ii) Referral service

(c) Providinguser with list of information sources — (iii) Informative Literacy

(d) Directing theuser of INFLIBNET to seek needed information — (iv) Reference service

Codes :	(a)	(b)	(c)	(d)
(A)	(iii)	(ii)	(i)	(iv)
(B)	(iv)	(ii)	(iii)	(i)
(C)	(ii)	(i)	(iv)	(iii)
(D)	(iv)	(iii)	(i)	(ii)

40. Match the following :

List-I	List-II
(a) Whitaker's Almanack	(i) Year of starting 'Publishers Weekly'
(b) Ulrich's International Periodicals Directory	(ii) Availability of V 50 of 'Library Journal'
(c) National Union Catalogue of Scientific Serials in India	(iii) Information on discontinuation of New Encyclopaedia Britannica
(d) Data India	(iv) Astronomical information

Codes :	(a)	(b)	(c)	(d)
(A)	(iv)	(i)	(ii)	(iii)
(B)	(ii)	(iv)	(i)	(iii)
(C)	(iii)	(ii)	(i)	(iv)
(D)	(i)	(iv)	(ii)	(iii)

41. Match the following :

	List-I		List-II
(a)	J. Thompson	(i)	Basic Statistics for Libraries
(b)	S. Halkett of J Laing	(ii)	Planning of Academic and Research Buildings
(c)	William A Katz	(iii)	Dictionary of anonymous and Pseudonymous literature
(d)	K.D. Metcalf	(iv)	Introduction to reference work

Codes :	**(a)**	**(b)**	**(c)**	**(d)**
(A)	(i)	(ii)	(iv)	(iii)
(B)	(i)	(iii)	(iv)	(ii)
(C)	(ii)	(iv)	(i)	(iii)
(D)	(iv)	(ii)	(iii)	(i)

42. Match the following :

	List-I		List-II
(a)	Budget prepared using previous period budget	(i)	Formula Budget
(b)	Budget based on norms and Standards	(ii)	Zero-based budget
(c)	Budget planned Integrating number of techniques	(iii)	Incremental Budget
(d)	Budget prepared identifying current tasks independent of previous year	(iv)	Planning programming budgeting system

Codes :	**(a)**	**(b)**	**(c)**	**(d)**
(A)	(iii)	(i)	(iv)	(ii)
(B)	(i)	(iii)	(iv)	(ii)
(C)	(iii)	(ii)	(i)	(iv)
(D)	(i)	(ii)	(iii)	(iv)

43. According to Machlup the difference between information and knowledge is
    (A) Information increases with use, whereas knowledge is constant.
    (B) Information is stimulatory, whereas knowledge is practical.
    (C) Information is shareable, whereas knowledge is one's property.
    (D) Information is piecemeal, fragmented, particular, whereas knowledge is structured, coherent and universal.

44. Transformation of traditional libraries to hybrid / digital libraries is
    (A) Crisis Management
    (B) Re-engineering
    (C) Change Management
    (D) Project Management

45. Access to back volumes of E-journals is known as ________.
    (A) Random Access (B) Perpetual Access
    (C) Online Access (D) Retrospective Access

46. Which of the following are library networks ?
    (i) Internet (ii) DELNET
    (iii) NICNET (iv) OCLC

Codes :

(A) (i) and (ii) are correct.

(B) (ii) and (iv) are correct.

(C) (i) and (iii) are correct.

(D) (i) and (iv) are correct.

47. Which of the following are Trade Bibliographies ?

(i) Books-in-Print

(ii) Indian Books-in-Print

(iii) Indian National Bibliography

(iv) British National Bibliography

Codes :

(A) (i) and (iii) are correct.

(B) (ii) and (iv) are correct.

(C) (i) and (ii) are correct.

(D) (ii) and (iii) are correct.

48. **Assertion (A) :** Distance education for LIS courses is gaining ground in India.

Reason (R) : Majority of people prefer it as an alternative channel of education.

Codes :

(A) (A) is true but (R) is false.

(B) (A) is false but (R) is true.

(C) Both (A) and (R) are correct.

(D) Both (A) and (R) are wrong.

49. **Assertion (A) :** Present decade has accepted E-journals as channels of fast communication.

Reason (R) : E-publications have added enormous quantity of literature but affected the quality of research.

Codes :

(A) (A) is true but (R) is false.

(B) (A) is false but (R) is true.

(C) Both (A) and (R) are true and (R) is the correct explanation.

(D) Both (A) and (R) are true, but (R) is not a correct explanation.

50. **Assertion (A) :** Metadata hold much promise for information retrieval and access in the digital age.

Reason (R) : Metadata can save a number of functions including description, resource discovery and management of resources.

Codes :

(A) (A) is true, but (R) is false.

(B) (A) is false, but (R) is true.

(C) Both (A) and (R) are true.

(D) Both (A) and (R) are false.

51. Match the following :

List - I	List - II
a. 'Guide to Use of Books and Libraries'	i. F.W. Lancaster
b. 'If You Want to Evaluate Your Library'	ii. A.C. Foskelt
c. 'Cuneiform to Computer : A History of Reference Sources'	iii. Jean K. Gates
d. 'Subject Approach to Information'	iv. William A. Katz

Codes :	**(a)**	**(b)**	**(c)**	**(d)**
(A)	ii	iii	iv	i
(B)	i	iv	iii	ii
(C)	iii	i	iv	ii
(D)	iv	ii	i	i

52. Match the following :

List - I	**List - II**
a. Directory	i. Information Please Almanac
b. Annuals	ii. Keesing's Record of World Events
c. Bibliography	iii. Encyclopaedia of Associations
d. News paper Digest	iv. Publishers' Weekly

Codes :	**(a)**	**(b)**	**(c)**	**(d)**
(A)	iii	i	iv	ii
(B)	i	iii	iv	ii
(C)	iii	ii	iv	i
(D)	iv	i	ii	iii

53. Match the following :

List - I	**List - II**
a. Guiding users to the place of information	i. Digest
b. Guiding users in the use of information	ii. User orientation
c. Alerting users with the latest arrivals	iii. Referral
d. Providing users with summarised information	iv. Current Awareness

Codes :	**(a)**	**(b)**	**(c)**	**(d)**
(A)	iii	iv	i	ii
(B)	iii	ii	iv	i

(C)	iv	i	iii	ii
(D)	ii	i	iii	i

54. Match the following :

	List - I		List - II
a.	B.S. Kesvan	i.	School of librarianship
b.	Paul Otlet	ii.	National Library of India
c.	W.C.B. Sayers	iii.	UDC
d.	M. Taube	iv.	Uniterm Indexing

Codes :	**(a)**	**(b)**	**(c)**	**(d)**
(A)	ii	iii	i	iv
(B)	iii	ii	i	iv
(C)	ii	iii	iv	i
(D)	iv	ii	iii	i

55. Match the following :

List - I	List - II
a. Theory of Motivation	i. Factor of planning
b. Unity of Command	ii. Efficiency and waste prevention
c. MBO	iii. Maslow
d. Forecasting	iv. Peter Drucker

Codes :	**(a)**	**(b)**	**(c)**	**(d)**
(A)	i	ii	iii	iv
(B)	iv	i	ii	iii
(C)	ii	iii	iv	i
(D)	iii	iv	i	ii

56. Match the following :

	List - I	List - II
a.	Classification	i. LISA
b.	Cataloguing	ii. UDC
c.	Subject Heading	iii. AACR
d.	Library Science Abstracts	iv. LCSH

Codes :	(a)	(b)	(c)	(d)
(A)	ii	i	iv	iii
(B)	ii	iii	iv	i
(C)	iv	iii	i	ii
(D)	ii	iv	i	ii

57. Match the following :

	List - I		List - II
a.	OCLC	i.	Bio-Med
b.	INFLIBNET	ii.	Web-Dewey
c.	IISC	iii.	N-List
d.	NLM	iv.	Digital Library of India

Codes :	(a)	(b)	(c)	(d)
(A)	ii	iii	iv	i
(B)	iii	i	ii	iv
(C)	iv	ii	iii	i
(D)	i	iii	iv	ii

58. E-Journal articles can be identified with the help of
    (A) Digital Journal Identifier
    (B) Journal Source Identifier
    (C) Journal Article Identifier
    (D) Digital Object Identifier

59. Research in automatic classification for information retrieval of term or cluster of terms is called
    (A) Evaluation theory (B) Theory of clumps
    (C) Time binding theory (D) Dynamic theory

60. As specified by AACR-II (R), the source of information for machine readable data file is
    (A) Internal user label (B) Title page
    (C) Colophone (D) Title frame

61. Name of the President of Sri Lankacan be found in
    (A) International who's who
    (B) Stateman's Yearbook
    (C) Who's who in the world
    (D) Wilson Biographies
62. Which of the following has stopped publishing in the print from since 2012 ?
    (A) Europa World Yearbook
    (B) Times of India Directory
    (C) New Encyclopedia Britannica
    (D) Keesing's Contemporary Archives
63. Which of the following is not providing encyclopedia type ofinformation ?
    (A) Encyclopedia of Associations
    (B) Compton's Encyclopedia
    (C) Worldbook Encyclopedia
    (D) Encyclopedia Americana
64. Who used the phrase 'control-access directional type sources' ?
    (A) R.E. Bopp (B) B.C. Wynar
    (C) W.A. Katz (D) R. Balay
65. Which of the following are the problems of present information environment ?
    (i) Information indiscipline
    (ii) Information literacy
    (iii) Information overload
    (iv) Information technology

    Codes :
    (A) (i), (iii) are correct
    (B) (i) and (iv) are correct

(C) (ii) and (iv) are correct

(D) (i) and (ii) are correct

66. Which of the following are not partners of National Programme on Technology Enhanced Learning (NPTEL) ?

(i) IIT Madras (ii) IIT Delhi

(iii) IIIT Bangalore (iv) NIT Rourkela

Codes :

(A) (iii) and (iv) (B) (i) and (iv)

(C) (ii) and (iii) (D) (i) and (ii)

67. **Assertion (A) :** Internet can replace libraries.

Reason (R) : Google searches will satisfy the maximum users needs.

Codes :

(A) Both (A) and (R) are true.

(B) Both (A) and (R) are false.

(C) (A) is true but (R) is false.

(D) (A) is false but (R) is true.

68. **Assertion (A) :** A combination of hypertext and Hypermedia contains text, images, sounds and other information.

Reason (R) : Hypermedia information is represented in alinear fashion.

Codes :

(A) (A) is true and (R) is false.

(B) Both (A) and (R) are true.

(C) (A) is false and (R) is true.

(D) Both (A) & (R) are false.

69. **Assertion (A) :** Book selection should be done judiciously.

Reason (R) : A library should acquire important and latest book selection tools.

Codes :

(A) (A) is true but (R) is false.

(B) (A) is false but (R) is true.

(C) Both (A) & (R) are true, but (R) is not the correctexplanation of (A).

(D) Both (A) & (R) are true and (R) is the correct explanation of (A).

70. **Assertion (A) :** TQM promotes the way in which a library is organised and perform its ICT functions.

Reason (R) : TQM is seen as ahindrance to library and information services.

Codes :

(A) Both (A) and (R) are true.

(B) Both (A) and (R) are false.

(C) (A) is false and (R) is true.

(D) (A) is true and (R) is false.

71. **Assertion (A) :** Informative abstracts provide a concise summary of the subject content of an article.

Reason (R) : These are title oriented than finding-oriented.

Codes :

(A) Both (A) and (R) are true.

(B) (A) is true but (R) is false.

(C) (A) is false but (R) is true.

(D) Both (A) and (R) are false.

72. Match the following :

List - I	List - II
a. Pen drive	i. Communication device
b. i-Pad	ii. Web server device
c. Wifi Modem	iii. Storage device
d. Cloud computing	iv. Computing device

Codes :	(a)	(b)	(c)	(d)
(A)	i	iii	ii	iv
(B)	iii	iv	i	ii
(C)	iv	iii	ii	i
(D)	iii	ii	i	iv

73. Match the following :

List - I	List - II
a. Information contribution to the GNP of anation	i. Social information
b. Information that changes human activity	ii. Technological information
c. Information that establishes interaction between government and people	iii. Economic information
d. Information that forms a modern society	iv. Political information

Codes :	(a)	(b)	(c)	(d)
(A)	iii	i	iv	ii
(B)	i	iii	iv	ii
(C)	iv	ii	i	iii
(D)	ii	iii	iv	i

74. "Poole's Index to Periodical Literature" was brought out by

(A) William Frederick (B) F.W. Lancaster
(C) Van Rijsbergen (D) H.P. Luhn

75. Walford's Guide to Reference Material is published by

(A) American Library Association, Chicago
(B) R.R. Bowkar, London
(C) Library Association Publishing, London
(D) Learned Information Ltd., New Jersey

76. Science Abstracts published by

(A) INSPEC (Institute of Electrical Engineering)
(B) Institute of Physics, London
(C) American Institute of Physics
(D) PSOJ (Physical Society of Japan)

77. LAMP stands for

(A) Library Archives Management Programme
(B) Laser Analysis and Multi-media Performance
(C) Linux Apache.MySQL Perl
(D) Library Automation Managem Protocol

78. "Information Literacy Competency Standards for Higher Education" is prepared by

(A) AASL (B) IFLA
(C) SCONUL (D) ACRL

79. Which reference tool defines Reference service as ".... that phase of work which is directly concerned with assistance to readers in securing information and in using the resources of the library in study and research" ?

(A) Encyclopaedia of Librarianship

(B) Encyclopaedia of Library and Information Science
(C) ALA Glossary of Library Terms
(D) ALA World Encyclopaedia of Library & Information Services

80. Indian National Advisory Board for Libraries was setup in 1966 by
(A) Association of Indian Universities
(B) Ministry of Education
(C) Planning Commission
(D) University Grants Commission

81. The process of establishing headings and providing 'Cross references' is called
(A) Access points (B) Headings
(C) Authority control (D) Bibliographic Records

82. Whose model of communication of knowledge suggests that communication as an open system may be regarded as subjective, selective, variable and yet unpredictable ?
(A) G. Gerbner (B) Juger Hebermans
(C) E Shanon & Weaver (D) M. Foucault

83. Who said that information is both a product and process ?
(A) S.R. Ranganathan (B) J. Martin
(C) D.J. Foskett (D) S.C. Bradford

84. The purposes of Metadata are
(i) Unique identification
(ii) Authentication of records
(iii) Shelf arrangement
(iv) Shows the collection of a library

Codes :

(A) (i), (ii) are correct.

(B) (ii), (iii) are correct.

(C) (iii), (iv) are correct.

(D) (iv), (i) are correct.

85. The primary difference between knowledge classification and library classification are

(i) Knowledge classification arranges knowledge itself.

(ii) Library classification arranges the expression of knowledge in the form of documents.

(iii) Knowledge classification is the basis of Library Classification.

(iv) Knowledge classification follows system of numbers, called notation.

Codes :

(A) (i) and (ii) are correct.

(B) (ii) and (iii) are correct.

(C) (i), (ii) and (iv) are correct.

(D) (i), (ii) and (iii) are correct.

86. Match the following :

List - I	List - II
a. Public Library Extension	i. KD Metcalf
b. Academic Library Management	ii. M A Gelfand
c. University Libraries for Developing Countries	iii. L R McColvin
d. Planning Academic and Research Library Buildings	iv. M B Line

Codes :	**(a)**	**(b)**	**(c)**	**(d)**
(A)	iii	iv	ii	i
(B)	iv	ii	i	iii
(C)	iii	i	iv	ii
(D)	ii	iii	i	iv

87. Match the following :

List - I	**List - II**
a. Indian Cultural Heritage	i. TKDL
b. Race & Brittle documents	ii. IGNCA
c. Traditional Knowledge	iii. C-DAC
d. Mobile Digital Library	iv. National Library

Codes :	**(a)**	**(b)**	**(c)**	**(d)**
(A)	i	iv	iii	ii
(B)	iv	iii	ii	i
(C)	ii	iv	i	iii
(D)	iii	ii	iv	i

88. **Assertion (A) :** The information seeking behaviour research at the current times is on the social and cultural context of human interaction with information.

Reason (R) : Attempt is being made to interpret social and cultural experiences of individuals with respect to their information seeking and searching experiences.

Codes :

(A) (A) is true and (R) is false.

(B) Both (A) and (R) are false.

(C) (A) is false and (R) is true.

(D) Both (A) and (R) are true.

89. **Assertion (A) :** With the emergence of Internet, there is no need for reference service in this technology-based era.

Reason (R) : Internet has allowed access to every one to seek his/her information from anywhere, any time.

Codes :

(A) Both (A) and (R) are true.

(B) Both (A) and (R) are false.

(C) (A) is false but (R) is partially true.

(D) (A) is true, but (R) is false.

90. Which of the following states don't have library legislation ?

(i) Haryana (ii) Delhi

(iii) J & K (iv) Manipur

Codes :

(A) (i) and (ii) are correct.

(B) (ii) and (iii) are correct.

(C) (i) and (iv) are correct.

(D) (ii) and (iii) are correct.

91. Limitations of Bibliometrics is/are

(i) Analysing research and development trends

(ii) Describing text, not necessarily meaning and context

(iii) Identifying the active areas of research

(iv) Citation bias

Codes :

(A) (ii) and (iv) are correct.

(B) (i) and (iii) are correct.

(C) (i), (ii) and (iv) are correct.

(D) (ii) and (iii) are correct.

92. Match the following :

	List - I		List - II
a.	Systematic Bibliography	i.	List of macro/micro ideas of articles
b.	Analytical or Critical Bibliography	ii.	Investigation of physical nature of books
c.	Historical Bibliography	iii.	Listing of items with minimum details
d.	Documentary Bibliography	iv.	Concerned withart of writing, printing and binding

Codes :	(a)	(b)	(c)	(d)
(A)	i	iv	iii	ii
(B)	ii	i	iv	iii
(C)	iii	ii	iv	i
(D)	ii	iv	iii	i

93. Match the following queries withtheir appropriate category of reference source :

List - I	List - II
a. Enrolment of students in a university	i. Yearbook
b. Weather of Denmark	ii. Statistical source
c. No. of foreigners visited World Book Fair in 2011	iii. Directory
d. No. of hospitals in China	iv. Geographical Source

Codes :	(a)	(b)	(c)	(d)
(A)	iv	iii	i	ii
(B)	i	iii	ii	iv
(C)	ii	iv	i	iii
(D)	iii	iv	i	ii

94. Give in sequence, the following inorder of their origin :

i. National Library

ii. Calcutta Public Library

iii. Imperial Library Act

iv. Imperial Library

Codes :

(A) ii iii iv i (B) i ii iii iv

(C) iii i iv ii (D) ii iv iii i

95. Arrange the following according to year of publication :

i. Colon Classification

ii. Prolegomena to Classification

iii. Five Laws of Library Science

iv. Classified Catalogue Code

Codes :

(A) iii iv i ii (B) iv ii i iii

(C) iii i iv ii (D) i ii iv iii

96. Who is the propounder of the term 'Information Transfer' ?

(A) Ranganathan (B) J. Martin

(C) Calvin Moores (D) Beesman

97. The online version of 'McGraw Hill Encyclopaedia of Science and Technology' is

(A) Access Science

(B) McGraw Hill Online

(C) Online Encyclopaedia of Science and Technology

(D) Science online

98. 'Indian National Bibliography' is arranged under two parts, General Publication and _____ Publications.

(A) Private (B) Electronic

(C) Governmental (D) Non-book

99. Match the following as per Ranganathan's Staff formula recommended for a university library :

List - I	List - II
a. Acquisition Section	i. 1 person for 1500 readers
b. Reference Section	ii. 1 person for 500 titles
c. Periodical Section	iii. 1 person for 6000 titles
d. Circulation Section	iv. 1 person for 50 readers

Codes :	(a)	(b)	(c)	(d)
(A)	i	iv	iii	ii
(B)	iii	iv	ii	i
(C)	iv	i	iii	ii
(D)	ii	iii	i	iv

100. Match the following standard sub-divisions from DDC :

List - I	List - II
a. Philosophy & Theory	i. 07
b. Serial Publications	ii. 05
c. Collections	iii. 01
d. Study and Teaching	iv. 08

Codes :	(a)	(b)	(c)	(d)
(A)	i	ii	iv	iii
(B)	iii	iv	ii	i
(C)	iii	ii	iv	i
(D)	ii	iv	i	iii

101. Give the following in sequence according to the year of their first publication :

(i) Bibliographic Classification

(ii) Universal Decimal Classification

(iii) Library of Congress Classification

(iv) Colon Classification

Codes :

(A) ii iii i iv (B) iv ii iii i

(C) i iii ii iv (D) iii ii iv i

102. Which one of the following is not the feature of H-index ?

(A) Mathematically simple index

(B) Applied to any level of aggregation

(C) Publication that are hardly ever cited don't influence it.

(D) Sensitive to performance change.

103. The intrinsic value of information lies in its

(A) Procurement

(B) Processing and Storage

(C) Communication and Retrieval

(D) Usage

104. Which of the following web resource for LIS has been compiled by academic librarians of universities of California ?

(A) Infomine

(B) Internet Public Library

(C) Internet Library for Librarians

(D) Current Informed Librarian

105. Who developed the sense making approach for human information behaviour which is implemented in terms of four constituent elements?

(A) T.D. Wilson (B) B. Dervin

(C) D. Ellis (D) C.C. Kuhlthau

106. Which of the following is/are the major activities/ services of a library and networks in India ?

(i) Consortium purchase
(ii) Indexing of Internet resources
(iii) Document delivery
(iv) Staff training

Codes :

(A) (i), (iii), (iv) are correct.
(B) (ii), (iii), (iv) are correct.
(C) (i), (ii), (iii) are correct.
(D) (i), (ii), (iii), (iv) are correct.

107. Match the following :

	List - I	List - II
a.	Cumulative Book Index	i. D.K. Publishers & Distributors
b.	Publisher's weekly	ii. Whitaker
c.	Publishing in India	iii. Wilson
d.	Book seller	iv. R.R. Bowker

Codes :	**(a)**	**(b)**	**(c)**	**(d)**
(A)	ii	i	iv	iii
(B)	iii	iv	i	ii
(C)	i	iii	ii	iv
(D)	iv	ii	i	ii

108. Match the following :

List - I	List - II
a. Information should be as accurate as possible	i. Broadus
b. Get the best title on any subject but add midiocres that are well read.	ii. Haines
c. Know the community's character and interest	iii. McColvin
d. Consider the duration as well as intensity of the demand	iv. Drury

Codes :	**(a)**	**(b)**	**(c)**	**(d)**
(A)	iii	iv	ii	i
(B)	ii	iii	i	iv
(C)	i	ii	iv	iii
(D)	iv	i	iii	ii

109. Match the functions performed by different layers of OSI model :

List - I	**List - II**
a. Delivery of Packets from source of destination	i. Application layer
b. Data transmission rate	ii. Data link layer
c. Access to network resources	iii. Network layer
d. Provide hop-to-pop delivery	iv. Physical layer

Codes :	**(a)**	**(b)**	**(c)**	**(d)**
(A)	i	iii	ii	iv
(B)	ii	iv	i	iii
(C)	iii	iv	i	ii
(D)	iii	i	iv	ii

110. Match the following :

List - I	**List - II**
a. Behaviour studies	i. Extent of use of facilities/services
b. Use studies	ii. Pattern of Science communication
c. User studies	iii. Interaction of user with communication system
d. Information flow studies	iv. Use of communication medium

Codes :	(a)	(b)	(c)	(d)
(A)	i	iv	ii	iii
(B)	iii	iv	i	ii
(C)	ii	iii	i	iv
(D)	ii	iv	iii	i

111. A rubber stamp impressed on the verso of title page giving information concerning the records and processing of each individual book acquired is called
    (A) Book stamp (B) Process stamp
    (C) Date stamp (D) Accession stamp

112. Which law states that "An information retrieval system will tend not to be used whenever it is more painful and trouble some for a customer to have information than for him not to have it" ?
    (A) Bradford's Law (B) Mooer's Law
    (C) Ziff's Law (D) Lotka's Law

113. Who is the compiler of Web- Bibliography of Rabindranath Tagore ?
    (A) Bengal Library Association
    (B) RRRLF
    (C) National Library of India
    (D) IASLIC

114. Who are the publishers of 'Year Book on Human Rights' ?
    (A) United Nations
    (B) Ministry of Law, Govt. of India
    (C) Europa Publishers
    (D) R.R. Bowker

115. ASTINFO stands for
    (A) Asian Scientific and Technological Information Network

(B) Association of Scientific and Technological Information Scientists in Asia

(C) International Network for Exchange of Science and Technology Information

(D) Regional Network for the Exchange of Information and Experience in Science and Technology in Asia and the Pacific

116. A characteristic in which information tends to leak and the more it leaks, the more we have, is

(A) Synergetic characteristics

(B) Diffusive characteristics

(C) Compressible characteristics

(D) Shareable characteristics

117. Which of the following facilitate informal communication on the web ?

(i) Split Screens (ii) Chat

(iii) Wikis (iv) RSS feeds

Codes :

(A) (i) & (iii) are correct

(B) (ii) & (iii) are correct

(C) (iii) & (iv) are correct

(D) (i) & (ii) are correct

118. Match the following :

List - I	List - II
a. Outdated Information	i. Information Diffusion
b. Condensed Information	ii. Obsolete Information
c. Message	iii. Compressible Information
d. Vintage model	iv. Understanding

Codes :	**(a)**	**(b)**	**(c)**	**(d)**
(A)	iv	iii	ii	i
(B)	i	ii	iv	iii
(C)	iii	iv	ii	i
(D)	ii	iii	iv	i

119. Match the following :

List - I	**List - II**
a. Technique for identifying the theme of a document	i. Cataloguing
b. Prussian Instruction	ii. Standard for encoding data on CD-ROM
c. ISO-9960	iii. Data Transmission Speed
d. Baud	iv. Bibliographic coupling

Codes :	**(a)**	**(b)**	**(c)**	**(d)**
(A)	iv	i	ii	iii
(B)	i	ii	iii	iv
(C)	ii	iii	iv	i
(D)	iii	ii	i	iv

120. Match the following :

List - I	**List - II**
a. Maurice B. Line	i. Resource Management in Academic Libraries
b. David Baker	ii. Planning Academic and Research Library Buildings
c. Peter Brophy	iii. Academic Library Management
d. K. D. Metcalf	iv. The Academic Libraries

Codes :	(a)	(b)	(c)	(d)
(A)	iii	i	iv	ii
(B)	i	ii	iii	iv
(C)	iv	i	ii	iii
(D)	ii	iii	i	iv

121. **Assertion (A) :** India's contribution to LIS literatures is decreasing.

Reason (R) : Authors find it more convenient to get their articles published in open access journals.

Codes :

(A) Both (A) and (R) are true.

(B) (A) is false, but (R) is true.

(C) Both (A) and (R) are false.

(D) (A) is true but (R) is false.

122. Name the scientist who said that Information Science is cluster of many disciplines where in the central core is 'Information'.

(A) B.C. Brooks (B) Fritz Machlup

(C) Daniel Bell (D) N.J. Belkin

123. Which approach of information is not given by Wersig and Neveling ?

(A) Structural Approach

(B) Knowledge Approach

(C) Meaning Approach

(D) Technique Approach

124. Which of the following citation style manuals are from the same publisher ?

(i) A.P.A. (ii) Turabian

(iii) Chicago (iv) M.L.A.

Codes :

(A) (i) and (ii) are correct.

(B) (ii) and (iii) are correct.

(C) (iii) and (iv) are correct.

(D) (ii) and (iv) are correct

125. An indispensable function of Thesaurus is to

(i) Knowledge Classification

(ii) Grouping the words together according to similarity of meaning

(iii) Representation of Relationship between concepts

(iv) Knowledge Engineering

Codes :

(A) (i) and (ii) are correct.

(B) (ii) and (iii) are correct.

(C) (iii) and (iv) are correct.

(D) (i) and (iv) are correct.

126. Which of the following are the models of communication ?

(i) Economic Theory Model

(ii) Stock Adjustment Model

(iii) Shanon Weaver Model

(iv) Schramm Model

Codes :

(A) (iii) and (iv) are correct.

(B) (ii) and (iii) are correct.

(C) (i) and (ii) are correct.

(D) (ii) and (iv) are correct.

127. Match the following :

	List - I	**List - II**
a.	User Education	i. James IWyer
b.	Conservative, Liberal and Moderate Theory of Reference Service	ii. Patricia B. Knapp
c.	Minimum, Middling and Maximum Theories of Reference Service	iii. Eugene P. Sheehy
d.	Guide to Reference Book	iv. Samuel Rothstein

Codes :	**(a)**	**(b)**	**(c)**	**(d)**
(A)	ii	i	iv	iii
(B)	i	ii	iv	iii
(C)	iii	ii	iv	i
(D)	iv	iii	i	ii

128. Match the following :

	List - I	**List - II**
a.	Encyclopaedia of Associations	i. Secondary sources
b.	Whitaker's Almanac	ii. Primary sources
c.	LISA	iii. Directories
d.	Economic Times	iv. Yearbooks

Codes :	**(a)**	**(b)**	**(c)**	**(d)**
(A)	iii	iv	i	ii
(B)	iv	iii	i	ii
(C)	ii	i	iv	iii
(D)	i	iv	iii	ii

129. Match the following :

List - I	List - II
a. Books in Print	i. National Bibliography
b. Social Science : A Bibliography of Doctoral Dissertations	ii. Trade Bibliography
c. Asian Social Science Bibliography	iii. National & Trade Bibliography
d. Cumulative Book Index	iv. Subject Bibliography

Codes :	**(a)**	**(b)**	**(c)**	**(d)**
(A)	ii	i	iv	iii
(B)	i	iii	ii	iv
(C)	iv	i	ii	iii
(D)	iii	ii	i	iv

130. Match the following :

List - I	List - II
a. Dictionary	i. Foreign Language
b. Glossary	ii. Synonymous terms
c. Thesaurus	iii. Words, Synonyms
d. Lexicon	iv. Specific subjects

Codes :	**(a)**	**(b)**	**(c)**	**(d)**
(A)	iii	iv	ii	i
(B)	iv	iii	i	ii
(C)	i	ii	iv	iii
(D)	ii	iv	iii	i

131. **Assertion (A) :** In the study of History, as an academic discipline, a primary source is an artefact, a document, a recording or other source of information that was created during the event or

immediately after the event.

Reason (R) : Primary sources are considered as original material or evidences about the topic and are fundamental to history.

Codes :

(A) (A) is true, but (R) is false.

(B) (A) is false, but (R) is true.

(C) Both (A) and (R) are true.

(D) Both (A) and (R) are false.

132. **Assertion (A) :** Indian National Bibliography is the most comprehensive source of Indian publications.

Reason (R) : National Library of Kolkata is entitled to receive one copy of each Indian publication under Delivery of Book Act.

Codes :

(A) (A) is true, but (R) is false.

(B) (A) is false, but (R) is true.

(C) Both (A) and (R) are true.

(D) Both (A) and (R) are false.

133. **Assertion (A) :** According to Horton and Merchant, information is a commodity like other resources.

Reason (R) : Information is a tangible commodity.

Codes :

(A) (A) is true, but (R) is false.

(B) Both (A) and (R) are false.

(C) Both (A) and (R) are true.

134. **Assertion (A) :** Newspaper Digests are the best sources of information to get current and authentic information like books.

Reason (R) : These sources are compiled by going through various newspapers.

Codes :

(A) Both (A) and (R) are true.

(B) (A) is partially true but (R) is true.

(C) Both (A) and (R) are false.

(D) (A) is true but (R) is partially true.

135. **Assertion (A) :** Encyclopaedias have been regarded as the substitute of all categories of reference sources as these provide all types of information.

Reason (R) : Encyclopaedias provide comprehensive information on all aspects which otherwise are scattered in different categories of reference sources.

Codes :

(A) (R) is true but (A) is false.

(B) Both (A) and (R) are true.

(C) (A) is true but (R) is false.

(D) Both (A) and (R) are false.

136. **Assertion (A) :** Information is commodity.

Reason (R) : Commodity is a marketable item produced to satisfy human wants or needs.

Codes :

(A) (A) is false, and (R) is true.

(B) (R) is false and (A) is true.

(C) Both (A) and (R) are false.

(D) Both (A) and (R) are true.

137. The important methods of measuring impact factor of any information retrieval system are :

(i) Expression Rate (ii) Precision Rate

(iii) Recall Rate (iv) Depression Rate

Codes:

(A) (i) and (iii) are correct.

(B) (ii) and (iv) are correct.

(C) (ii) and (iii) are correct.

(D) (iii) and (iv) are correct.

138. Which of the following are standard TQM tools ?

(i) Pie chart (ii) Zigzag chart

(iii) Fishbone diagram (iv) Pareto chart

Codes:

(A) (i), (iv) are correct.

(B) (ii), (iii), (iv) are correct.

(C) (i), (iii), (iv) are correct.

(D) (iii), (iv) are correct.

139. Which of the following organizations are contributing to the implementation of standards for networked information system ?

(i) CNI (ii) W3C

(iii) IANA (iv) IEEE

Codes:

(A) (i) and (iii) are correct.

(B) (ii) and (iv) are correct.

(C) (ii) and (iii) are correct.

(D) (i), (ii) are correct.

140. **Assertion (A) ;** The value of information depends on its age and the time it is sold.

Reason (R) : Newer information tends to have more value.

Codes :

(A) Both (A) and (R) are true.

(B) Both (A) and (R) are false.

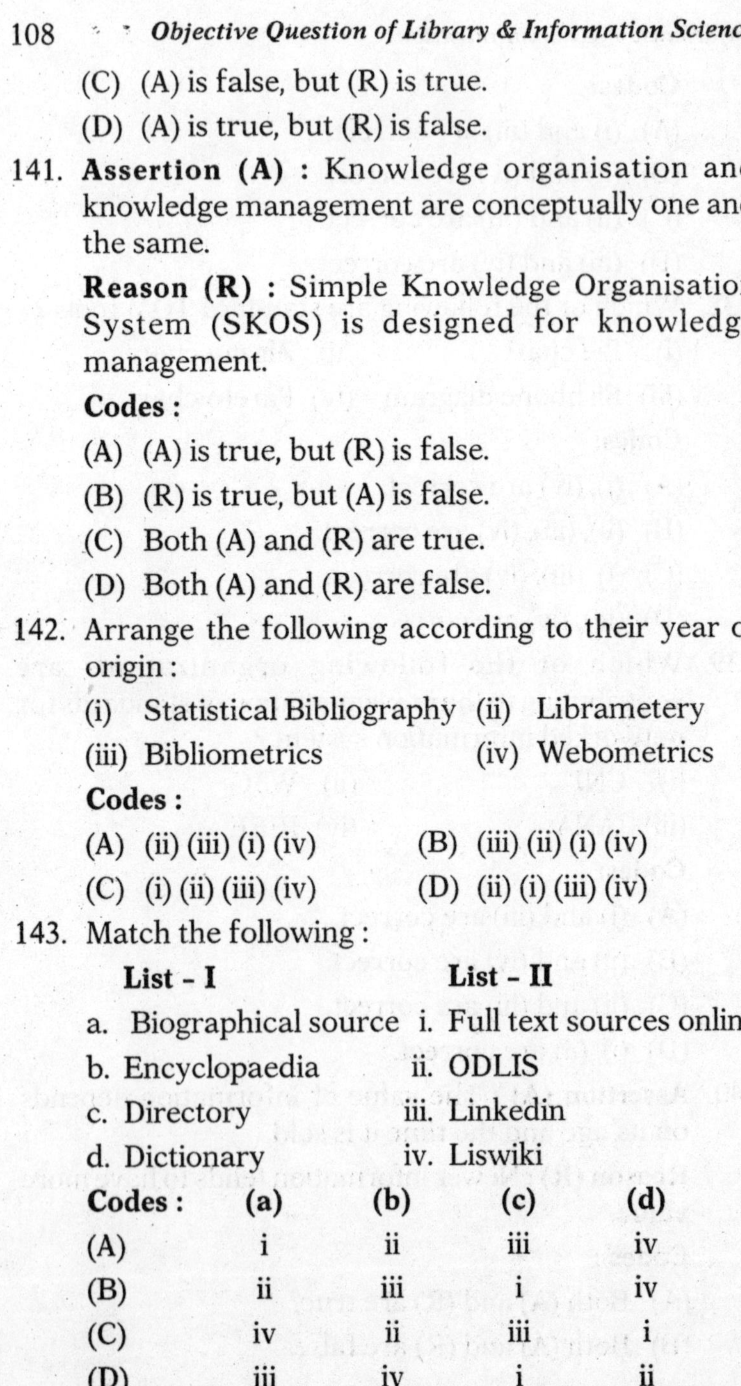

(C) (A) is false, but (R) is true.

(D) (A) is true, but (R) is false.

141. **Assertion (A) :** Knowledge organisation and knowledge management are conceptually one and the same.

Reason (R) : Simple Knowledge Organisation System (SKOS) is designed for knowledge management.

Codes :

(A) (A) is true, but (R) is false.

(B) (R) is true, but (A) is false.

(C) Both (A) and (R) are true.

(D) Both (A) and (R) are false.

142. Arrange the following according to their year of origin :

(i) Statistical Bibliography (ii) Librametery

(iii) Bibliometrics (iv) Webometrics

Codes :

(A) (ii) (iii) (i) (iv) (B) (iii) (ii) (i) (iv)

(C) (i) (ii) (iii) (iv) (D) (ii) (i) (iii) (iv)

143. Match the following :

List - I	**List - II**
a. Biographical source	i. Full text sources online
b. Encyclopaedia	ii. ODLIS
c. Directory	iii. Linkedin
d. Dictionary	iv. Liswiki

Codes :	**(a)**	**(b)**	**(c)**	**(d)**
(A)	i	ii	iii	iv
(B)	ii	iii	i	iv
(C)	iv	ii	iii	i
(D)	iii	iv	i	ii

144. A non-linear model of information seeking behaviour was presented by

(A) T.D. Wilson (B) Ellis

(C) Kulthou (D) Allen Foster

145. What type of bibliography is 'Indian National Bibliography' ?

(A) Enumerative (B) Analytical

(C) Descriptive (D) Textual

146. Which of the following facilitate formal communication on the web ?

i. Wikis ii. Chat

iii. RSS feeds iv. Split screens

Codes :

(A) i & ii are correct. (B) ii &iii are correct.

(C) i & iii are correct. (D) iii & iv are correct.

147. Which of the following source(s) you refer to get information on old namefor 'Zaire' ?

i. Encyclopaedias ii. Yearbooks

iii. Gazetteers iv. Directories

Codes :

(A) (i) and (ii) are correct.

(B) (i), (ii) and (iii) are correct.

(C) (i) and (iii) are correct.

(D) (ii), (iii) and (iv) are correct.

148. Which of the following methods are adopted for offering information literacy ?

i. Stand alone course

ii. Integrated with curriculum

iii. Online course

iv. Internship

Codes :

(A) i and ii (B) i, ii and iii

(C) ii and iv (D) i, ii and iv

149. Match the following :

List - I	List - II
a. Information Literacy Competency Standards for Higher Education	i. IFLA
b. Seven Pillars of Information literacy	ii. CAUL
c. Guidelines on Information Literacy for Life Long Learning	iii. ACRL
d. Information Literacy Working Group	iv. SCONUL

Codes :	(a)	(b)	(c)	(d)
(A)	iii	iv	i	ii
(B)	iv	ii	iii	i
(C)	iii	i	ii	iv
(D)	ii	iii	i	iv

150. Match the following :

List - I	List - II
a. Behaviour Science	i. Cognitive Process of Information
b. Philosophical Studies	ii. Studies on Epistomology
c. Ontology	iii. Information Processing in living things
d. Biological Science	iv. Study of nature of existence

Codes :	**(a)**	**(b)**	**(c)**	**(d)**
(A)	iv	iii	i	ii
(B)	iii	ii	iv	i
(C)	ii	i	iii	iv
(D)	i	ii	iv	iii

151. Match the following for locating the information :

List - I	**List - II**
a. Information on recent Nobel Prize winners	i. Bibliographic Service
b. Current developments in Library & Information Science	ii. Indexing Services
c. Books on Economic Policies of India	iii. Trend Sources
d. Articles on Cloud Computing	iv. Digest Services

Codes :	**(a)**	**(b)**	**(c)**	**(d)**
(A)	iv	iii	i	ii
(B)	iii	i	iv	ii
(C)	ii	iii	iv	i
(D)	i	ii	iii	iv

152. **Assertion (A) :** Information Literacy is a technique and skill known by the information literate for utilizing the wide range of information sources and tools.

Reason (R) : It discourages the use of libraries and information centres and makes the patron independent in identifying, locating and using information sources without depending upon an intermediary.

Codes :

(A) Both (A) and (R) true.

(B) Both (A) and (R) are false.

(C) (A) is true, but (R) is false.

(D) (A) is false, but (R) is true.

153. Which information theory focuses on the purpose of communication is, to inform, instruct or motivate the receiver ?

(A) Shannon's Theory (B) Weaver's Theory

(C) Ackoff's Theory (D) Yovit's Theory

154. 'Noise' in Information retrieval is due to

(A) Precision

(B) Recall

(C) Relevant Information

(D) Redundant Information

155. Whose model of communication of knowledge suggests that communication is an open system ?

(A) G. Garbner

(B) Juger Hebermans

(C) Shannon & Weaver

(D) M. Foucault

156. 'Trans Border Data Flow' means

(A) Exchange of documentsbetween countries

(B) Free flow of informationbetween countries

(C) Flow of information betweencountries

(D) Exchange of electronicinformation between countries

157. Which of the following are reasons for obsolescence of information ?

(i) Information is considered invalid.

(ii) Information is valid but mostly available online.

(iii) Works are extensively cited.

(iv) Information is valid butinadequate for exploration.

Codes :

(A) (i) and (ii) are correct.

(B) (ii) and (iii) are correct.

(C) (i) and (iv) are correct.

(D) (ii) and (iv) are correct.

158. Which of the following are news summaries ?

(i) Data India

(ii) Times of India Index

(iii) New York Times Index

(iv) Asian Recorder

Codes :

(A) (i), (ii) and (iii) are correct.

(B) (ii) and (iii) are correct.

(C) (ii) (iii) and (iv) are correct.

(D) (i) and (iv) are correct.

159. Which of the following are not the Models of communication ?

(i) Vintage Model (ii) Lasswell's Model

(iii) Epidemic Model (iv) Garbner's Model

Codes :

(A) (i) & (iv) are correct.

(B) (ii) & (iii) are correct.

(C) (i) & (iii) are correct.

(D) (iii) & (iv) are correct.

160. Match the following :

	List - I	List - II
a.	Phenomenon	i. Physical Media for grouping of Information
b.	Spectrum	ii. Facts or Occurrence
c.	Modes	iii. Transfer Process
d.	Diffusion	iv. A broad range of varied but relatedideas

Codes :	**(a)**	**(b)**	**(c)**	**(d)**
(A)	i	iii	iv	ii
(B)	ii	iv	i	iii
(C)	ii	iii	iv	i
(D)	iv	i	iii	ii

161. Match the following :

List - I	List - II
a. Union Catalogue	i. Primary sources
b. Pamphlets & Brochures	ii. Unpublished sources
c. Indexing & Abstracting Sources	iii. Tertiary sources
d. Memoirs of diaries	iv. Secondary sources

Codes :	**(a)**	**(b)**	**(c)**	**(d)**
(A)	iv	iii	ii	i
(B)	ii	iv	iii	i
(C)	iii	i	iv	ii
(D)	i	ii	iv	iii

162. Name the characteristics of information in which the more information we have, the more we use, the more it becomes useful.

(A) Synergetic Characteristics

(B) Diffusive Characteristics

(C) Compressible Characteristics

(D) Shareable Characteristics

163. Identify the correct sequence of elements of communication :

(A) Channel-Decoder-Destination-Encoder-Message-Source

(B) Decoder-Channel-Destination-Message-Source-Encoder

(C) Source-Encoder-Message-Channel-Decoder-Destination

(D) Encoder-Decoder-Source-Message-Channel-Destination

164. From which year the Encyclopaedia Britannica ceased its print version ?

(A) 2009 (B) 2010

(C) 2011 (D) 2012

165. Which of the following are features of 'Open Journal System' ?

i. License to access content

ii. Access restricted to limited group

iii. Online submission

iv. Subscription module with delayed open access options

Codes :

(A) i and ii are correct.

(B) ii and iii are correct.

(C) iii and iv are correct.

(D) ii and iv are correct.

166. What are the approaches to plagiarism check of academic publications ?

i. String matching ii. Bag of words analysis

iii. Citation analysis iv. Parse trees

Codes :

(A) ii, iv are correct. (B) i, ii, iii are correct.

(C) i, iv are correct. (D) i, iii, iv are correct.

167. Identify the abilities of an information literate person :

i. the ability to find information

ii. the ability to prepare bibliographic description of information

iii. the ability to use information

iv. the ability to evaluate information

Codes :

(A) i, ii, iii are correct. (B) i, iii, iv are correct.

(C) i, ii, iv are correct. (D) ii, iii, iv are correct.

168. Which of the following are threats to information security ?

i. Personal firewalls ii. Compromise to IPR

iii. Anti-spyware iv. Acts of espionage

Codes :

(A) i, ii, iii are correct. (B) ii, iii are correct.

(C) ii, iv are correct. (D) ii, iii, iv are correct.

169. Match the following :

List - I	**List - II**
a. Informing about best books	i. Support service
b. Guidance to use citation manual	ii. Bibliography
c. Providing prints for downloads	iii. Readers advisory
d. Providing list of URLs	iv. Users education

Codes :	**(a)**	**(b)**	**(c)**	**(d)**
(A)	ii	iii	i	iv
(B)	iii	iv	i	ii
(C)	iv	ii	iii	i
(D)	ii	iv	iii	i

170. Match the following :

	List - I	**List - II**
a.	Market segmentation	i. User behaviour
b.	Consumer analysis	ii. Market mix
c.	Market positioning	iii. Category of users
d.	Market program	iv. Prioritising users

Codes :	**(a)**	**(b)**	**(c)**	**(d)**
(A)	i	iii	ii	iv
(B)	iii	i	iv	ii
(C)	ii	iv	i	iii
(D)	iv	ii	iii	i

171. With whom would you relate 'Dissertation Abstracts International'?

(A) Pro-quest (B) Springer
(C) Emerald (D) OUP

172. When was Encyclopedia Britannica first published?

(A) 1758 (B) 1768
(C) 1865 (D) 1875

173. Which one of the following reference source attempts to explain theliterary terms and works ?

(A) Oxford Dictionary of Quotations
(B) Who's Who of Indian Writers
(C) Information please Almanac
(D) Benet's Reader's Encyclopedia

ANSWERS

1. B	2. D	3. B	4. D	5. A/B	6. B
7. C	8. B	9. A	10. D	11. D	12. B
13. C	14. A	15. C	16. A	17. B	18. C
19. A	20. C	21. C	22. A	23. C	24. D
25. B	26. A	27. A	28. D	29. C	30. C
31. A	32. A	33. C	34. B	35. A	36. B
37. C	38. B	39. D	40. A	41. B	42. A
43. D	44. C	45. B	46. B	47. B	48. C
49. C	50. C	51. C	52. A	53. B	54. A
55. D	56. B	57. A	58. D	59. B	60. A
61. B	62. C	63. A	64. C	65. A	66. A
67. B	68. A	69. C	70. D	71. B	72. B
73. A	74. A	75. C	76. A	77. C	78. D
79. C	80. B	81. C	82. A	83. B	84. A
85. D	86. A	87. C	88. D	89. C	90. B
91. A	92. C	93. D	94. D	95. C	96. D
97. A	98. C	99. B	100. C	101. D	102. D
103. D	104. A	105. B	106. A	107. B	108. A
109. C	110. B	111. D	112. B	113. B	114. A
115. D	116. B	117. D	118. D	119. A	120. A
121. B	122. B	123. D	124. B	125. B	126. A
127. A	128. A	129. A	130. A	131. C	132. B
133. A	134. B	135. C	136. D	137. C	138. C
139. D	140. C	141. D	142. C	143. D	144. D
145. A	146. C	147. B	148. B	149. A	150. D
151. A	152. C	153. C	154. D	155. A	156. C/D
157. C	158. D	159. C	160. B	161. C	162. A
163. C	164. D	165. C	166. B	167. B	168. C
169. B	170. B	171. A	172. B	173. D	

4

Information Processing

1. Which of the following are 'Open Source Content Management Systems' ?

   (i) Drupal (ii) Atex
   (iii) Joomla (iv) OpenCms

   Codes :

   (A) (i), (ii) and (iv) are correct
   (B) (i), (ii) and (iii) are correct
   (C) (ii), (iii) and (iv) are correct
   (D) (i), (iii) and (iv) are correct

2. Which of the following are not styles of citation ?

   (i) Anglo American Cataloguing Rules
   (ii) MLA Handbook for Writers of Research Papers
   (iii) Chicago Manual of Style
   (iv) Little Science Big Science

   Codes :

   (A) (i) and (ii) are correct
   (B) (iii) and (iv) are correct
   (C) (i) and (iv) are correct
   (D) (ii) and (iii) are correct

3. **Assertion (A) :** Abstracting services facilitate literature review.

   Reason (R) : Literature review summarises major findings of various studies.

   Codes :

   (A) (A) is true, but (R) is false
   (B) (A) is false, but (R) is true
   (C) Both (A) and (R) are true
   (D) Both (A) and (R) are false

4. "Prevention of Cholera in India" generates following index terms according to modified 'Chain Indexing', arrange themin correct order

   (i) India (ii) Cholera
   (iii) Disease (iv) Treatment
   (v) Medicine

   Codes :

   (A) (iii), (iv), (i), (ii), (v)
   (B) (ii), (i), (iii), (iv), (v)
   (C) (iv), (iii), (ii), (v), (i)
   (D) (i), (iii), (iv), (v), (ii)

5. Match the following :

List - I	**List - II**
(a) User orientation	(i) Bibliographic service
(b) Information repackaging	(ii) Reference service
(c) Translation	(iii) Digest series
(d) Indexing	(iv) Support service

Codes :	**(a)**	**(b)**	**(c)**	**(d)**
(A)	(i)	(iv)	(iii)	(ii)
(B)	(iii)	(ii)	(i)	(iv)
(C)	(iv)	(i)	(ii)	(iii)
(D)	(ii)	(iii)	(iv)	(i)

6. Match the following :

List - I	**List - II**
(a) Hubs	(i) A physical layer device used to interconnect the media segments of an extended network
(b) Repeater	(ii) A physical layer device that connects Multiple computer seach via a dedicated cable
(c) Bus Topology	(iii) Multiple bridges known for transfer of Data between different parts
(d) Switches	(iv) A straight line data highway that carries network information from one network station to another

Codes :	**(a)**	**(b)**	**(c)**	**(d)**
(A)	(iii)	(iv)	(ii)	(i)
(B)	(ii)	(i)	(iv)	(iii)
(C)	(iv)	(i)	(iii)	(ii)
(D)	(i)	(iii)	(ii)	(iv)

7. Inference Engine is a part of which information system ?
   (A) Management information System
   (B) Decision Support System
   (C) Expert System
   (D) Open System

8. Even though 'Xerography' is a photocopying method, but it is called
   (A) Diazographic (B) Thermographic
   (C) Electrofax (D) Electrostatic

9. 'CODEN' is connected with
   (A) Books (B) Serials
   (C) Reports (D) Gray Literature

10. Radio Frequency Identification is used in library for:
    (i) Circulation of Documents
    (ii) Cataloguing of Documents
    (iii) Security of Documents
    (iv) Acquisition of Documents

    Codes :
    (A) (i) and (ii) are correct
    (B) (ii) and (iv) are correct
    (C) (iii) and (ii) are correct
    (D) (i) and (iii) are correct

11. A version of KWIC augmented with author/name is called
    (A) WADEX (B) KWOC
    (C) KWAC (D) KWIC

12. **Assertion (A) :** Knowledge is growing exponentially.
    Reason (R) : Number of researchers have increased.

    Codes :
    (A) Both (A) & (R) are true.
    (B) Both (A) and (R) are false.
    (C) (A) is false but (R) is true.
    (D) (A) is true but (R) is false.

13. Arrange the following according to their year of origin :
    (i) UNICODE (ii) XML
    (iii) HTML (iv) SGML
    Codes :
    (A) (iv), (iii), (i), (ii) (B) (iii), (iv), (ii), (i)
    (C) (ii), (iv), (i), (iii) (D) (i), (ii), (iii), (iv)
14. Metadata Dublin core refers to
    (A) Data elements in database
    (B) Bibliographic elements indatabase
    (C) Field elements in database
    (D) Subject elements in database
15. The physical and chemical treatment of materials to retard their further deterioration refers to
    (A) Conservation (B) Rescuing
    (C) Prevention (D) Restoration
16. Read the following example and indicate the name of the indexing system used : 'Remuneration of teachers in French universities.'
    The index headings are set as the following two lines:
    France
    Universities → Teachers → Remuneration
    Universities → France → Teachers → Remuneration
    (A) Chain procedure (B) POPSI
    (C) PRECIS (D) KWIC
17. NICRYS is information system for
    (A) Machine tools (B) Food science
    (C) Crystallography (D) Drugs
18. Report on 'the development of digital libraries of the past decade' is categorized as

(A) Review Report (B) Trend Report
(C) Research Report (D) State of the art report

19. Digital library function in corporate :
    (i) Creating and capturing
    (ii) Storage and management
    (iii) Search and access
    (iv) Abstracting and reviewing

    Codes :
    (A) (i), (ii) and (iii) are correct.
    (B) (i), (iii) and (iv) are correct.
    (C) (ii), (iii) and (iv) are correct.
    (D) (i), (ii) and (iv) are correct.

20. Vocabulary in a database is controlled by :
    (i) Thesaurus files (ii) Import files
    (iii) Standard files (iv) Authority files

    Codes :
    (A) (i) and (ii) are correct.
    (B) (iii) and (iv) are correct.
    (C) (i) and (iii) are correct.
    (D) (ii) and (iii) are correct.

21. CCF for bibliographic record referst o
    (i) Data transfer
    (ii) Data storage
    (iii) Standard tags of data identification
    (iv) Formatting of records

    Codes :
    (A) (i) and (iii) are correct.
    (B) (i), (ii) and (iv) are correct.
    (C) (ii) and (iii) are correct.
    (D) (iii), (i) and (ii) are correct.

22. Magazines are suitable for
    (i) Leisure and entertainment
    (ii) Scholarly information
    (iii) Popular information
    (iv) Subject information

    Codes :
    (A) (i), (ii) and (iii) are correct.
    (B) (ii), (iii) and (iv) are correct.
    (C) (i) and (iii) are correct.
    (D) (ii) and (iv) are correct.

23. Which of the following are the fundamental conditions for a subject to be protected by IPR ?
    (i) The work must be original
    (ii) The work must be man made
    (iii) The work must be intelligible
    (iv) The work must be recorded/fixed

    Codes :
    (A) (i), (ii) and (iii) are correct.
    (B) (i), (iii) and (iv) are correct.
    (C) (ii), (iii) and (iv) are correct.
    (D) (i), (ii) and (iv) are correct.

24. **Assertion (A) :** E-publications have added enormous quantity of literature but adversely affected the quality of literature.

    Reason (R) : Present decade has accepted E-publication as channels of fast communication.

    Codes :
    (A) (A) is true (R) is false.
    (B) (A) is false, but (R) is correct.
    (C) Both (A) & (R) are false.
    (D) Both (A) & (R) are true.

25. **Assertion (A) :** Encyclopedias are not relevant for finding geographically information.

    Reason (R) : Encyclopedias are the substitute for all categories of reference sources.

    Codes :

    (A) (A) is false but (R) is true.

    (B) Both (A) and (R) are true.

    (C) Both (A) and (R) are false.

    (D) (A) is true but (R) is false.

26. What is the correct order of SCONUL's "Seven Pillar Model of Information Skills" ?

    (i) Recognise information need

    (ii) Construct strategies for locating

    (iii) Compare and evaluate

    (iv) Locate and access

    Codes :

    (A) (i), (ii), (iii), (iv) (B) (ii), (iii), (iv), (i)

    (C) (i), (ii), (iv), (iii) (D) (ii), (iii), (i), (iv)

27. Identify the correct order as per increasing data storage capacity :

    (A) CDROM, DVD, Cartridge, Blue Ray Disc

    (B) DVD, Cartridge, Blue Ray Disc, CDROM

    (C) Cartridge, CDROM, DVD, Blue Ray Disc

    (D) Blue Ray Disc, DVD, Cartridge, CDROM

28. Match the following :

List - I	List - II
a. Communication Barrier	i. Radio
b. Communication Medium	ii. Shanon & Weaver
c. Communication Model	iii. Video conferencing
d. Interactive Communication	iv. Noise

Codes :	**(a)**	**(b)**	**(c)**	**(d)**
(A)	i	ii	iii	iv
(B)	iv	i	ii	iii
(C)	ii	iii	iv	i
(D)	iii	ii	i	iv

29. Starting, Chaining, Browsing, Differentiating, Monitoring, Extracting, Verification and Ending are important stages of which information seeking behaviour model ?
   (A) Dervin's Model
   (B) Ellis Model
   (C) Marchionnini Model
   (D) Kuhlthan Model
30. What kind of arrangement is followed in LISA ?
   (A) Alphabetical (B) Chronological
   (C) Classified (D) Geographical
31. An online search in which all aspects of the records innatural language may be used as sought terms is
   (A) Alphabetical collateral search
   (B) Multi-aspect search
   (C) Free text searching
   (D) Streaming search
32. Which of the following is/are not database object(s)?
   (A) Tables (B) Queries
   (C) Relationships (D) Report
33. Name a technique used for searching sorted data in a database
   (A) Boolean operator (B) Inverting file
   (C) Indexing (D) Binary

34. The process of surrogation, repackaging and compaction of the primary literature that results in creation of secondary journals, is
    (A) Newsletter
    (B) Abstracting and Indexing Periodical
    (C) House Journals
    (D) Electronic Journal
35. One of the authorized user makes bulk downloading of a Journal using robots and consequently licensor blocks access of the journal. What may be the most appropriate action(s) that librarian should initiate ?
    (i) Cancellation of authentication of the said user.
    (ii) Asking the licensor for blocking up the access without prior information.
    (iii) Investigate and take corrective measures.
    (iv) Notify user community of user restrictions.

    Codes :
    (A) (ii), (iv) are correct.
    (B) (ii), (iii) are correct.
    (C) (i), (iii) are correct.
    (D) (i), (ii) are correct.
36. Which of the following activities are supported by UGC ?
    (i) Facilitating increased access to information.
    (ii) Monitoring the implementation of revised curriculum.
    (iii) Making policies for human resource development.
    (iv) Funding all academic libraries.

Codes :

(A) (i) and (ii) are correct.

(B) (i) and (iii) are correct.

(C) (ii) and (iii) are correct.

(D) (i) and (iv) are correct.

37. The alternatives and modifications to H-Index are

(i) I-index

(ii) Pure-h Index

(iii) Scimgo Journal Rank

(iv) European Impact Factor

Codes :

(A) (i) & (iii) are correct.

(B) (i) & (ii) are correct.

(C) (i) and (iv) are correct.

(D) (ii) & (iii) are correct.

38. Digitization of various cultural resources is possible through

(i) Scanners

(ii) Digital cameras

(iii) Video cameras

(iv) Smart & Mobile phones

Codes :

(A) (i), (ii) are correct.

(B) (iv), (iii) are correct.

(C) (iii), (iv) are correct.

(D) (i), (ii), (iii) & (iv) are correct.

39. Match the following :

	List - I		List - II
a.	INFLIBNET	i.	Digital Library
b.	INDEST-AICTE	ii.	Resource aggregator
c.	DELNET	iii.	E-consortia
d.	e-Gyankosh	iv.	Organisation

Codes :	(a)	(b)	(c)	(d)
(A)	i	ii	iii	iv
(B)	iv	iii	ii	i
(C)	iii	ii	i	iv
(D)	ii	iii	iv	i

40. Match the booksagainst their authors :

	List - I		List - II
a.	Introduction to Modern Information Retrieval (McGraw Hill)	i.	H. Borko & C. Bernier
b.	Indexing Concepts and Methods (Academic Press)	ii.	G. Salton & M.J. McGill
c.	Thesaurus Construction : A Practical Manual (Aslib)	iii.	J.E. Rowley & R. Hartley
d.	Organising Knowledge : An Introduction to Managing Access to Information (Ashgate)	iv.	J. Aitchison & A. Gilchrist

Codes :	(a)	(b)	(c)	(d)
(A)	i	ii	iii	iv
(B)	ii	i	iv	iii
(C)	iv	i	ii	iii
(D)	iii	i	iv	ii

41. **Assertion (A) :** Colon classification is popular in online catalogues.

    Reason (R) : Traditional classification systems are used in online searching advantageously.

    Codes :

    (A) (A) is true, but (R) is false.

    (B) Both (A) & (R) are true, but (R) is not the correct explanation of (A).

    (C) (A) is false, but (R) is true.

    (D) Both (A) & (R) are true.

42. **Assertion (A) :** Technical writing standards, style manuals and citation standards are very essential in structuring the research report.

    Reason (R) : Value will get enhanced by standardising the structure of research report.

    Codes :

    (A) (A) is true and (R) is partially true.

    (B) Both (A) and (R) are true.

    (C) Both (A) and (R) are false.

    (D) (A) is true and (R) is false.

43. **Assertion (A) :** The encouraging environment of all time, full reading halls with the students in the libraries is diminishing day by day.

    Reason (R) : All the reading material is easily available and accessible on Internet to all the students.

    Codes :

    (A) Both (A) and (R) are true.

    (B) Both (A) and (R) are false.

    (C) (A) is true, but (R) is false.

    (D) (A) is false, but (R) is true.

44. **Assertion (A) :** There is a tremendous increase in number of doctoral degrees being awarded in library and information science.

Reason (R) : Any academician in LIS holding a Ph.D degree is entitled to supervise research programme.

Codes :

(A) (A) is true and (R) is partially true.

(B) Both (A) and (R) are true.

(C) Both (A) and (R) are false.

(D) (A) is false and (R) is true.

45. **Assertion (A) :** Maximizing the access to information in higher education is the motto of UGC-INFONET Project.

Reason (R) : The financial grants of UGC-INFONET are not being fully utilized by all University Libraries for the assigned purpose.

Codes :

(A) Both (A) and (R) are false.

(B) (A) is true and (R) is partially true.

(C) (A) is true and (R) is false.

(D) (A) is false and (R) is true.

46. **Assertion (A) :** The effective reprographic service in libraries indirectly demotivates the user for tearing/theft of reading material.

Reason (R) : The user gets the photocopy of reading materials free of cost.

Codes :

(A) (A) is false and (R) is true.

(B) Both (A) and (R) are true.

(C) (A) is true and (R) is false.

(D) Both (A) and (R) are false.

47. The distinct characteristic(s) ofdigital objects are
    (A) Physical Medium
    (B) Logical process
    (C) Conceptual recognition and transaction
    (D) All the above
48. METS stands for
    (A) Machine EncodedTransmission System
    (B) Metadata Encoded for Textual Sources
    (C) Machine Encoded Textual Standard
    (D) Metadata Encoding Transmission Standard
49. "Control, Disease, Malaria, Brain" indicates that it is
    (A) Raw Title (B) Expressive Title
    (C) Kernel Title (D) Transformed Title
50. A graphical representation using symbols to represent operations, data, flow, etc. is
    (A) Logical Chart
    (B) Flow Chart
    (C) System Flow Chart
    (D) Network Chart
51. The 12 rules for relational database were given by
    (A) E.F. Codd (B) Charles Babbage
    (C) James Weyer (D) Tim Berners Lee
52. Historical/Government records related to an organisation are maintained in
    (i) Archieves (ii) Museums
    (iii) Repositories (iv) Government libraries
    Codes :
    (A) (i) and (ii) are correct.
    (B) (ii) and (iii) are correct.
    (C) (i) and (iii) are correct.
    (D) (ii) and (iv) are correct.

53. Vocabulary in a database is controlled by

(i) Thesaurus files (ii) Dictionary files

(iii) Standard files (iv) Authority files

Codes :

(A) (i) and (ii) are correct.

(B) (iii) and (iv) are correct.

(C) (i) and (iii) are correct.

(D) (i) and (iv) are correct.

54. Which of the following are prohibited under copyright ?

(i) Downloading a document, printing multiple copies

(ii) Placing a copyright protected document on web-server

(iii) Downloading a document and save it in folder

(iv) Downloading a document with license to use and E-mailing it

Codes :

(A) (i), (iii) and (iv) are correct.

(B) (i), (ii) and (iii) are correct.

(C) (iii), (iv) and (ii) are correct.

(D) (i), (ii) and (iv) are correct.

55. Match the following :

List - I	**List - II**
a. 1st Law of Library Science	i. Real time access
b. 2nd Law of Library Science	ii. Search engine & subject gateways
c. 3rd Law of Library Science	iii. Web access to resources
d. 4th Law of Library Science	iv. Open access initiatives

Codes :	**(a)**	**(b)**	**(c)**	**(d)**
(A)	iii	iv	ii	i
(B)	iv	i	ii	iii
(C)	i	iii	ii	iv
(D)	ii	iv	i	iii

56. **Assertion (A) :** Library Science profession in India enjoys thestatus at par with medical, legaland management professions.

    Reason (R) : S.R. Ranganathan's contributions and teachings for Indian librarianship secured a status to the profession.

    Codes :

    (A) (A) is true, but (R) is false.

    (B) (A) is false, but (R) is true.

    (C) Both (A) and (R) are true.

    (D) Both (A) and (R) are false.

57. The "citation indexes" are now available online as

    (A) Web of Science (B) JCCC

    (C) Scopus (D) EBSC

58. Which among the following is free Audio book site?

    (A) Ebrary (B) Virtua

    (C) Librivox (D) Google Books

59. 'Open Journal Access System' in India is mainly managed by

    (A) NIC (B) CSIR

    (C) ICSSR (D) INFLIBNET

60. TKDL is developed and managed by

    (A) National Library and RRRLF

    (B) CSIR and RRRLF

    (C) CSIR and AYUSH

    (D) AYUSH and National Library

61. Which of the following guides are used in maintenance section of the library ?

(i) Gangway guides (ii) Shelf guides

(iii) Tier guides (iv) User guides

Codes :

(A) (i), (ii) and (iv) are correct.

(B) (i), (ii) and (iii) are correct.

(C) (ii), (iii) and (iv) are correct.

(D) (i), (iii) and (iv) are correct.

62. As per Voigt's study, which are the approaches of the scientists towards information ?

(i) Current (ii) Everybody

(iii) Exhaustive (iv) Browsing

Codes :

(A) (ii), (iii) and (iv) are correct.

(B) (i), (iii) and (iv) are correct.

(C) (i), (ii) and (iii) are correct.

(D) (i), (ii) and (iv) are correct.

63. Why to cite ?

(i) Acknowledging the source

(ii) Crediting the original ideas

(iii) Substantiate findings

(iv) For popularising cited sources

Codes :

(A) (i), (ii) and (iv) are correct.

(B) (i), (ii) and (iii) are correct.

(C) (ii), (iii) and (iv) are correct.

(D) All are correct.

64. Match the following :

List - I	List - II
a. Scientific Management	i. Max Weber
b. System School	ii. Mary Follett
c. Human Behaviour School	iii. Henry Fayol
d. Classical School	iv. Louis Brandeis

Codes :	**(a)**	**(b)**	**(c)**	**(d)**
(A)	iv	i	ii	iii
(B)	iv	ii	i	iii
(C)	ii	i	iii	iv
(D)	i	iv	ii	i

65. **Assertion (A) :** It would be logical to replace catalogue with metadata.

Reason (R) : Metadata is useful for organising and managing information resources.

Codes :

(A) (A) is false and (R) is true.

(B) (A) and (R) are true.

(C) (A) is true and (R) is false.

(D) (A) and (R) are false.

66. Which of the bibliometric law describes the frequency of publications by author ?

(A) Zipf's law (B) Bradford's law

(C) Lotka's law (D) None of the above

67. Indian patents on all areas are published in

(A) India : A reference annual

(B) Indian chemical patent index

(C) Gazette of India, Part-III

(D) None of the above

68. "World directory of sources of Patents" is published by
    (A) Bowker-Saur, U.S.A.
    (B) WIPO
    (C) Patent Information System, India
    (D) Derwent, London
69. 'Web of Science' covers
    (A) Sciences (B) Social Sciences
    (C) Arts of Humanities (D) All the above
70. Identification of an e-article and paying for full-text is known as
    (A) Pay-per-view (B) Consortium
    (C) Campus license (D) E-subscription
71. The formula $K(S) + \Delta I = K(S + \Delta S)$ for summation of information is propounded by
    (A) Claude Shannon (B) George Gerbner
    (C) Charles Osgood (D) Mandy Broo
72. "Pro Quest" is ________.
    (A) Traditional Commercial Publisher
    (B) Scholarly Society Publisher
    (C) Electronic Aggregator
    (D) Publisher of Higher Learning Institutions
73. Which of the following is/are part(s) of classified catalogue ?
    (A) An author-title file
    (B) Subject file arranged by library classification
    (C) An alphabetical index to the subject file
    (D) All of the above
74. Which one of the following is not an operation involved in quality circles ?

(A) Problem identification

(B) Problem selection

(C) Solution recommendation

(D) Problem shifting

75. In a database table, the category of information is called ______.

(A) Tuple (B) Field

(C) Record (D) All the above

76. MARC records contain

(i) Description of library materials

(ii) Searchable headings

(iii) Elements to organize collection

(iv) List of index terms

Codes :

(A) (i), (ii), (iii) are correct.

(B) (ii), (iii), (iv) are correct.

(C) (iii), (iv), (i) are correct.

(D) (iv), (i), (ii) are correct.

77. RDBMs are advantageous as they :

(i) Manage and Maintain

(ii) Represent data in the form of tables

(iii) Facilitate handling of objects rather than records

(iv) Are developed with mathematic theory of relations

Codes :

(A) (i), (iv) are correct. (B) (ii), (iii) are correct.

(C) (ii), (iv) are correct. (D) (iii), (iv) are correct.

78. Match the following :

List - I	List - II
a. Special library	i. Provides bibliographical services
b. Public library	ii. Conservation of knowledge
c. National library	iii. Popularisation of Govt. information
d. Academic library	iv. Critical compilation

Codes :	**(a)**	**(b)**	**(c)**	**(d)**
(A)	i	iii	iv	ii
(B)	ii	iv	i	iii
(C)	iii	iv	i	ii
(D)	iv	iii	i	ii

79. Match the following :

List - I	List - II
a. Information over load	i. Indexing and abstracting
b. Variation in quality and reliability	ii. Translation
c. Multiplicity of language	iii. Reviews and digests
d. Information scatter	iv. Alert services

Codes :	**(a)**	**(b)**	**(c)**	**(d)**
(A)	i	ii	iii	iv
(B)	iv	iii	ii	i
(C)	ii	iv	iii	i
(D)	iii	i	ii	i

80. Match the following :

List - I	List - II
a. Information Theory	i. Ogden and Richards
b. Theory of Signs	ii. Locke
c. Triadic Relationships	iii. Shannon
d. Doctrine of Signs	iv. Morris

Codes :	**(a)**	**(b)**	**(c)**	**(d)**
(A)	ii	iii	iv	i
(B)	iii	iv	i	ii
(C)	i	iii	iv	ii
(D)	ii	i	iii	iv

81. **Assertion (A) :** Colon classification is the most successful classification schemes in India.

Reason (R) : The most important factor behind the success of any classification scheme is the revision and publication of different editions at regular intervals.

Codes :

(A) Both (A) and (R) are true.

(B) (A) is true but (R) is false.

(C) (A) is false but (R) is true.

(D) Both (A) and (R) are false.

82. **Assertion (A) :** Scholar frequency to visit academic libraries has decreased tremendously over the period of last two decades.

Reason (R) : E-scholarly resources are easily accessible to everyone from anywhere anytime.

Codes :

(A) Both (A) and (R) are true.

(B) Both (A) and (R) are false.

(C) (A) is true, but (R) is false.

(D) (A) is false, but (R) is true.

83. **Assertion (A)** : H-index lacks sensitivity to performance changes.

Reason (R) : It can never decrease and is insensitive to number of citations received.

Codes :

(A) Both (A) and (R) are false.

(B) Both (A) and (R) are true.

(C) (A) is true but (R) is false.

(D) (A) is false, but (R) is true.

84. A Boolean query using only AND and NOT is

(A) Fuzzy query (B) Conjunctive query

(C) Routing query (D) Probabilistic query

85. Ontology is

(A) A Documentation service

(B) An Indexing method

(C) Classification of Internet based documents

(D) Cataloguing of Internet based documents

86. In colon classification, which mnemonic is displayed in the use of digit '4' as for pathology, disease, transport, hybrid etc. ?

(A) Seminal (B) Systematic

(C) Scheduled (D) Alphabetical

87. Name the similarity measure in which similarity of a document is adjusted such that the similarity of a document to itself is 1.

(A) Cosine measure

(B) Distance measure

(C) Swet's measure

(D) Normalised similarity measure

88. Which of the following are the core content of ISI web of knowledge ?

(i) Current Contents
(ii) ISI proceedings
(iii) Derwent Information Index
(iv) AGRICOLA

Codes :

(A) (i), (iv) and (iii) (B) (i), (ii) and (iii)
(C) (ii), (iii) and (iv) (D) (i), (ii) and (iv)

89. Arrange the following according to their year of emergence :

i. LISA
ii. Dissertation Abstracts International
iii. Indian Science Abstracts
iv. Indian Library & Information Science Abstracts

Codes :

(A) iii iv ii i (B) iv iii i ii
(C) ii i iii iv (D) i ii iii iv

90. In colon classification which indicator has been used for indicating interpolation ?

(A) Comma (B) Hyphen
(C) Astericks (D) Ampersand

91. What is Denudation ?

(A) Is dividing classes to decreasethe extension.
(B) Is dividing classes to increasethe extension.
(C) Is dividing classes to increase intension and decrease extension.
(D) Is dividing classes to decrease intension.

92. Pre co-ordinate Indexing system perceives :

(i) Syntax (ii) Semantic
(iii) Context (iv) Relation

Codes :

(A) (i) and (iv) are correct
(B) (i), (ii) and (iii) are correct
(C) (ii), (iii) and (iv) are correct
(D) (ii) and (iv) are correct

93. Which of the following are the basic components of expert system ?

(i) User interface
(ii) Knowledge base
(iii) Inference Mechanism
(iv) Schema

Codes :

(A) (i), (ii) and (iii) (B) (ii), (iii) and (iv)
(C) (iii), (iv) and (i) (D) (iv), (iii) and (ii)

94. What is the correct sequence of the following sections of the main entry as per classified catalogue code (CCC) ?

(i) Note Section (ii) Leading Section
(iii) Heading Section (iv) Title Section

Codes :

(A) (i) (iv) (iii) (ii) (B) (ii) (iii) (iv) (i)
(C) (iii) (iv) (ii) (i) (D) (iv) (i) (iii) (ii)

95. Arrange the following indexing sources according to the year of their first publication :

(i) Biological Abstracts
(ii) Chemical Abstracts
(iii) Index Medicus
(iv) Poole's Index to Periodical Literature

Codes :

(A) (i) (ii) (iii) (iv) (B) (iv) (iii) (ii) (i)
(C) (iv) (ii) (i) (iii) (D) (i) (iv) (iii) (ii)

96. Match the following :

	List - I	**List - II**
a.	Facts on File Directory	i. Periodical
b.	World of Learning	ii. Index
c.	Concordance Digest	iii. Newspaper
d.	Willing's Press Guide	iv. Directory

Codes :	**(a)**	**(b)**	**(c)**	**(d)**
(A)	i	iii	iv	ii
(B)	ii	i	iii	iv
(C)	iii	iv	ii	i
(D)	iv	ii	i	iii

97. Match the following :

List - I	**List - II**
a. McGroger Theory X	i. Less External Control
b. McGroger Theory Y	ii. PERT
c. Unity of Command	iii. Workers' Participation in Decision Making
d. Time and Cost	iv. All Powers in One Person

Codes :	**(a)**	**(b)**	**(c)**	**(d)**
(A)	iii	i	iv	ii
(B)	iv	i	iii	ii
(C)	ii	iv	iii	i
(D)	i	iii	ii	iv

98. **Assertion (A) :** Knowledge Management involves a number of assets and value added to them.

Reason (R) : Knowledge Management is the core activity of information transfer.

Codes :

(A) (A) is true, but (R) is false.

(B) (A) is true, but (R) is partiallytrue.

(C) Both (A) and (R) are true.

(D) (A) is partially true but (R) istrue.

99. Identify content management software from the following :

(i) Evergreen (ii) Drupal

(iii) Joomla (iv) New Genlib

Codes:

(A) (i) and (ii) are correct.

(B) (ii) and (iii) are correct.

(C) (iii) and (iv) are correct.

(D) (i) and (iv) are correct.

100. Identify open source softwares for library management.

(i) New Genlib (ii) SOUL

(iii) LIBSYS (iv) KOHA

Codes:

(A) (i) and (ii) are correct.

(B) (ii) and (iii) are correct.

(C) (iii) and (iv) are correct.

(D) (i) and (iv) are correct.

101. **Assertion (A) :** An electronic library may have both born digital and converted digital documents.

Reason (R) : A document stored in Unicode is same as storing the scanned image of the document.

Codes :

(A) (A) is false, but (R) is true.

(B) (A) is true, but (R) is false.

(C) Both (A) and (R) are true.

(D) Both (A) and (R) are false.

102. Arrange the following web browsers in chronological order :

(i) Safari (ii) Chrome

(iii) Netscape Navigator (iv) Firefox

Codes :

(A) (iv) (i) (ii) (iii) (B) (i) (ii) (iii) (iv)

(C) (ii) (i) (iv) (iii) (D) (iii) (i) (iv) (ii)

103. Arrange the following in chronological order :

(i) MEDLINE (ii) Pub-Med

(iii) Index Medicus (iv) MEDLARS

Codes :

(A) (iii) (iv) (i) (ii) (B) (iv) (i) (iii) (ii)

(C) (i) (iii) (ii) (iv) (D) (iii) (ii) (iv) (i)

104. Match the following :

	List - I		List - II
a.	Systematic indexing	i.	Derek Austin
b.	PRECIS	ii.	Mortimer Taube
c.	Uniterm	iii.	J. Kaiser
d.	Chain Procedure	iv.	S.R. Ranganathan

Codes :	**(a)**	**(b)**	**(c)**	**(d)**
(A)	ii	i	iv	iii
(B)	iv	iii	ii	i
(C)	i	ii	iii	iv
(D)	iv	i	iii	ii

105. Match the following :

	List - I		**List - II**
a.	Internet	i.	Knowledge navigation
b.	Computing	ii.	Collection of E-resources
c.	WWW	iii.	Tools and Techniques for accessing
d.	Digital Library	iv.	Delivery Mechanism

Codes :	**(a)**	**(b)**	**(c)**	**(d)**
(A)	iv	i	iii	ii
(B)	iv	iii	i	ii
(C)	ii	i	iii	iv
(D)	iii	iv	ii	i

106. What is the relationship between ISBD and cataloguing codes ?
   (A) They are not related to each other
   (B) ISBD includes cataloguing rules
   (C) ISBD can replace cataloguing rules
   (D) Anglo-American codes include bibliographic description

107. Who first used the phrase 'Bibliographical Control'?
   (A) Paul Otlet (B) Henry La Fontaine
   (C) Luther Evans (D) Konrad Gesner

108. Cost recovery and profit making aspects in relation to gathering information, organization, services and usage, etc. refer to
   (A) Economy evaluation
   (B) Coverage evaluation
   (C) Workforce evaluation
   (D) User evaluation

109. Which of the following are the characteristic features of Post coordinate indexing system ?

i. Index terms are pre-determined
ii. Coordination of terms done byusers
iii. No fixed citation order
iv. Multiple entries prepared foreach document

Codes :

(A) i and ii are correct. (B) ii and iii are correct.
(C) i and iii are correct. (D) ii and iv are correct.

110. Shannon's model of information theory is criticized for which of the following reasons ?

i. Concern on semantic issues
ii. Engineering bias
iii. Concern for technical transmission
iv. Emphasis on effectiveness

Codes :

(A) i and ii are correct.
(B) ii and iii are correct.
(C) iii and iv are correct.
(D) i and iii are correct.

111. Arrange the following stages of knowledge representation in order :

i. Gather data ii. Knowledge database
iii. Codification iv. Content mapping

Codes :

(A) iv, iii, i, ii (B) iii, i, iv, ii
(C) ii, iv, i, iii (D) i, iii, ii, iv

112. Match the following :

	List - I		List - II
a.	N. Grogan	i.	Scientific & Technical Libraries
b.	J. Saha	ii.	Scientific & technical libraries; an introduction to literature
c.	Nilfred Ashworth	iii.	Handbook of special librarianship & information work
d.	L.J. Strauss	iv.	Special libraries and information services in India & USA

Codes :	(a)	(b)	(c)	(d)
(A)	ii	iv	iii	i
(B)	i	ii	iv	iii
(C)	ii	i	iii	iv
(D)	iv	ii	i	iii

113. Match the following implications with the respective laws of library science :

	List - I		List - II
a.	Location of the library	i.	Second Law
b.	Obligation of the State	ii.	Third Law
c.	Publicity	iii.	Fifth Law
d.	Strength of Library Staff	iv.	First Law

Codes :	(a)	(b)	(c)	(d)
(A)	iv	ii	i	iii
(B)	iv	i	ii	iii
(C)	ii	i	iii	iv
(D)	ii	iii	iv	i

114. Match the following biographical publications from India with the respective compilers :

List - I	List - II
a. India, Who's Who	i. S.P. Sen
b. Who's Who in India	ii. J.S. Sharma
c. Dictionary of Indian Biography	iii. Business Press, Mumbai
d. National Biographical Dictionary of India	iv. INFA Pub., New Delhi

Codes :	(a)	(b)	(c)	(d)
(A)	iii	iv	ii	i
(B)	i	ii	iii	iv
(C)	ii	iii	i	iv
(D)	iv	iii	i	ii

115. Match the following :

List - I	List - II
a. Principle of Osmosis	i. Security
b. Theory of Literary Warrants	ii. Sinha Committee
c. Public Libraries are stagnating pools of books	iii. Reclassification
d. Firewall	iv. Dr. S.R.Ranganathan

Codes :	(a)	(b)	(c)	(d)
(A)	iv	ii	iii	i
(B)	iii	iv	ii	i
(C)	iv	iii	i	ii
(D)	i	ii	iv	iii

116. Match the following MARC 21 tags with respective fields :

List - I	List - II
a. 020	i. Publication and Distribution
b. 100	ii. Series Statement
c. 260	iii. ISBN
d. 440	iv. Personal name

Codes :	**(a)**	**(b)**	**(c)**	**(d)**
(A)	i	ii	iii	iv
(B)	ii	iv	iii	i
(C)	iii	ii	iv	i
(D)	iii	iv	i	ii

117. **Assertion (A) :** Inverse document frequency is the logarithm of the reciprocal of the number of documents in a collection that contains a given term.

Reason (R) : Inverse document frequency measure is computed from term frequency and inverse document frequency.

Codes :

(A) Both (A) and (R) are true.
(B) Both (A) and (R) are false.
(C) (A) is true, but (R) is false.
(D) (A) is false, but (R) is true.

118. **Assertion (A) :** Subject gateways are suitable for all types of user for finding their information.

Reason (R) : Subject gateways are developed by subject and computer experts.

Codes :

(A) (A) is true, but (R) is false.
(B) (A) is false, but (R) is true.
(C) Both (A) & (R) are true.
(D) Both (A) & (R) are false.

119. **Assertion (A) :** The principle of canonical sequence states when subjects in a array of subjects are traditionally referred to in a specific sequence, it will be convenient to conform to this traditional sequence.

Reason (R) : In classification scheme, the principle of canonical sequence is mainly followed to arrange the array of subjects.

Codes :

(A) Both (A) and (R) are true.

(B) (A) is false, but (R) is true.

(C) (A) is true, but (R) is false.

(D) Both (A) and (R) are false.

120. **Assertion (A) :** Acceptance of First Law of library Science "Books are for Use" has brought forth far reaching change in the present digital environment.

Reason (R) : Online access, open access, virtual reference are the results of this acceptance.

Codes :

(A) (A) is true, but (R) is false.

(B) (A) is false, but (R) is true.

(C) Both (A) and (R) are false.

(D) Both (A) and (R) are true.

121. **Assertion (A) :** PANDEX is a indexing system which sometimes allows changing the lead term to a standard form in order to provide better collocation of terms.

Reason (R) : It facilitates the first input string to be truncated after 18 characters and second after 11 characters.

Codes :

(A) Both (A) and (R) are true.

(B) Both (A) and (R) are false.

(C) (A) is false, but (R) is true.

(D) (A) is true, but (R) is false.

122. **Assertion (A) :** The diary technique enables the researcher to keep record of information activities of the users for a specified period of time.

Reason (R) : The diary technique is the most suitable technique of user studies over other techniques.

Codes :

(A) Both (A) and (R) are false.

(B) (A) is true, but (R) is false.

(C) Both (A) and (R) are true.

(D) (A) is false, but (R) is true.

123. Books of Unknown or doubtful authorship is known as :

(A) Apograph (B) Incunabulla

(C) Apocryphal books (D) Blue Books

124. Arrange the following in the ascending order of their first year of publication :

(i) BNB

(ii) INB

(iii) Compendex

(iv) Roget's Thesaurus of Englishwords

Codes :

(A) (iv), (iii), (i), (ii) (B) (iii), (ii), (iv), (i)

(C) (ii), (iv), (i), (iii) (D) (i), (iii), (ii), (iv)

125. Arrange the following ISBDs according to their year of formulation :

(i) ISBD (PM) (ii) ISBD (CF)
(iii) ISBD (M) (iv) ISBD (S)

Codes :

(A) (iii), (ii), (i), (iv) (B) (iii), (iv), (i), (ii)
(C) (iv), (i), (iii), (ii) (D) (iv), (ii), (iii), (i)

126. Arrange the following in the chronological order of their first year of publication :

(i) Arts and Humanities Index
(ii) Social Science Citation Index
(iii) ISI Web of Science
(iv) Science Citation Index

Codes :

(A) (iv), (ii), (i), (iii) (B) (ii), (iii), (iv), (i)
(C) (iii), (ii), (i), (iv) (D) (iv), (i), (iii), (ii)

127. Match the following :

List - I	**List - II**
a. Information on important recent happenings of India	i. India – A Reference Annual
b. Total number of foreigners visited in India in 2012	ii. Keesing's Record of World Events
c. Name of Prime Minister of India	iii. Statistical Yearbook
d. Postal Address of Anna Hazare	iv. Who's Who

Codes :	**(a)**	**(b)**	**(c)**	**(d)**
(A)	iv	i	ii	iii
(B)	ii	iii	i	iv
(C)	iii	ii	i	iv
(D)	i	iv	iii	ii

128. Match the following :

	List - I		**List - II**
a.	Scaler Chain	i.	Direct dealing with subordinates
b.	Espirit deCorps	ii.	Production, efficiency and prevention of waste
c.	Scientific Management	iii.	Emphasis on Team Work
d.	Span of control	iv.	Top to Bottom

Codes :	**(a)**	**(b)**	**(c)**	**(d)**
(A)	iv	iii	ii	i
(B)	iii	iv	i	ii
(C)	iv	ii	iii	i
(D)	ii	iii	i	iv

129. **Assertion (A) :** Intellectual Property Rights facilitate free flow of information.

Reason (R) : Effective free flow of information is the pre-requisite for knowledge society.

Codes :

(A) (A) is true, but (R) is false.

(B) (A) is false, but (R) is true.

(C) Both (A) and (R) are true.

(D) Both (A) and (R) are false.

130. **Assertion (A) :** The total output of Indian publications is reflected in 'Indian National Bibliography'.

Reason (R) : A number of publishers in India are defaulters and do not deposit their publications as per Delivery of Books and Newspapers (Public Libraries) Act.

Codes :

(A) Both (A) and (R) are true.

(B) Both (A) and (R) are false.

(C) (A) is true, but (R) is false.

(D) (A) is false, but (R) is true.

131. **Assertion (A) :** No library is self-sufficient in terms of resources even in electronic age.

Reason (R) : Resource sharing and consortia initiatives are essential to meet user needs.

Codes :

(A) (A) is true and (R) is false.

(B) (A) is false and (R) is true.

(C) Both (A) and (R) are true.

(D) Both (A) and (R) are false.

132. The class index entries which are derived from the class number of a document are based upon :

(A) Unsought links (B) Missing links

(C) False links (D) Sought links

133. Which of the following does not belong to the set of canons for the characteristics ?

(A) Canon of Differentiation

(B) Canon of Ascertainability

(C) Canon of Currency

(D) Canon of Relevance

134. Semouv Lubutzsky and Mary Piggot are associated with which of the following ?

(A) Classification (B) Cataloguing

(C) Indexing (D) Management

135. **Assertion (A) :** Multilingual dictionaries provide equivalent words in three or more languages.

Reason (R) : They generally do not define the words but they give equivalent words in one or more foreign languages.

Codes :

(A) Both (A) and (R) are true.

(B) Both (A) and (R) are false.

(C) (A) is true, but (R) is false.

(D) (A) is false, but (R) is true.

136. **Assertion (A) :** Wikis have provided everybody an opportunity for authoring, editing and publishing.

Reason (R) : Web has provided very generic rules for creation, maintenance and development of Wikis.

Codes :

(A) (A) is true, but (R) is false.

(B) (A) is false, but (R) is true.

(C) Both (A) and (R) are true.

(D) Both (A) and (R) are false.

137. **Assertion (A) :** Knowledge Management is an extension of conventional library management.

Reason (R) : Knowledge Management deals with elements like content, technology and culture.

Codes :

(A) (A) is true, but (R) is false.

(B) Both (A) and (R) are true.

(C) (A) is false, but (R) is true.

(D) Both (A) and (R) are false.

138. **Assertion (A) :** To increase accessibility to information for differently abled users we need to accept assistive technologies.

Reason (R) : Information for all.

Codes :

(A) Both (A) and (R) are true, but (R) is not the correct explanation of (A).

(B) Both (A) and (R) are true and (R) is the correct explanation of (A).

(C) (A) is true, but (R) is false.

(D) (A) is false, but (R) is true.

139. **Assertion (A)** : The plagiarism detection software implements a generic detection approach for all types of materials.

Reason (R) : There is no difference between text and source code plagiarism.

Codes :

(A) (A) is true, but (R) is false.

(B) (A) is false, but (R) is true.

(C) Both (A) and (R) are true.

(D) Both (A) and (R) are false.

140. **Assertion (A)** : According to National Knowledge Commission, 'the library and information services sector in India has not kept pace with the paradigmatic changes taking place in society'.

Reason (R) : There is no proportionate growth in library resources.

Codes :

(A) Both (A) and (R) are true.

(B) (A) is true, but (R) is false.

(C) Both (A) and (R) are false.

(D) (A) is false, but (R) is true

141. Arrange the following in chronological order :

i. Delivery of Books and Newspapers Act
ii. RTI Act
iii. Imperial Library Act
iv. IT (Amendment) Act

Codes :

(A) i, iv, ii, iii (B) iii, i, ii, iv
(C) iii, ii, i, iv (D) iv, iii, i, ii

142. Arrange the following in chronological order :

i. Rome convention
ii. WIPO copyright treaty
iii. Universal copyright convention
iv. Berne convention

Codes :

(A) i, iv, iii, ii (B) iv, i, ii, iii
(C) iv, iii, i, ii (D) iii, i, iv, ii

143. Arrange the following according to their date of origin :

i. Librametry ii. Statistical bibliography
iii. Statistical analysis iv. Bibliometrics

Codes :

(A) i, iii, ii, iv (B) ii, iii, i, iv
(C) iii, i, ii, iv (D) iii, ii, i, iv

144. Arrange the following activities in the order as given by Ellis in his model of information seeking behaviour :

i. Browsing ii. Monitoring
iii. Extracting iv. Differentiating

Codes :

(A) ii, i, iv, iii (B) i, iv, ii, iii

(C) iii, ii, i, iv (D) ii, i, iii, iv

145. Arrange the following steps in the order of accessioning the book :

i. Arrange books as per bill

ii. Check books as per order placed

iii. Enter the accession number in the register

iv. Write accession number on back of title page of other relevant pages

Codes :

(A) i, ii, iii, iv (B) ii, iii, i, iv

(C) iii, i, ii, iv (D) ii, i, iii, iv

ANSWERS

1. D	2. C	3. D	4. C	5. D	6. B
7. C	8. D	9. B	10. D	11. A	12. A
13. A	14. A	15. A	16. C	17. C	18. B
19. A	20. B	21. A	22. C	23. D	24. D
25. B	26. C	27. C	28. B	29. B	30. C
31. C	32. C	33. D	34. B	35. D	36. B
37. B	38. D	39. B	40. B	41. C	42. A
43. C	44. A	45. B	46. C	47. D	48. D
49. C	50. B	51. A	52. C	53. B	54. D
55. A	56. B	57. A	58. C	59. D	60. C
61. B	62. C	63. B	64. A	65. A	66. C
67. C	68. B	69. D	70. A	71. D	72. C
73. D	74. D	75. B	76. A	77. C	78. D
79. B	80. B	81. C	82. C	83. B	84. B
85. C	86. A	87. D	88. B	89. C	90. C
91. C	92. C	93. A	94. B	95. B	96. C
97. A	98. B	99. B	100. D	101. B	102. D

103. A	104. D	105. B	106. D	107, C	108. A
109. B	110. B	111. D	112. A	113. B	114. D
115. B	116. D	117. A	118. B	119. A	120. D
121. D	122. B	123. C	124. A	125. B	126. A
127. B	128. A	129. B	130. D	131. C	132. D
133. C	134. B	135. A	136. C	137. C	138. D
139. D	140. A	141. B	142. C	143. D	144. B
145. D					

5

Research in LIS & Statistical Methods

1. Which of the following tests can be employed for hypothesis testing ?
   (A) F – test (B) Chi – square test
   (C) t – test (D) All of the above
2. Which of the following is not related to case study approach in a research design ?
   (A) In depth Study
   (B) Study of one/limited cases
   (C) General study
   (D) Little concern about generalisation to a large population
3. "Students' visit to Library is influenced by the availability of Internet". State "Students' visit to library" is which kind of variable ?
   (A) Independent Variable
   (B) Intervening Variable
   (C) Dependent Variable

(D) Intercept Variable

4. Idiographic hypothesis is directed to wards predicting the behaviour of

(A) An Individual

(B) Group of People

(C) Masses

(D) People from same school ofthought

5. In the process of reasoning when westart with a specific statement, and conclude to a general statement, it iscalled

(A) Deductive Reasoning

(B) Inductive Reasoning

(C) Abnormal Reasoning

(D) Transcendental Reasoning

6. Solomon Four group design is related to

(A) Field studies

(B) Pretest-post test control groupdesign

(C) Data Analysis Model

(D) Statistical Technique

7. Which sources would you consult to know the "Impact Factor" of Journal publications ?

(i) Web of Science (ii) Science Direct

(iii) SCOPUS (iv) EBSCO

Codes :

(A) (i) and (iv) (B) (ii) and (iii)

(C) (i) and (iii) (D) (iii) and (iv)

8. Research is conducted to :

(i) Generate new knowledge

(ii) Develop a theory

(iii) Develop communication skills

(iv) Re-interpret existing knowledge

Codes :

(A) (i), (iii) and (ii) are correct

(B) (iii), (ii) and (i) are correct

(C) (i), (ii) and (iv) are correct

(D) (i), (iii) and (iv) are correct

9. Match the following :

List-I	List-II
(a) Thurston scale	(i) Sharing individual preference in agroup
(b) Semantic Differential Scale	(ii) Group of Judges
(c) Likert Scale	(iii) Selection from two opposite position
(d) Sociometric scale	(iv) Intensity structure

Codes :	**(a)**	**(b)**	**(c)**	**(d)**
(A)	(i)	(iv)	(ii)	(iii)
(B)	(ii)	(iii)	(iv)	(i)
(C)	(iv)	(i)	(iii)	(ii)
(D)	(iii)	(ii)	(iv)	(i)

10. Match the following :

List-I	List-II
(a) Vidyanidhi	(i) Institutional Repository
(b) TKDL	(ii) Electronic Theses & Dissertations
(c) DOAJ	(iii) Digital Library of Journals
(d) E-Prints @IISc	(iv) Digital Archive

Codes :	**(a)**	**(b)**	**(c)**	**(d)**
(A)	(ii)	(iv)	(iii)	(i)
(B)	(iii)	(ii)	(i)	(iv)
(C)	(iv)	(iii)	(ii)	(i)
(D)	(i)	(ii)	(iv)	(iii)

11. The chi-square technique is used to compare the observed data with that of

(A) Collected raw data (B) Expected data

(C) Analysed data (D) Graphical data

12. **Assertion (A) :** Random samples are not representative of the whole population.

Reason (R) : Random numbers are used in forming a random sample.

Codes :

(A) (A) is true, but (R) is false.

(B) (A) is false, but (R) is true.

(C) Both (A) and (R) are true.

(D) Both (A) and (R) are false.

13. Match the following :

List - I (Budgetary technique)	**List - II (Limitation of budgetary technique)**
a. Line	i. Detailed information required
b. Formula	ii. Time consuming
c. PPBS	iii. Do not permit variation
d. Zero-based	iv. Do not suggest future

Codes :	**(a)**	**(b)**	**(c)**	**(d)**
(A)	ii	i	iv	iii
(B)	iii	ii	i	iv
(C)	iv	iii	i	ii
(D)	i	iv	ii	iii

14. Which of the factor is not helping in limiting the external validity ?
    (A) Reactive effect
    (B) Ecological validity
    (C) Interaction between selection bias of experimental variables
    (D) Ecological effect
15. Semantic differential scale isconcerned with
    (A) Pool of items
    (B) Selection from two opposite positions
    (C) Five point scale
    (D) Selection from a check list
16. In spiral of scientific method, thespan of Zenith to descendent is
    (A) Empirical phase (B) Hypothesizing phase
    (C) Deductive phase (D) Verification phase
17. Which of the following variable cannot be expressed in quantitative terms ?
    (A) Socio-Economic status
    (B) Marital status
    (C) Numerical Aptitude
    (D) Professional Attitude
18. Z39.50 is a standard for
    (A) Communication formats
    (B) Search and Retrieval services
    (C) Cataloguing Web Resources
    (D) Library Management Services
19. In context to modulation, PCM stands for
    (A) Pulse Code Modulation
    (B) Phase Control Modulation

(C) Popular Code Modulation

(D) Penultimate Code Modulation

20. The stages in the product life cycle curve are

(A) Introduction, Growth, Maturity,Decline

(B) Introduction, Growth, Maturity,Profit

(C) Growth, Maturity, Profit, Decline

(D) Introduction, Growth, Maturity,Saturation

21. Match the following :

List - I	**List - II**
a. Mean value	i. Most frequently occurring
b. Mode	ii. Average
c. Median	iii. Measure ofdispersion
d. Standard Deviation	iv. Middle Value

Codes :	**(a)**	**(b)**	**(c)**	**(d)**
(A)	iii	iv	i	ii
(B)	ii	i	iv	iii
(C)	iv	iii	i	ii
(D)	ii	iii	iv	i

22. Match the following :

List - I	**List - II**
a. Bradford	i. Citation indexing
b. Lotka	ii. Distribution of articles published in periodicals
c. Zipf	iii. Scientific productivity of author
d. Garfield	iv. Frequency of word occurrence in a text

Codes :	**(a)**	**(b)**	**(c)**	**(d)**
(A)	iv	i	iii	ii
(B)	ii	iii	iv	i

(C)	iii	iv	i	ii
(D)	iv	iii	ii	i

23. Match the following :

List - I	List - II
a. Chain indexing	i. Derek Austin
b. Relational indexing	ii. S. R. Ranganathan
c. Subject Indexing	iii. J. E. L. Farradane
d. PRECIS	iv. E. J. Coats

Codes :	**(a)**	**(b)**	**(c)**	**(d)**
(A)	i	ii	iv	iii
(B)	ii	iii	iv	i
(C)	i	ii	iii	iv
(D)	ii	iv	i	iii

24. Match the following :

List - I	List - II
a. Collateral classes	i. Class comprising two or more entities
b. Multiple classes	ii. Classes of the same order but not belonging to one in the same order
c. Chain of classes	iii. A subject fixed with others in the universal of subject
d. Co-ordinate classes	iv. A sequence of classes made up of any given class and its universe

Codes :	**(a)**	**(b)**	**(c)**	**(d)**
(A)	ii	iv	i	iii
(B)	i	iii	ii	iv
(C)	ii	i	iv	iii
(D)	i	iv	ii	iii

25. Match the following :

List – I	List – II
a. Osgood and Schramm	i. General Model
b. Berlo	ii. Mathematical Model
c. Shannon and Weaver	iii. Circular Model
d. George Gerbner	iv. S-M-C-RModel

Codes :	(a)	(b)	(c)	(d)
(A)	i	ii	iii	iv
(B)	ii	iii	iv	i
(C)	iii	iv	ii	i
(D)	iv	i	ii	iii

26. Work study, standardised tools, selecting and training of workers are the contributions of
    (A) Louis Brndeis (B) F.W. Taylor
    (C) Henry Fayol (D) Lyndall Urwick

27. When the population is heterogenous, which of the following methods give better results ?
    (A) Purposive Sampling
    (B) Quota Sampling
    (C) Random Sampling
    (D) Stratified Random Sampling

28. "Scitation" is the online host service of
    (A) American Institute of Physics
    (B) University of Maryland
    (C) Society for Industrial Research
    (D) Oxford University

29. The process of planning, allocating, organizing and evaluating library tasks and activities within the

framework of major objectives, mission and policy refers to

(A) Functional control

(B) Functionai Classification

(C) Functional Approach

(D) Functional Authority

30. Match the following :

List - I	List - II
a. Amenable to further algebraic treatment	i. Mean deviation
b. Estimated without knowing values of extreme items	ii. Median
c. Mathematically and logically incorrect	iii. Inter-quartile deviation
d. The dispersion does not cover all items of a series	iv. Arithmetic means

Codes :	(a)	(b)	(c)	(d)
(A)	iv	ii	i	iii
(B)	iii	ii	i	iv
(C)	ii	iv	iii	i
(D)	i	iii	iv	i

31. Match the following :

List - I	List - II
a. Statistical Quality/ Process Control (SQC/SPC)	i. Identify the intensity of each problem in the production process
b. Check Sheets	ii. Selected variables checked

c. Pareto Chart iii. Identify the relationship between problems and causes

d. Fish Bone Diagram iv. Record variables in the production process

Codes :	**(a)**	**(b)**	**(c)**	**(d)**
(A)	ii	iv	i	iii
(B)	iv	ii	iii	i
(C)	iii	iv	i	ii
(D)	i	ii	iv	ii

32. Match the following :

List - I	**List - II**
a. Finding solution to the problem of pilferage in libraries	i. Historical Research
b. Implementation of cloud computing services in special libraries	ii. Action Research
c. A study of mathematician turned librarian	iii. Experimental Research
d. Use of web resources in Central Universities of India	iv. Survey Research

Codes :	**(a)**	**(b)**	**(c)**	**(d)**
(A)	ii	iii	i	iv
(B)	iii	ii	iv	i
(C)	iv	i	ii	iii
(D)	i	iv	iii	ii

33. Match the following :

	List - I		**List - II**
a.	Classical Models	i.	Ruesch and Bateson's Functional Model
b.	Linear Model	ii.	Aristotle
c.	Non-linear Model	iii.	Lasswell
d.	Multi-dimensional	iv.	Westley and Mackan's Conceptual Model

Codes :	**(a)**	**(b)**	**(c)**	**(d)**
(A)	ii	iii	iv	i
(B)	ii	iv	i	iii
(C)	i	ii	iii	iv
(D)	iii	ii	iv	i

34. Match the following :

	List - I		**List - II**
a.	Carol Kuhlthau	i.	8 stages
b.	David Ellis	ii.	ISB is a 6 stage process
c.	M.J. Belkin	iii.	ISB is of 8 key activities
d.	Marchionnini	iv.	ISB is 4 dimension characteristic

Codes :	**(a)**	**(b)**	**(c)**	**(d)**
(A)	ii	iii	iv	i
(B)	ii	iii	i	iv
(C)	iii	i	iv	ii
(D)	iv	ii	i	ii

35. **Assertion (A) :** Institutions generate information through research and development activities.

Reason (R) : All such generated information forms the grey literature.

Codes :

(A) Both (A) and (R) are true.

(B) Both (A) and (R) are false.

(C) (A) is true, (R) is partially true.

(D) (A) is false, (R) is true.

36. Impact factor is devised by

(A) Eugene Garfield (B) Alan Pritchard

(C) David Hume (D) Louis Brandeis

37. A skilful method of providing means,mechanism and structural elements tostreamline organizational work isknown as

(A) Role Analysis

(B) Strategic Planning

(C) Work Culture

(D) Autonomous Planning

38. ETD database in India is maintainedby

(i) Shodhgangotri

(ii) Vidyanidhi

(iii) Shodhganga

(iv) INDEST-AICTE consortium

Codes :

(A) (i) and (iii) are correct.

(B) (ii), (iii) and (iv) are correct.

(C) (ii) and (iii) are correct.

(D) (iii) and (iv) are correct.

39. Match the following :

List - I	**List - II**
a. Key to a given collection	i. Abstract
b. Key to literary sources on a subject	ii. Index

c. Representation of subject concept — iii. Catalogue

d. Condensation of a document — iv. Bibliography

Codes :	**(a)**	**(b)**	**(c)**	**(d)**
(A)	iii	iv	ii	i
(B)	ii	iii	iv	i
(C)	i	ii	iii	iv
(D)	iv	i	ii	iii

40. **Assertion (A) :** In conducting research, Social Sciences are not considered at par with natural sciences.

Reason (R) : Research in Social Sciences can't be performed sorigorously as can be in Natural Sciences.

Codes :

(A) Both (A) and (R) are true.

(B) Both (A) and (R) are false.

(C) (A) is true, but (R) is false.

(D) (A) is false, but (R) is true.

41. **Assertion (A) :** Research starts inmind first and then inlaboratories.

Reason (R) : Systematically conducted research leads to generalization.

Codes :

(A) (A) is true, but (R) is false.

(B) (A) is false, but (R) is true.

(C) Both (A) and (R) are true.

(D) Both (A) and (R) are false.

42. **Assertion (A) :** Systematic and efficient use of statistical tools in research helps in precise

interpretation of research results.

Reason (R) : Statistical tools cannotgive specific explanations ofthe data.

Codes :

(A) Both (A) and (R) are true.

(B) (A) is true and (R) is false.

(C) Both (A) and (R) are false.

(D) (A) is false and (R) is true.

43. 'Research-in-progress' database in India is________.

(A) Vidyanidhi

(B) Shodhganga

(C) Shodhgangotri

(D) Indian National Depository Library

44. Web impact factor is developed by

(A) P. Ingwersen (B) L. Bornebora

(C) M. Thelwall (D) R. Rousseau

45. Which of the following are 'TQM' tools ?

(i) Fishbone Diagram (ii) Histogram

(iii) Pie Chart (iv) Run Charts

Codes :

(A) (i), (iii) and (iv) are correct.

(B) (i), (ii), (iii) and (iv) are correct.

(C) (ii), (iii) and (iv) are correct.

(D) (i), (ii) and (iv) are correct.

46. Library Ethics is a combination of what ?

(i) Responsibility (ii) Accountability

(iii) Commitment (iv) Decision Making

Codes :

(A) (i), (ii) and (iii) are correct.

(B) (ii), (iii) and (iv) are correct.

(C) (i), (iii) and (iv) are correct.

(D) (i), (ii) and (iv) are correct.

47. Match the following :

	List - I		**List - II**
a.	DCMES	i.	Defined Functional Requirements of Records
b.	MARC	ii.	Rules for Bibliographic Records
c.	RDA	iii.	Retrieval and Data Exchange
d.	FRBR	iv.	Coding Scheme for computerised Bibliographic Records

Codes :	**(a)**	**(b)**	**(c)**	**(d)**
(A)	iii	iv	ii	i
(B)	iv	ii	iii	i
(C)	i	ii	iii	iv
(D)	ii	iv	i	ii

48. Match the following :

	List - I		**List - II**
a.	POSDCORB	i.	Robert McNamara
b.	TQM	ii.	Peter Phyrr
c.	ZBB	iii.	Gulick F. Urwick
d.	PPBS	iv.	Edward Deming

Codes :	**(a)**	**(b)**	**(c)**	**(d)**
(A)	iv	iii	i	ii
(B)	iii	iv	ii	i
(C)	iii	i	ii	iv
(D)	ii	i	iii	i

49. Match the following :

List - I	List - II
a. Remote resource sensing satellite	i. Processing data
b. Memory chips	ii. Transportation of data
c. VLSI chips	iii. Capture data
d. Optical fibre	iv. Storage data

Codes :	**(a)**	**(b)**	**(c)**	**(d)**
(A)	i	ii	iii	iv
(B)	iv	iii	ii	i
(C)	ii	iii	iv	i
(D)	iii	iv	i	ii

50. Match the following :

List - I	List - II
a. f(r) = K/r	i. Bradford
b. xny = C	ii. Zipf's
c. L : n : n2	iii. Pareto
d. 80 – 20	iv. Lotka

Codes :	**(a)**	**(b)**	**(c)**	**(d)**
(A)	iv	ii	iii	i
(B)	ii	iii	iv	i
(C)	ii	iv	i	iii
(D)	i	iii	ii	iv

51. **Assertion (A) :** All research require hypotheses to be proposed and tested.

Reason (R) : No research is complete without testing of hypotheses.

Codes :

(A) (A) is false but (R) is true.

(B) Both (A) and (R) are false.

(C) (A) is true but (R) is false.

(D) Both (A) and (R) are true.

52. Assertion (A) : There is criticism by academicians and scientists on the use of impact factor as a measure of importance.

    Reason (R) : Impact factor is a journal metrics and can not be used to assess quality of individual research.

    Codes :

    (A) (A) is false but (R) is true.
    (B) Both (A) and (R) are true.
    (C) Both (A) and (R) are false.
    (D) (A) is true but (R) is false.

53. The correlational coefficient is
    (A) A strength of relationship between two variables.
    (B) A typical relationship between two variables.
    (C) A linear relationship between two variables.
    (D) Non-linear relationship between two variables.

54. Which of the following does not protect intellectual property ?
    (A) Encryption of data
    (B) Digital watermark
    (C) Uniquely encoded licences
    (D) Plug-ins

55. What does encrypting a file mean ?
    (A) Set the read only property
    (B) Hiding the file
    (C) Set a password
    (D) Scrambling the contents

56. Papyras was used as a writing material by
    (A) Summarians (B) Italians
    (C) Egyptians (D) Assyrians

57. The normal curve in a distribution is
    (i) Symmetrical, bell shaped continuously curve
    (ii) Asymmetrical, bell shaped continuously curve
    (iii) Symmetrical, bell shaped curve which does not touch the 'X' axis
    (iv) Bell shaped curve

    Codes :
    (A) (i) and (iv) are correct.
    (B) (i) and (iii) are correct.
    (C) (ii) and (iv) are correct.
    (D) (i) is correct.

58. Arrange the following MARC formats in order of year of their emergence :
    (i) CAN MARC (ii) US MARC
    (iii) LC MARC (iv) MARC 21

    Codes :
    (A) i ii iii iv (B) ii iii iv i
    (C) iii i ii iv (D) iv ii iii i

59. Match the following :

List - I	**List - II**
a. Every unit of population has equal chance of being selected	i. Systematic sampling
b. Every n^{th} case is selected from the list of population	ii. Cluster sampling
c. Units are randomly selected from the subgroups	iii. Random sampling
d. Geographic area based units	iv. Stratified sampling

Codes :	**(a)**	**(b)**	**(c)**	**(d)**
(A)	i	iv	iii	ii
(B)	iv	ii	i	iii
(C)	iii	i	iv	ii
(D)	ii	iii	iv	i

60. Match the following :

List - I	**List - II**
a. Approach of measuring two opposite sets of items	i. Semantic-differential scale
b. Approach of measurement yielding a single score	ii. Cumulative scale
c. Approach of measurement adopting bipolar objective rating to study a social phenomenon	iii. Sociometric scale
d. Approach to measure interaction pattern among close associates in a variety of groups	iv. Summated scale

Codes :	**(a)**	**(b)**	**(c)**	**(d)**
(A)	ii	iii	i	iv
(B)	iii	i	iv	ii
(C)	i	ii	iv	iii
(D)	iv	ii	i	ii

61. Match the following :

List - I	**List - II**
a. Σ\11/110-EF2	i. df (degree of freedom)
b. ΣXN	ii. S.D. (Standard Deviation)
c. (R – 1) (C – 1)	iii. Mean
d. ΣX2N	iv. Chi-square

Codes :	**(a)**	**(b)**	**(c)**	**(d)**
(A)	iv	i	iii	ii
(B)	iv	iii	i	ii
(C)	iii	i	ii	iv
(D)	ii	i	iii	iv

62. Match the following language and their function :

List - I	**List - II**
a. Procedural	i. Scan arbitrary files and extra information
b. Special purpose	ii. Manipulate data and change memory
c. Practical extraction report	iii. Create documents to view with web server
d. Hyper text mark up	iv. Data base queries

Codes :	**(a)**	**(b)**	**(c)**	**(d)**
(A)	ii	iv	i	iii
(B)	i	iii	ii	iv
(C)	iii	iv	i	ii
(D)	ii	iii	iv	i

63. Match the following :

	List - I	List - II
a.	Intra-Facet Relation	i. S : 5210t3
b.	Intra-Array Phase Relation	ii. Q 20 m4
c.	Intra-Facet Phase Relation	iii. SO b2
d.	Inter-Subject Phase Relation	iv. X.440j56

Codes :	**(a)**	**(b)**	**(c)**	**(d)**
(A)	iv	i	ii	iii
(B)	iv	ii	iii	i
(C)	ii	iii	i	iv
(D)	i	iv	iii	i

64. Match the following :

List - I	List - II
a. Organisational chart	i. Identification of responsibility for specific tasks
b. Flow charts	ii. Examine specific detailed procedure
c. Activity charts	iii. Division of responsibility & functions
d. Decision table	iv. Diagrams composed of symbols and directional lines

Codes :	**(a)**	**(b)**	**(c)**	**(d)**
(A)	i	iv	ii	iii
(B)	ii	iii	iv	i
(C)	iii	iv	i	ii
(D)	iv	ii	iii	i

65. Match the following :

List - I	List - II
a. Gender	i. Dependent variable
b. Information Technology	ii. Variable
c. Usership in libraries	iii. Binomial variable
d. Logical set of attributes	iv. Independent variable

Codes :	**(a)**	**(b)**	**(c)**	**(d)**
(A)	i	iv	ii	iii
(B)	iii	iv	i	ii
(C)	ii	i	iv	iii
(D)	iv	iii	ii	i

66. Match the following :

List - I	List - II
a. The assessment device that appears to measure the subject matter it purports to	i. Content validity
b. The assessment device in which individual's test score predicts the probable behaviour on a second variable	ii. Construct validity
c. The assessment device which adequately measures the major dimensions of the behaviour under consideration	iii. Criterion-related validity
d. The assessment device which appears to measure the general elements it purports to measure	iv. Face validity

Codes :	**(a)**	**(b)**	**(c)**	**(d)**
(A)	i	ii	iv	iii
(B)	ii	i	iii	iv
(C)	iv	iii	i	ii
(D)	iii	i	ii	iv

67. Match the following :

	List - I		**List - II**
a.	Halftone	i.	Translate instructions from original software to new platforms
b.	Threshold	ii.	Imaging with varying densities
c.	Emulation	iii.	Transfer of digital materials
d.	Migration	iv.	Minimum level to detect a signal

Codes :	**(a)**	**(b)**	**(c)**	**(d)**
(A)	i	iii	iv	ii
(B)	iii	ii	iv	i
(C)	ii	iv	i	iii
(D)	ii	i	iii	i

68. **Assertion (A) :** The entire scholarly publishing system is in danger of eroding due to increasing influence of predatory publishing.

Reason (R) : Many prey on Junior researchers and graduate students with personalised messages praising their earlier work and inviting them to submit a new manuscript.

Codes :

(A) (A) is true but (R) is false.

(B) (A) is false but (R) is true.

(C) Both (A) and (R) are false.

(D) Both (A) and (R) are true.

69. **Assertion (A)** : Metrics based evaluation is not suitable for assessing research performance of individual.

Reason (R) : Construction of citation profiles depend upon the databases used.

Codes :

(A) Both (A) and (R) are true.

(B) Both (A) and (R) are false.

(C) (A) is true, but (R) is false.

(D) (A) is false, but (R) is true.

70. **Assertion (A) :** Effective methods of communicating in H.R. Management of libraries still remains elusive.

Reason (R) : The management do not have the needed direction of approach, precision of thoughts and their expression and empathy.

Codes :

(A) (A) is true, (R) is false.

(B) Both (A) and (R) are false.

(C) (A) is true, (R) is partially true.

(D) (A) is false, (R) is true.

71. A chart in which some figures are broken down into its constituent parts is

(A) Bar chart (B) Column chart

(C) Pie chart (D) Band chart

72. The use of more words or symbols than are necessary to convey a meaning results in

(A) Efficiency (B) Accuracy

(C) Redundancy (D) Precision

73. The measure of certainty or predictability is called as

(A) Entropy (B) Feedback

(C) Redundancy (D) Distortion

74. Identify the methods used for plagiarism detection:
    (i) Term occurrence analysis
    (ii) API Testing
    (iii) Citation-based plagiarism detection
    (iv) Local similarity assessment

    Codes :
    (A) (i), (ii) and (iv) are correct.
    (B) (i), (iii) and (iv) are correct.
    (C) (ii), (iii) and (iv) are correct.
    (D) (i), (ii) and (iii) are correct.

75. Which of the following are the main role operators of PRECIS ?
    (i) Key System (ii) Action
    (iii) Performer of action (iv) Form of Document

    Codes :
    (A) (i), (ii) and (iii) (B) (ii), (i) and (iv)
    (C) (i), (iii) and (iv) (D) (ii), (iii) and (i)

76. Which of the following are the International Cooperative Serials Control Program ?
    (i) CONSER (ii) BIBCO
    (iii) SERLINE (iv) CATLINE

    Codes :
    (A) (i) & (ii) are correct.
    (B) (ii) & (iii) are correct.
    (C) (i) & (iii) are correct.
    (D) (ii) & (iv) are correct.

77. Which of the following are called 'path finders' to the literature ?
    (i) Bibliography (ii) Catalogue
    (iii) Shelf List (iv) Indices and Abstracts

Codes :

(A) (i) & (ii) are correct

(B) (i), (ii) & (iv) are correct

(C) (i) & (iv) are correct

(D) (ii) & (iii) are correct

78. The sources of hypothesis, as enunciated by P.V. Young are

(i) Genealogy (ii) Culture

(iii) Experiment (iv) Analogy

Codes :

(A) (i), (ii) and (iii) are correct

(B) (i), (iii) and (iv) are correct

(C) (i), (ii) and (iv) are correct

(D) (ii), (iii) and (iv) are correct

79. Systematic sampling is

(i) A type of probability sampling.

(ii) A type of non-probability sampling.

(iii) In which first unit is selected randomly.

(iv) Selected on the basis of specified characteristics.

Codes :

(A) (i) and (iii) are correct

(B) (i) and (iv) are correct

(C) (iii) and (iv) are correct

(D) (ii) and (iv) are correct

80. Match the following :

List - I	**List - II**
a. Survey of requirements	i. Design phase
b. Determining cost efficiency & effectiveness	ii. Installation phase

c. Review of the programs and their goals — iii. Analysis phase

d. Complete change over basics of system — iv. Evaluation phase

Codes :	**(a)**	**(b)**	**(c)**	**(d)**
(A)	i	ii	iii	iv
(B)	ii	iii	iv	i
(C)	iii	iv	i	ii
(D)	iv	i	ii	iii

81. Match the following :

List - I	**List - II**
a. Nadir to Ascending	i. Hypothesizing
b. Ascending to Zenith	ii. Verification
c. Zenith to Descending	iii. Deductive
d. Descending to Nadir	iv. Empirical

Codes :	**(a)**	**(b)**	**(c)**	**(d)**
(A)	i	iii	ii	iv
(B)	ii	iv	i	iii
(C)	iii	i	iv	ii
(D)	iv	i	iii	ii

82. Match the following characteristics of DBMS with respective activity :

List - I	**List - II**
a. Reduction of redundancy	i. Encryption
b. Data sharing	ii. Centralized control
c. Data integrity	iii. No. of application programs
d. Data security	iv. Accurate and consistent data

Codes :	**(a)**	**(b)**	**(c)**	**(d)**
(A)	ii	iii	iv	i
(B)	iv	iii	ii	i
(C)	iii	iv	i	ii
(D)	i	ii	iv	iii

83. Match the following :

List - I	**List - II**
a. Social Microscope	i. Cluster Technique
b. Fundamental Research	ii. No control over variance
c. Ex-post facto research	iii. Case study method
d. Multi stage random sampling	iv. Knowledge for knowledge sake

Codes :	**(a)**	**(b)**	**(c)**	**(d)**
(A)	i	ii	iii	iv
(B)	iii	iv	ii	i
(C)	ii	iii	i	iv
(D)	iv	i	ii	iv

84. Match the following :

List - I	**List - II**
a. Estimation of future expenditure on the basis of previous year expenditure	i. Programme
b. '15 per studentand' 200/- per teacher	ii. Comparison
c. 6.5%-10% of university budget for the development of library	iii. Per capita
d. Activities to be accomplished by the library	iv. Proportional

Codes :	**(a)**	**(b)**	**(c)**	**(d)**
(A)	ii	iii	iv	i
(B)	i	ii	iii	iv
(C)	iii	iv	i	ii
(D)	iv	i	ii	iii

85. Match the following :

List - I	**List - II**
a. Identification of user categories	i. Market positioning
b. Prioriting user groups and services	ii. Segmentation
c. Information seeking be haviour of users	iii. Marketing Mix
d. Product, price, place, promotion	iv. Consumer analysis

Codes :	**(a)**	**(b)**	**(c)**	**(d)**
(A)	i	ii	iii	iv
(B)	ii	i	iv	iii
(C)	iii	iv	i	ii
(D)	iv	iii	ii	i

86. Match the following :

List - I	**List - II**
a. Measure of similarity between two documents	i. Proportion of coefficient association
b. Similarity measure based on overlap interms between two documents	ii. Rectangular distance coefficient
c. Documents imilarity based solely on the occurrence of words	iii. Coefficient of association

d. Similarity measure which is based on the city block distance between two documents — iv. Lexical similarity

Codes :	**(a)**	**(b)**	**(c)**	**(d)**
(A)	i	iii	ii	iv
(B)	iii	i	ii	iv
(C)	iii	i	iv	ii
(D)	ii	iii	iv	i

87. Match the following authors with their statements on information characteristics :

	List - I		**List - II**
a.	Peter Drucker	i.	Human andshareable
b.	Borlando Cleveland	ii.	Quantity, Quality, Life
c.	K.J. McGarry	iii.	Natural and man-made physical resources
d.	Williams	iv.	Resources by analogy with classic resources of labour

Codes :	**(a)**	**(b)**	**(c)**	**(d)**
(A)	iii	i	iv	ii
(B)	iii	ii	i	iv
(C)	i	iii	iv	ii
(D)	i	iv	ii	iii

88. **Assertion (A) :** Approaches to Research is not dependent on Epistemologies.

Reason (R) : Scientific research relies on the application of the scientific method.

Codes :

(A) Both (A) and (R) are true.

(B) Both (A) and (R) are false.

(C) (A) is true and (R) is false.

(D) (R) is true and (A) is false.

89. **Assertion (A) :** Mean, median and mode are the simple techniques to get exact averages for data analysis in research.

Reason (R) : These are the well accepted statistical techniques of research for data analysis of historical data.

Codes :

(A) (A) is false, but (R) is true.

(B) Both (A) and (R) are true.

(C) (A) is true but (R) is false.

(D) Both (A) and (R) are false.

90. Which of the following are the types factors studies under ANOVA ?

(i) Fixed (ii) Frequency

(iii) Calculated (iv) Random

Codes :

(A) (ii) and (iii) are correct.

(B) (i) and (iv) are correct.

(C) (i) and (iii) are correct.

(D) (ii) and (iv) are correct.

91. **Assertion (A) :** As per the generally accepted principles of construction of statistical tabulation, every table should have a clear, concise and adequate title so as to make the table intelligible without reference to the text and this titles hould always be placed just below the body of the table.

Reason (R) : A statistical table which reflects its title just above the table and supply information about several interrelated characteristics of data makes thetable unwield and inconvenient.

Codes :

(A) Both (A) and (R) are true.

(B) Both (A) and (R) are false.

(C) (A) is true, but (R) is false.

(D) (A) is false, but (R) is true.

92. **Assertion (A) :** Chi-square is an important non-parametric test which does not require rigid assumptions in respect of the type of population being studied.

Reason (R) : Since ÷2 is a non parametric test, it requires onlythe degrees of freedom (implicitly, the size of the population) for using the test.

Codes :

(A) (A) is true, but (R) is false.

(B) Both (A) and (R) are true.

(C) (A) is false but (R) is true.

(D) Both (A) and (R) are false.

93. A cross reference that gives an indexer complete control over the cross references of an index is known as :

(A) see also cross reference

(B) check also cross reference

(C) see cross reference

(D) inverted cross reference

94. DMAIC is the acronym for :

(A) Define, Measure, Access, Improve and Control

(B) Define, Measure, Analyse, Improve and Control

(C) Describe, Measure, Analyse, Improve and Control

(D) Define, Measure, Access, Instruct and Control

95. 'Delphi Technique' was first discussed in a monograph by

(A) O. Helmer (B) E. Nagel

(C) D.M. Potter (D) J.H. Shera

96. The service that helps the students to acquire soft skills, writing skills and job-oriented skills is

(A) Reader's advisory (B) Career guidance

(C) Referral service (D) User education

97. Which of the following are characteristics of a review ?

(i) Analyses research topic

(ii) Indicates inter-relation of ideas

(iii) Presents an integrated picture of development and program

(iv) Provides only current information

Codes :

(A) (ii), (iii), (iv) are correct.

(B) (i), (iii), (iv) are correct.

(C) (i), (ii), (iii) are correct.

(D) (i), (ii), (iv) are correct.

98. **Assertion (A) :** Abstracts are precise representation of the content of a document.

Reason (R) : Researcher have time constraints to go through the original articles.

Codes :

(A) (A) is true, but (R) is false.

(B) Both (A) and (R) are true.

(C) (A) is false, but (R) is true.

(D) Both (A) and (R) are false.

99. **Assertion (A) :** To increase the specificity, we need to accept long notations.

Reason (R) : An important quality of notation is brevity.

Codes :

(A) Both (A) and (R) are true and (R) is the correct explanation of (A).

(B) (A) is false, but (R) is true.

(C) (A) is true, but (R) is false.

(D) Both (A)and (R) are true, but (R) is not the correct explanation of (A).

100. **Assertion (A) :** In a particular study, we may reject the alternative hypothesis.

Reason (R) : In the same study the null hypothesis is not rejected.

Codes :

(A) (A) is true, but (R) is false.

(B) (A) is false, but (R) is true.

(C) Both (A) and (R) are true and (R) is the correct explanation of (A).

(D) Both (A) and (R) are true, but (R) is not the correct explanation of (A).

101. Arrange the stages in the preparation of State-of the Art Report.

(i) Consultation with subject expert

(ii) Scope determination

(iii) Appraisal of information

(iv) Identification of the collection

Codes :

(A) (ii) (iv) (iii) (i)
(B) (iv) (ii) (iii) (i)
(C) (iii) (i) (iv) (ii)
(D) (i) (ii) (iii) (iv)

102. Match the following :

	List - I		List - II
a.	Nominal variable	i.	Temperature in centigrade
b.	Interval variable	ii.	Students and Faculty
c.	Ordinal variable	iii.	Classification of gender
d.	Ratio	iv.	Grades of students

Codes :	(a)	(b)	(c)	(d)
(A)	ii	iii	i	iv
(B)	iii	i	iv	ii
(C)	i	iv	iii	ii
(D)	iv	ii	iii	i

103. Which form of reasoning is the process of drawing a specific conclusion from a set of premises ?
(A) Rationalism
(B) Deductive reasoning
(C) Inductive reasoning
(D) Probabilistic

104. A systematic method and process of studying and evaluating whether the expenditure for products, materials, or services is justified by the benefitsis
(A) Break Even Analysis
(B) Cost-Effective Analysis
(C) System Analysis
(D) Administrative Analysis

105. LIPHIS (Linked Phrase Indexing System) was developed by
(A) T.C. Craven (B) J. Farradane
(C) J.C.R. Yeats (D) P. Ekern

106. Which of the following gives complete control over the cross references of anindex to the Indexer ?

(A) See also cross reference

(B) check also cross reference

(C) See cross reference

(D) Inverted cross reference

107. Which of the following are plagiarism detection software ?

(i) Turnitin (ii) Ithenticate

(iii) Tulips (iv) Veri Guide

Codes :

(A) (i) and (ii) (B) (i), (ii) and (iii)

(C) (i), (ii) and (iv) (D) (ii) and (iii)

108. Which of the following are direct methods of user study ?

i. Reading habits

ii. Analysis of library records

iii. Service preferences

iv. User needs

Codes :

(A) ii & iii (B) ii & iv

(C) i & iv (D) iii & iv

109. Which of the following are the steps in operational research process ?

i. Construction of mathematicalmodel

ii. Deriving solution from themodel.

iii. Graphic representation of workon a time scale.

iv. Developing network diagram showing inter relationships.

Codes :

(A) i and ii are correct. (B) ii and iii are correct.

(C) iii and iv are correct. (D) iv and i are correct.

110. Which of the following are statistical programming software ?

i. GAUSS
ii. SAS
iii. SPSS
iv. SLIM

Codes :

(A) i, iii and iv
(B) i, ii and iii
(C) i, ii and iv
(D) ii, iii and iv

111. Arrange the following steps in Flow-Chart in order :

i. Modularity
ii. Data Structure
iii. Identifying problems into subproblems
iv. Loops and Termination ofloops

Codes :

(A) iii, iv, i, ii
(B) iii, ii, iv, i
(C) ii, iii, iv, i
(D) iv, ii, i, iii

112. Match the following tools used in Total Quality Management :

List - I	**List - II**
a. Statistical Quality Control	i. Conformance and Maintain sticks
b. Check Sheets	ii. To identify relationship between problem and cause
c. Pareto Charts	iii. Checking variables
d. Fish bone diagram	iv. To identify intensity of problem

Codes :	**(a)**	**(b)**	**(c)**	**(d)**
(A)	ii	i	iv	iii
(B)	iii	i	iv	ii
(C)	i	iii	ii	iv
(D)	iv	i	iii	ii

113. Match the following :

List - I (Hypothesis)	**List - II (Characteristics)**
a. Null	i. Statement of expectations
b. Working (Directional)	ii. Relational propositions
c. Explanatory	iii. No relation between variables
d. Descriptive	iv. Existence ofvariables

Codes :	**(a)**	**(b)**	**(c)**	**(d)**
(A)	i	iv	ii	iii
(B)	iii	iv	ii	i
(C)	iii	ii	i	iv
(D)	iii	i	ii	iv

114. Match the following :

List - I	**List - II**
a. Theory of Hygiene & Motivation	i. Likerts
b. Maturity Theory	ii. Vroomand Lawler
c. Expectancy Theory	iii. Herzberg
d. Analysis Theory	iv. Argyris

Codes :	**(a)**	**(b)**	**(c)**	**(d)**
(A)	ii	iii	iv	i
(B)	iii	iv	ii	i
(C)	ii	i	iii	iv
(D)	iv	i	ii	iii

115. Match the following :

List - I	List - II
a. Harrold Koontz	i. MBO
b. Rensis Likert	ii. Three leadership styles
c. Peter Drucker	iii. Four systems management
d. Georgen Haber	iv. Problem solving Vs. Decision making

Codes :	**(a)**	**(b)**	**(c)**	**(d)**
(A)	i	ii	iii	iv
(B)	iii	iv	i	ii
(C)	iv	iii	ii	i
(D)	ii	iii	i	iv

116. Which of the following are non probability sampling?

(i) Quota sampling (ii) Judgement Sampling
(iii) Cluster Sampling (iv) Multi-stage sampling

Codes :

(A) (i) and (iv) are correct.
(B) (ii) and (iii) are correct.
(C) (i) and (ii) are correct.
(D) (iii) and (iv) are correct.

117. Arrange the following processes of research in order:

(i) Theory Building
(ii) Reflecting and Integrating of Idea
(iii) Research Design
(iv) Review of Literature

Codes :

(A) (iv), (iii), (ii), (i) (B) (iii), (i), (iv), (ii)
(C) (ii), (iv), (iii), (i) (D) (i), (ii), (iv), (iii)

118. Match the following :

	List - I		**List - II**
a.	Skewness	i.	Numbers of frequently appearing variables
b.	Modality	ii.	Degree of association between two/more variables
c.	F distribution	iii.	Structure of distribution
d.	Correlation	iv.	Ratio of two Chi square variables

Codes :	**(a)**	**(b)**	**(c)**	**(d)**
(A)	i	iv	ii	iii
(B)	iii	i	iv	ii
(C)	iv	ii	iii	i
(D)	ii	iii	i	iv

119. **Assertion (A) :** Mail survey, a data collection technique in which questionnaires are mailed to potential respondents, who in then fill and return at their convenience become obsolete.

Reason (R) : Survey-Monkey, the free online survey tool has totally replaced the traditional Mail survey.

Codes :

(A) (A) is true, but (R) is false.

(B) (A) is false, but (R) is true.

(C) Both (A) and (R) are true.

(D) Both (A) and (R) are false.

120. **Assertion (A) :** Case situations are seldom comparable and as such the information gathered in case studies is often not comparable.

Reason (R) : The subject under case study are usually described in terms of the characteristics exhibited by the subject/case itself.

Codes :

(A) Both (A) and (R) are true.

(B) Both (A) and (R) are false.

(C) (A) is true, but (R) is false.

(D) (A) is false, but (R) is true.

121. **Assertion (A)** : Interviewing is essential to supplement the research data collected through questionnaire.

Reason (R) : Interview is the most suitable technique to collect data as all respondents cooperate more during interview.

Codes :

(A) (A) is false, but (R) is true.

(B) Both (A) and (R) are true.

(C) Both (A) & (R) are false.

(D) (A) is true, but (R) is false.

122. **Assertion (A)** : Indexing and abstracting services fulfil the 4th Law of Library Science.

Reason (R) : These services serve asthe substitute to the primaryjournals.

Codes :

(A) (A) is true, but (R) is false.

(B) Both (A) & (R) are false.

(C) Both (A) & (R) are true.

(D) (A) is false, but (R) is true.

123. Who advocated the seven basic statistical tools for quality control ?

(A) Joseph Juran (B) Phillip Crosby

(C) Kauro Ishikawa (D) C.A. Cutter

124. The 'Principle of Facet Sequence' includes

i. Cow-calf principle
ii. Wall-picture principle
iii. Whole organ principle
iv. Principle of osmosis

Codes :

(A) i, ii and iv are correct.
(B) i, ii and iii are correct.
(C) i, iii and iv are correct.
(D) ii and iv are correct.

125. Which of the following are the types of validity of measurement ?

i. Construct　　ii. Current
iii. Content　　iv. Predictive

Codes :

(A) i, ii, iii are true.　　(B) ii, iii, iv are true.
(C) i, iii, iv are true.　　(D) i, ii, iv are true.

126. **Assertion (A) :** DOI is the identification system for the intellectual property in the digital environment.

Reason (R) : DOI is developed by WIPO.

Codes :

(A) (A) is true, but (R) is false.
(B) Both (A) and (R) are true.
(C) Both (A) and (R) are false.
(D) (R) is true, but (A) is false.

127. **Assertion (A) :** A database can be searched with a query language.

Reason (R) : A database can store a large amount of data.

Codes :

(A) Both (A) and (R) are true, but (R) is not the correct explanation of (A).

(B) Both (A) and (R) are true and (R) is the correct explanation of (A).

(C) (A) is true, but (R) is false.

(D) (A) is false, but (R) is true.

128. **Assertion (A) :** Bibliometric study is the popular area of research on which maximum number of Ph.D degree have been awarded in India.

Reason (R) : Bibliometric study adds to the extension of fundamental research.

Codes :

(A) Both (A) and (R) are true.

(B) (A) is true, but (R) is false.

(C) Both (A) and (R) are false.

(D) (R) is true, but (A) is false.

129. Match the following :

	List - I		List - II
a.	India	i.	Agglomeration
b.	Agriculture of wheat	ii.	Fusion
c.	Bio-chemistry	iii.	Denudation
d.	Biological sciences	iv.	Lamination

Codes :	**(a)**	**(b)**	**(c)**	**(d)**
(A)	iii	iv	ii	i
(B)	iv	ii	iii	i
(C)	ii	iii	i	iv
(D)	i	ii	iv	iii

130. Match the following :

List - I	List - II
a. Standing order	i. For serial publications till cancellation
b. Blanket order	ii. Routine publications on order
c. Firm order	iii. For publications on recommendation
d. Approval order	iv. For supply of institutional publications as and when published

Codes :	(a)	(b)	(c)	(d)
(A)	iv	ii	i	iii
(B)	iii	ii	i	iv
(C)	i	iv	ii	iii
(D)	ii	iv	i	iii

131. Match the following :

	List - I		List - II
a.	Simple random	i.	Natural order
b.	Systematic random	ii.	Representative
c.	Stratified random	iii.	Equal chance
d.	Judgement	iv.	Sub-groups

Codes :	(a)	(b)	(c)	(d)
(A)	ii	i	iii	iv
(B)	iii	i	iv	ii
(C)	iv	ii	i	iii
(D)	iii	ii	iv	i

132. Match the following :

	List - I	**List - II**
a.	Semantic differential scale	i. Graded structure
b.	Thurston scale	ii. Opposition positions
c.	Interval scale	iii. Group of Judgement
d.	Likert scale	iv. Equal units of measurement

Codes :	**(a)**	**(b)**	**(c)**	**(d)**
(A)	iv	iii	i	ii
(B)	i	iv	iii	ii
(C)	iii	ii	i	iv
(D)	ii	iii	iv	i

133. Match the following :

	List - I	**List - II**
a.	Barren Hypothesis	i. Indian men marry at 26-28 years age
b.	Idiographic Hypothesis	ii. Seema will top this year
c.	Nomothetic Hypothesis	iii. Loss of limbs
d.	Crude Hypothesis	iv. Quality of collection

Codes :	**(a)**	**(b)**	**(c)**	**(d)**
(A)	iv	iii	i	ii
(B)	iii	ii	iv	i
(C)	ii	i	iii	iv
(D)	i	iv	ii	iii

134. Match the following :

	List - I	**List - II**
a.	Multiple choice questions	i. Personal opinion of interviewer
b.	Loaded questions	ii. No sets of answers
c.	Contingency questions	iii. Alternative answers
d.	Open ended questions	iv. Sub-group of respondents

Codes :	**(a)**	**(b)**	**(c)**	**(d)**
(A)	i	iv	iii	ii
(B)	iv	ii	iii	i
(C)	iii	i	iv	ii
(D)	ii	iii	i	iv

135. Match the following :

	List - I	**List - II**
a.	Mean	i. Σ(O–E)2E
b.	Degree of freedom (df)	ii. n + 12
c.	Median	iii. (r – 1) (c – 1)
d.	Chi-square (χ^2)	iv. Σxn

Codes :	**(a)**	**(b)**	**(c)**	**(d)**
(A)	ii	iv	i	iii
(B)	iii	ii	i	iv
(C)	iv	iii	ii	i
(D)	i	ii	iv	iii

136. Which of the following can not be considered as probability sampling ?
(A) Lottery method of sampling
(B) Systematic sampling
(C) Snowball sampling
(D) Cluster sampling

137. Who provided the first explication of a theory of scales for the measurement of operational variables?
(A) E.S. Pearson (B) S.S. Stevens
(C) F.W. Lancaster (D) Steve Leach

138. The standard deviation of apopulation is :
(A) Mean of the squared deviations
(B) Mean deviation

(C) Simply the variance

(D) Simply the square root of theVariance

139. Systems study involves :

(A) Analysis only

(B) Analysis, evaluation and design

(C) Analysis and design only

(D) Analysis and evaluation only

140. The concept of systematic indexing was devised by:

(A) E.J. Coates (B) J.E.L. Farradane

(C) H.P. Luhn (D) J. Keiser

141. 'Shodhagangotri' Project isconcerned with :

(A) Theses (B) Synopsis of Theses

(C) Books (D) E-Journals

142. The formula for the Chi-square testis :

(A) a2 (B) b2

(C) _2 (D) c2

143. Identify the Dublin Core metadata element that is not relatedto the resource as intellectual property :

(A) Creator (B) Publisher

(C) Title (D) Contributor

144. Which indexing system uses a single term and an accession number of thedocument as an indicator of reference ?

(A) POPSI (B) KWIC

(C) Index of DDC (D) Relative Index

145. Lotka's law of scientific productivity is expressed by the equation :

Y = C/Xn Here Y represents :

(A) Frequency of authors making X contribution

(B) The number of articles

(C) Frequency of authors writingonly one paper

(D) The year of publication

146. Identify the factor that may cause in consistency in indexing :

(A) When number of concepts represented are less

(B) When the indexer is a very experienced person

(C) When number of concepts represented are more

(D) When a thesaurus is used tocontrol the vocabulary

147. Data mining is :

(A) A technique for searching large scale databases

(B) A database used for reporting

(C) A repository of an organisation's stored data

(D) The process of designing, building and maintaining and organisation's database

148. Match List-I and List-II and choose the correct answer by using the codes given below :

List-I	List-II
(i) E spirit-de-corps	(a) Herzberg
(ii) Theory X and theory Y	(b) Maslow
(iii) Hierarchy of human needs	(c) Douglas McGregor
(iv) Hygiene-motivation theory	(d) Henry Fayol

Codes :	**(i)**	**(ii)**	**(iii)**	**(iv)**
(A)	(a)	(b)	(c)	(d)
(B)	(b)	(c)	(d)	(a)
(C)	(c)	(d)	(a)	(b)
(D)	(d)	(c)	(b)	(a)

149. In experimental research method treatment is administered to members of the :
   (A) Control Group
   (B) Both Experimental and Control Group
   (C) Experimental Group
   (D) To neither of the two groups
150. When the value of the correlation coefficient r is near –1 (i.e., minusone), it indicates ?
   (A) A perfect inverse relationship
   (B) A perfect direct relationship
   (C) A strong inverse relationship
   (D) No correlation
151. The concept of 'Bibliographic Coupling' was given by :
   (A) Small and Griffith (B) M.M. Kessler
   (C) Allan Pritchard (D) Melvin Weinstock
152. In the hypothesis, "shelf height isa major determining factor of bookuse", shelf height is :
   (A) The dependent variable
   (B) Independent variable
   (C) It is not a variable
   (D) It is a sample
153. Which of the following canons of cataloguing prescribes that the information found on title and its over flow pages should be used for preparing main entry ?
   (A) Canon of context
   (B) Canon of prepotence
   (C) Canon of Ascertainability
   (D) Canon of Sought Heading

154. Match List-I and List-II and choosethe correct answer by using thecodes given below :

List-I	List-II
(i) Fusion	(a) Metaphysics
(ii) Fission	(b) Humanities
(iii) Cluster	(c) Indology
(iv) Agglomeration	(d) Astrophysics

Codes :	**(i)**	**(ii)**	**(iii)**	**(iv)**
(A)	(b)	(d)	(a)	(c)
(B)	(a)	(b)	(c)	(d)
(C)	(d)	(c)	(b)	(a)
(D)	(d)	(a)	(c)	(b)

155. Invisible colleges are :

(A) Network of individuals interested in a subject field

(B) Group of scientific meetings

(C) Both (A) and (B)

(D) Neither (A) nor (B)

156. Match List-I and List-II and choose the correct answer by using the codes given below :

List-I	List-II
(i) Primary document	(a) LISA
(ii) Geographical source	(b) Library Herald
(iii) Abstracting service	(c) Bibliography of Bibliographies
(iv) Tertiary document	(d) Fodor's India

Codes :	**(i)**	**(ii)**	**(iii)**	**(iv)**
(A)	(b)	(d)	(a)	(c)
(B)	(a)	(d)	(b)	(c)
(C)	(d)	(b)	(c)	(a)
(D)	(b)	(d)	(c)	(a)

157. **Statement (1) :** Unity of Direction implies one manager and one plan for all the operations which have the same objective in view.

 Statement (2) : This principle isuseful for creating departments and subdepartments for designing and functioning of the organization structure.

 In the above statements.

 (A) Both (1) and (2) are true

 (B) (1) is true but (2) is false

 (C) (1) is false but (2) is true

 (D) Both (1) and (2) are false

158. Which of the following sequences iscorrect about Maslow's hierarchy of needs ?

 (A) Physiological, social, security, esteem and selfactualization

 (B) Security, physiological, social, self-actualization and esteem

 (C) Physiological, security, social, self-actualization and esteem

 (D) Physiological, security, social, esteem and self actualization

159. Match List-I and List-II and choose the correct answer by using the codes given below :

List-I	List-II
(i) Hawthorne studies	(a) Maslow
(ii) Theory X and Theory Y	(b) George Elton Mayo
(iii) Hierarchy of Needs	(c) R. Likert
(iv) Leadership Styles	(d) Douglas McGregor

Codes :	**(i)**	**(ii)**	**(iii)**	**(iv)**
(A)	(a)	(c)	(d)	(b)
(B)	(b)	(d)	(a)	(c)
(C)	(a)	(b)	(d)	(c)
(D)	(b)	(c)	(d)	(a)

160. The Intellectual property that does not come under copyright is :
    (A) Paintings
    (B) Databases
    (C) Computer Programmes
    (D) Industrial Designs
161. Methods of experimental enquiry were advocated by :
    (A) Charles Darwin (B) Copernicus
    (C) J.S. Mill (D) Plato
162. What is not true about spamming ?
    (A) The most widely recognized form of spam is e-mail spam.
    (B) It is the abuse of electronic messaging systems
    (C) Spamming is expensive to advertisers
    (D) Spamming costs huge in terms of loss of productivity

ANSWERS

1. D	2. C	3. C	4. A	5. B	6. B
7. C	8. C	9. B	10. A	11. B	12. B
13. C	14. D	15. B	16. C	17. D	18. B
19. A	20. A	21. B	22. B	23. B	24. C
25. C	26. B	27. D	28. A	29. C	30. A
31. A	32. A	33. A	34. A	35. C	36. A
37. B	38. C	39. A	40. A	41. C	42. A
43. C	44. A	45. D	46. A	47. A	48. B

49. D	50. C	51. B	52. B	53. A	54. D
55. D	56. C	57. B	58. C	59. C	60. D
61. B	62. A	63. A	64. C	65. B	66. C
67. C	68. D	69. A	70. C	71. C	72. C
73. C	74. B	75. A/D	76. C	77. C	78. C
79. A	80. C	81. D	82. A	83. B	84. A
85. B	86. C	87. A	88. A	89. C	90. B
91. B	92. B	93. D	94. B	95. A	96. B
97. C	98. B	99. D	100. C	101. A	102. B
103. B	104. B	105. A	106. D	107. C	108. C
109. A	110. B	111. B	112. B	113. D	114. B
115. D	116. C	117. A	118. B	119. D	120. A
121. D	122. A	123. C	124. B	125. C	126. A
127. A	128. B	129. A	130. C	131. B	132. D
133. B	134. C	135. C	136. C	137. B	138. D
139. B	140. D	141. B	142. C	143. C	144. B
145. A	146. C	147. A	148. D	149. C	150. C
151. B	152. B	153. C	154. D	155. C	156. A
157. A	158. D	159. B	160. D	161. C	162. C

6

Information Products, Services

1. Digital Reference Service can beoffered through
   (A) FAX (B) OPAC
   (C) Ask your librarian (D) Consortia
2. Relational Database is
   (A) A work which has some relationship to another work
   (B) A symbol representing relationship between two concepts
   (C) Manipulation commands which relate records in different fields
   (D) All of the above
3. Which principles are corollary to Wall-picture principle ?
   (i) Cow-calf principle
   (ii) Principle of later-in-time
   (iii) Whole – organ principle
   (iv) All of the above

Codes :

(A) (i) and (ii) are correct

(B) (ii) and (iii) are correct

(C) (i) and (iii) are correct

(D) (i) and (iv) are correct

4. **Assertion (A) :** "Name Authority File" should be used in a library.

   Reason (R) : All works of an author should be collocated.

   Codes :

   (A) (A) is true, but (R) is false

   (B) Both (A) and (R) true and (R) isthe correct explanation of (A).

   (C) (A) is false, but (R) is true

   (D) Both (A) and (R) are false

5. Arrange the following according totheir year of enactment in India :

   (i) Freedom of Information Act

   (ii) Right to Information Act

   (iii) Copyright Act (Revised)

   (iv) Information Technology Act

   Codes :

   (A) (iv), (ii), (i), (iii) (B) (iii), (iv), (i), (ii)

   (C) (ii), (iii), (iv), (i) (D) (i), (iv), (ii), (iii)

6. Arrange the following publications according to their year of origin.

   (i) Social Science Citation Index

   (ii) L I S A

   (iii) Library Literature and Information Science

   (iv) Library Journal

Codes :

(A) (i), (iii), (iv), (ii) (B) (ii), (i), (iii), (iv)

(C) (iv), (iii), (ii), (i) (D) (iii), (ii), (iv), (i)

7. Arrange the following according to their year of origin :

(i) Bradford's Law

(ii) Lotka's Law

(iii) Statistical Bibliography

(iv) Zipf's Law

Codes :

(A) (i), (iii), (iv), (ii) (B) (i), (ii), (iv), (iii)

(C) (iv), (iii), (i), (ii) (D) (iii), (ii), (iv), (i)

8. Which one of the following is a Bulletin Board Service on Internet ?

(A) Picaso (B) Google talk

(C) Blog (D) Oovoo

9. BIOS contains :

(i) Operating System Program

(ii) Bootstrap Program

(iii) Application System Program

(iv) Convert Character to CodeProgram

Codes :

(A) (i) and (ii) are correct

(B) (ii) and (iii) are correct

(C) (iii) and (iv) are correct

(D) (ii) and (iv) are correct

10. **Assertion (A) :** An indexing language is an artificial language and it uses controlled vocabulary.

Reason (R) : Controlled vocabulary provides relation between and among terms.

Codes :

(A) Both (A) and (R) are true.

(B) (A) is true, but (R) is false.

(C) (A) is false, but (R) is true.

(D) Both (A) and (R) are false.

11. **Assertion (A) :** Marketing of Information products is the need of the day.

Reason (R) : Information is aresource which consumes lot of time and money.

Codes :

(A) (A) is true, but (R) is false.

(B) (A) is false, but (R) is true.

(C) Both (A) and (R) are true.

(D) Both (A) and (R) are false.

12. **Assertion (A) :** INFLIBNET provides document delivery service to all types of libraries in India.

Reason (R) : Modern technologies made it possible for electronic transmission of required documents.

Codes :

(A) Both (A) and (R) are correct.

(B) (A) is wrong, but (R) is correct.

(C) Both (A) and (R) are wrong.

(D) (A) is correct and (R) is wrong.

13. Match the following :

List-I	**List-II**
(a) FaceBook	(i) Video Networking site
(b) Research Gate	(ii) Social Networking site
(c) Oovoo	(iii) Academic Networking site
(d) Flicker	(iv) Photo Networking site

Codes :	**(a)**	**(b)**	**(c)**	**(d)**
(A)	(i)	(iii)	(ii)	(iv)
(B)	(iv)	(i)	(ii)	(iii)
(C)	(ii)	(iii)	(i)	(iv)
(D)	(iii)	(iv)	(i)	(ii)

14. Which of the following are review type services ?
    (i) Current Awareness
    (ii) Trend Reports
    (iii) News Clippings
    (iv) State of the Art Report

    Codes :
    (A) (i), (ii), (iii) are correct.
    (B) (i), (iii), (iv) are correct.
    (C) (ii) & (iv) are correct.
    (D) (ii) & (iii) are correct.

15. Which one of the following is not a virtual library ?
    (A) Without walls.
    (B) With distributed physicallocations.
    (C) Providing integrated and unified remote access to geographically distributed collections.
    (D) Which does not exist in reality.

16. Which of the following are not reference service ?
    (i) Preparation of user profile
    (ii) Initiation of freshman
    (iii) Compilation of documentation list
    (iv) Readers Advisory

    Codes :
    (A) (i) and (ii) (B) (ii) and (iii)
    (C) (i) and (iii) (D) (iii) and (iv)

17. Which of the following functions are analysed by ALA as reference service functions ?
    (i) Consultation function
    (ii) Guidance function
    (iii) Instruction function
    (iv) Bibliographic function

    Codes :
    (A) (i), (ii) and (iii) are correct.
    (B) (ii), (iii) and (iv) are correct.
    (C) (i), (ii) and (iv) are correct.
    (D) (i), (iii) and (iv) are correct.

18. Match the following :

List - I	**List - II**
a. Altavista	i. Subject search engine
b. Lycos	ii. Meta search engine
c. Geo index	iii. Regional search engine
d. Savvy search	iv. General search engine

Codes :	**(a)**	**(b)**	**(c)**	**(d)**
(A)	iii	ii	i	iv
(B)	iii	iv	ii	i
(C)	iv	iii	i	ii
(D)	iv	i	ii	iii

19. Match the following :

List - I	**List - II**
a. Informix	i. Image software
b. OmniPage	ii. Remote login software
c. TIFF viewer	iii. DBMS software
d. TeamViewer	iv. OCR software

Codes :	**(a)**	**(b)**	**(c)**	**(d)**
(A)	ii	i	iii	iv
(B)	iii	iv	i	ii
(C)	i	ii	iii	iv
(D)	iv	iii	ii	i

20. Match the following :

List - I	**List - II**
a. William Martin	i. Little Science Big Science
b. Alvin Toffler	ii. Information society
c. Eric J deSolla Price	iii. Documentation
d. S.C.Bradford	iv. The Third Wave

Codes :	**(a)**	**(b)**	**(c)**	**(d)**
(A)	ii	iv	iii	i
(B)	iv	ii	iii	i
(C)	ii	iv	i	iii
(D)	i	iv	ii	iii

21. **Assertion (A) :** Micrographic services have lost acceptance for preservation and dissemination of archival material.

Reason (R) : ICT has brought in cost effective alternatives and replaced micrographic services.

Codes :

(A) (A) is true and (R) is partially true.

(B) Both (A) & (R) are false.

(C) (A) is true, (R) is false.

(D) (A) is false, (R) is true.

22. Which is not a reprographic service ?

(A) Micro Copying (B) Blue Printing

(C) Paper Printing (D) Thermo Copying

23. A technique displaying graphic information on

screen, pixel by pixel with bits held in main memory is

(A) Bit handling (B) Bit mapping

(C) Bit pattern (D) Bit matrix

24. Identify the technique(s) to collectthe data regarding the number of persons visited the periodical section of the library at different hours of the day.

(i) Questionnaire (ii) Interview

(iii) Observation (iv) Library records

Codes :

(A) (i) and (ii) are correct.

(B) (ii) and (iii) are correct.

(C) (iii) and (iv) are correct.

(D) (ii) and (iv) are correct.

25. **Assertion (A) :** Digitization has proved to be possible for every format and medium held by library.

Reason (R) : All libraries are making their text and visual collections digitized.

Codes :

(A) (A) is true, but (R) is false.

(B) (A) is false, but (R) is true.

(C) Both (A) and (R) are true.

(D) Both (A) and (R) are false.

26. **Assertion (A) :** In spite of political, economic and technological support, the growth of Public Library System is lopsided.

Reason (R) : The public libraries are totally depending on cess/taxamounts.

Codes :

(A) Both (A) and (R) are true.

(B) Both (A) and (R) are false.

(C) (A) is true, but (R) is false.
(D) (A) is false, but (R) is true.

27. The concept of 'Reference Service' is given by
(A) J.H. Shera (B) A. Strauss
(C) S.R. Ranganathan (D) Samuel Green

28. Which of the following is not an alerting service ?
(A) CAS
(B) SDI
(C) Document Delivery Service
(D) Electronic Clipping Service

29. The following is a collaborative network of Reference Librarians
(A) Worldcat (B) INDEST
(C) Question point (D) Global scholar

30. Which of the following is not a synchronous virtual reference service ?
(A) Chat
(B) E-mail
(C) Video-conferencing
(D) Voice over IP

31. Which of the following are value added information services ?
(i) Aggregator Service
(ii) Referral Service
(iii) Document Delivery Service
(iv) Research Reports/Market Survey Reports

Codes :
(A) (i) and (iii) are correct
(B) (ii) and (iv) are correct
(C) (ii) and (iii) are correct
(D) (i) and (iv) are correct

32. Arrange in sequence the medium used for 'Virtual Reference' in the order of their progress.

    i. Web form

    ii. Ask a Service

    iii. E-mail

    iv. Social Networking

    Codes :

    (A) i ii iii iv (B) ii iii iv i

    (C) iii i ii iv (D) iv ii i iii

33. **Assertion (A) :** All reference sources provide up to date information in their respective categories.

    Reason (R) : As these are compiled from primary sources of information.

    Codes :

    (A) Both (A) and (R) are true.

    (B) Both (A) and (R) are false.

    (C) (A) is false but (R) is partiallytrue.

    (D) (A) is true but (R) is false.

34. **Assertion (A) :** Online Reference Service can be offered using IMs, SMs, VoIP, Video, Blogs, Websites and host of such other mechanisms.

    Reason (R) : Majority of academic libraries in India are equipped with required infrastructure.

    Codes :

    (A) Both (A) and (R) are true.

    (B) (A) is true, (R) is false.

    (C) (A) is false, (R) is true.

    (D) Both (A) and (R) are false.

35. **Assertion (A) :** For providing an effective reference service, best & up to date reference collection is not as important as is the competent reference librarian.

Reason (R) : An efficient reference librarian can serve the users more effectively even in the absence of best reference collection.

Codes :

(A) (A) is true but (R) is false.

(B) Both (A) and (R) are true.

(C) (A) is false but (R) is true.

(D) Both (A) and (R) are false.

36. **Assertion (A)** : Reference section in a Library became insignificant.

Reason (R) : The Web. 2.0 services replaces the reference desk services.

Codes :

(A) (A) is true, but (R) is false.

(B) Both (A) and (R) are true.

(C) Both (A) and (R) are false.

(D) (A) is false and (R) is true.

37. A situation where a digital resource is no longer readable is called

(A) Digital Divide

(B) Digital Representation

(C) Digital Rendering

(D) Digital Obsolescence

38. EUAL stands for

(A) E-monitoring library forAcademics

(B) End User Logistics Association

(C) Electronic Usage of LibraryAcquisitions

(D) End User License Agreement

39. **Assertion (A)** : The objective of "Cross Ref" is to improve access to published scholarly works through collaborative technologies.

Reason (R) : "Cross Ref" is a non-profit membership association founded and directed by publishers.

Codes :

(A) Both (A) and (R) are true.

(B) Both (A) and (R) are true, but (R) is not the correct explanation.

(C) (A) is true, but (R) is false.

(D) (A) is false, but (R) is true.

40. **Assertion (A) :** Social networking tools are very effective for marketing of library products and services.

Reason (R) : It does not help to reach out the patrons any where any time.

Codes :

(A) (A) is true, but (R) is false.

(B) (A) is false, but (R) is true.

(C) Both (A) and (R) are true.

(D) Both (A) and (R) are false.

41. Index Translationum is a world bibliography of translations of :

(A) Periodical articles

(B) Books

(C) Books and periodical articles

(D) Patents

42. INSPEC database records ....

(A) Full text (B) Index and Abstract

(C) Numerical (D) Abstract and Full text

43. Which of the following journals is available only in electronic form ?

(A) D-Lib Magazine

(B) Journal of Documentation

(C) Library Quarterly

(D) Library Trends

44. In the context of extension services mark the odd one :

(A) Public lectures and talks byeminent persons

(B) Celebration of festivals

(C) Arranging the music show etc.

(D) Providing information pinpointedly

45. Which of the following is a primary document ?

(A) Science

(B) Indian Science Abstracts

(C) Science Citation Index

(D) Chemical Abstracts Service

46. Match the following List-I and List-II and choose the correct answer by using the codes given below:

List-I	**List-II**
(i) DOAJ	(a) Science Direct
(ii) Thomson Reuters	(b) Web of Science
(iii) Elsevier	(c) Open Access Journals
(iv) ASLIB Proceedings	(d) Emerald

Codes :	**(i)**	**(ii)**	**(iii)**	**(iv)**
(A)	(b)	(d)	(c)	(a)
(B)	(a)	(c)	(d)	(b)
(C)	(c)	(b)	(a)	(d)
(D)	(d)	(c)	(a)	(b)

47. General Information Programmewas launched by :

(A) UNESCO (B) IFLA

(C) FID (D) ISO

48. What does TLC stand for:

(A) Telecommunication and Documentation

(B) Traning In Librarianship
(C) Traning In Documentation For Librarianship
(D) Total Library Development Programme

49. Which of the following is an example of Associative relationship ?
(A) Vertebrates—Mammals
(B) Photocopies—Xeroxes
(C) Polling—Public Opinion
(D) Polyvinyl Chloride/PVC

50. In an Empirical study on impact of internet on reading, 'reading' would be :
(A) An independent variable
(B) The dependent variable
(C) An intervening variable
(D) The continuous variable

51. Match List-I and List-II and choose the correct answer by using the codes given below :

List-I	List-II
(i) Fusion	(a) Metaphysics
(ii) Fission	(b) Humanities
(iii) Cluster	(c) Indology
(iv) Agglomeration	(d) Astrophysics

Codes :	(i)	(ii)	(iii)	(iv)
(A)	(b)	(d)	(a)	(c)
(B)	(a)	(b)	(c)	(d)
(C)	(d)	(c)	(b)	(a)
(D)	(d)	(a)	(c)	(b)

52. Invisible colleges are :
(A) Network of individuals interested in a subject field

(B) Group of scientific meetings

(C) Both (A) and (B)

(D) Neither (A) nor (B)

53. Match List-I and List-II and choose the correct answer by using the codes given below :

List-I	List-II
(i) CeRA	(a) Education
(ii) FORSA	(b) Agriculture
(iii) INDEST	(c) Astrophysics
(iv) ERIC	(d) Engineering

Codes :	**(i)**	**(ii)**	**(iii)**	**(iv)**
(A)	(a)	(d)	(c)	(b)
(B)	(d)	(a)	(b)	(c)
(C)	(c)	(b)	(d)	(a)
(D)	(b)	(c)	(d)	(a)

54. In Building Block Search Strategy adding an extra facet would result in :

(A) Higher recall

(B) Higher precision

(C) Increase in recall as well as precision

(D) Lower precision

55. Which is not applicable to extensible Mark up Language ?

(A) It is compatible with SGML

(B) It is usable over Internet

(C) XML documents are easy to create

(D) It has to do with semantics to Data

56. **Statement (1) :** Cross-reference entry of the classification catalogue code is a number entry.

Statement (2) : It is entered under the dominant class of the document.

In the above statements :

(A) Both (1) and (2) are true

(B) (1) is true but (2) is false

(C) (1) is false but (2) is true

(D) Both (1) and (2) are false

57. Arrange the following Public Library Acts according to their year of enactment.

(i) Mizoram Public Libraries Act

(ii) Tamil Nadu Public Libraries Act

(iii) Haryana Public Libraries Act

(iv) Orissa Public Libraries Act

Codes :

(A) (iv) (iii) (i) (ii) (B) (ii) (iii) (i) (iv)

(C) (ii) (i) (iv) (iii) (D) (iii) (ii) (i) (iv)

58. ....Search gives more information output :

(A) Boolean 'And' (B) Boolean 'Or'

(C) Boolean 'Not' (D) Phrase Search

59. **Assertion (A) :** Loose Assemblage is the process of linking together different classes.

Reason (R) : The number of subjects are restricted.

In the above statements :

(A) (A) is true but (R) is false

(B) (A) is false but (R) is true

(C) Both (A) and (R) are true

(D) Both (A) and (R) are false

60. Identify the MARC tag that is used for variable fields containing data related to subject access to the document :

(A) 7 XX (B) 6 XX

(C) 5 XX (D) 2 XX

61. Which of the following is not the characteristics of the information society ?

(A) Information used as an economic source

(B) People use information intensively in their activities

(C) Information sector within the economy is developed

(D) Dependence on traditional Knowledge

62. How to write the size of book having height 21.5 cm and width 30 cm ina catalogue entry according toAACR II ?

(A) 21 cm (B) 22 cm

(C) 21 × 30 cm (D) 22 × 30 cm

63. According to ISBD format the GMDis recorded :

(A) After the statement of responsibility

(B) After the title proper

(C) After the subtitle

(D) After the series statement

64. Match List-I and List-II and choose the correct answer by using the codes given below :

List-I	**List-II**
(i) Maslow	(a) Hygienic factors
(ii) McGregor	(b) Immaturity /Maturity
(iii) Argyris	(c) Theory Y
(iv) Herzberg	(d) Hierarchy of needs

Codes :	**(i)**	**(ii)**	**(iii)**	**(iv)**
(A)	(a)	(b)	(c)	(d)
(B)	(d)	(a)	(b)	(c)
(C)	(d)	(c)	(b)	(a)
(D)	(d)	(c)	(a)	(b)

65. Which one of the following is the function of a library committee ?
    (A) To produce useful reading material
    (B) To lay down general library policy
    (C) To render adequate reference service
    (D) To arrange for resource sharing and interlibrary loan

66. Match List-I and List-II and choose the correct answer by using the codes given below :

List-I	**List-II**
(i) Primary document	(a) LISA
(ii) Geographical source	(b) Library Herald
(iii) Abstracting service	(c) Bibliography of Bibliographies
(iv) Tertiary document	(d) Fodor's India

Codes :	**(i)**	**(ii)**	**(iii)**	**(iv)**
(A)	(b)	(d)	(a)	(c)
(B)	(a)	(d)	(b)	(c)
(C)	(d)	(b)	(c)	(a)
(D)	(b)	(d)	(c)	(a)

67. Arrange the following classification schemes in their chronological order of origin :
    (i) Bibliographic Classification
    (ii) Colon Classification
    (iii) Universal Decimal Classification
    (iv) Dewey Decimal Classification

Codes :
(A) (i) (ii) (iii) (iv) (B) (iii) (iv) (ii) (i)
(C) (iv) (iii) (ii) (i) (D) (i) (iv) (iii) (ii)

68. Which of the following is an indicator of dispersion for a set of observations ?
   (A) Central tendency
   (B) Correlation coefficient
   (C) Regression line
   (D) Standard Deviation

69. **Statement (1) :** Unity of Direction implies one manager and one plan for all the operations which have the same objective in view.

   Statement (2) : This principle is useful for creating departments and sub departments for designing and functioning of the organization structure.

   In the above statements.
   (A) Both (1) and (2) are true
   (B) (1) is true but (2) is false
   (C) (1) is false but (2) is true
   (D) Both (1) and (2) are false

70. Which of the following sequences is correct about Maslow's hierarchy of needs ?
   (A) Physiological, social, security, esteem and self actualization
   (B) Security, physiological, social, self-actualization and esteem
   (C) Physiological, security, social, self-actualization and esteem
   (D) Physiological, security, social, esteem and self actualization

71. Match List-I and List-II and choose the correct answer by using the codes given below :

	List-I	List-II
(i)	Hawthorne studies	(a) Maslow
(ii)	Theory X and Theory Y	(b) George Elton Mayo
(iii)	Hierarchy of Needs	(c) R. Likert
(iv)	Leadership Styles	(d) Douglas McGregor

Codes :	**(i)**	**(ii)**	**(iii)**	**(iv)**
(A)	(a)	(c)	(d)	(b)
(B)	(b)	(d)	(a)	(c)
(C)	(a)	(b)	(d)	(c)
(D)	(b)	(c)	(d)	(a)

72. Arrange the following in chronological sequence of their year of establishment :

(i) IASLIC (ii) IATLIS

(iii) SIS (iv) ILA

Codes :

(A) (iv) (i) (ii) (iii) (B) (i) (ii) (iv) (iii)

(C) (ii) (i) (iv) (iii) (D) (i) (iii) (iv) (ii)

73. The Intellectual property that does not come under copyright is :

(A) Paintings

(B) Databases

(C) Computer Programmes

(D) Industrial Designs

74. Methods of experimental enquiry were advocated by :

(A) Charles Darwin (B) Copernicus

(C) J.S. Mill (D) Plato

75. What is not true about spamming ?

(A) The most widely recognized form of spam is e-mail spam.

(B) It is the abuse of electronic messaging systems

(C) Spamming is expensive to advertisers

(D) Spamming costs huge in terms of loss of productivity

ANSWERS

1. C	2. C	3. C	4. B	5. B	6. C
7. D	8. C	9. A	10. A	11. C	12. B
13. C	14. C	15. B	16. C	17. B	18. C
19. B	20. C	21. A	22. C	23. B	24. C
25. A	26. C	27. D	28. C	29. C	30. B
31. D	32. C	33. C	34. B	35. B	36. D
37. D	38. D	39. A/B	40. A	41. B	42. B
43. A	44. D	45. A	46. C	47. A	48. B
49. C	50. B	51. D	52. C	53. D	54. B
55. D	56. B	57. B	58. B	59. A	60. B
61. D	62. D	63. B	64. C	65. B	66. A
67. C	68. D	69. A	70. D	71. B	72. A
73. D	74. C	75. C			

7

Application of Information Technology

1. "Biotechnology" is formed as a result of
   (A) Fusion (B) Lamination
   (C) Fission (D) Agglomeration
2. The information network that connects Universities and Colleges in United Kingdom :
   (A) JANET (B) SERCNET
   (C) OCLC (D) BONET
3. Internet filtering is
   (A) A form of censorship
   (B) Acceptable user policy
   (C) Access to inappropriate material
   (D) Blocking internet facility
4. Virus is a software which can
   (A) Manipulate data (B) Replicate itself
   (C) Damage computer (D) All the above

5. Which one of the following protocol isused in file transfer over internet ?

(A) FTP (B) SMTP

(C) POP (D) TCP/IP

6. **Assertion (A)** : Modern Integrated Library Management Softwares offer user friendly Graphical UserInterfaces (GUI) on the web.

Reason (R) : Almost every module of modern Integrated Library Management Software isaccessible through the internet.

Codes :

(A) Both (A) and (R) are correct.

(B) (A) is correct but (R) is wrong.

(C) Both (A) and (R) are wrong.

(D) (A) is wrong but (R) is correct.

7. **Assertion (A) :** Open Systems Interconnection allows connectivity of ICT components.

Reason (R) : Network Printer goesslow if it is OSI compatible.

Codes :

(A) Both (A) and (R) are true.

(B) Both (A) and (R) are false.

(C) (A) is false, but (R) is true.

(D) (A) is true, but (R) is false.

8. **Assertion (A)** : Browne charging system is simple and less time consuming.

Reason (R) : There is permanent issue record available.

Codes :

(A) (A) is false, but (R) is true.

(B) (A) is true, but (R) is false.

(C) Both (A) and (R) are true.

(D) Both (A) and (R) are false.

9. Match the following :

List-I	**List-II**
(a) HTMLFile	(i) Text Format
(b) PDF File	(ii) Film Format
(c) JPG File	(iii) Web Format
(d) AVI File	(iv) Image Format

Codes :	**(a)**	**(b)**	**(c)**	**(d)**
(A)	(i)	(ii)	(iv)	(iii)
(B)	(iii)	(i)	(iv)	(ii)
(C)	(i)	(iv)	(ii)	(iii)
(D)	(iv)	(iii)	(i)	(ii)

10. Match the following :

List-I	**List-II**
(a) DRUPAL	(i) Integrated Library Management Software
(b) Moodle	(ii) Digital Library Software
(c) D space	(iii) Content Management Software
(d) New GenLib	(iv) Learning Management Software

Codes :	**(a)**	**(b)**	**(c)**	**(d)**
(A)	(iv)	(iii)	(ii)	(i)
(B)	(ii)	(i)	(iv)	(iii)
(C)	(iii)	(iv)	(ii)	(i)
(D)	(i)	(ii)	(iii)	(iv)

11. "Web of Science" is

(A) A Citation Index

(B) A Bibliography

(C) An Abstracting Service

(D) All of the above

12. "Facts on File" can be grouped under

(A) Primary source (B) Secondary source

(C) Tertiary source (D) None of the above

13. In MARC 21, subject access fields are

(A) 3xx (B) 4xx

(C) 5xx (D) 6xx

14. Which one of the following is not a switching system?

(A) Packet (B) Circuit

(C) Router (D) Message

15. The basic characteristics of a system are

(i) Interrelated components

(ii) Independent and can stand alone

(iii) Arranged in hierarchical order

(iv) Inputs, processes, outputs & feed back

Codes :

(A) (i), (ii), (iii) are correct.

(B) (i), (ii), (iv) are correct.

(C) (ii), (iii), (iv) are correct.

(D) (i), (iii), (iv) are correct.

16. The general image file formats are :

(i) TIFF (ii) JPEG

(iii) MPEG (iv) PNG

Codes :

(A) (i), (ii) and (iii) are correct.

(B) (i), (iii) and (iv) are correct.

(C) (i), (ii) and (iv) are correct.

(D) (ii), (iii) and (iv) are correct.

17. Which of the following are common types of protocols ?

(i) HTTP (ii) FTP

(iii) Telnet (iv) Gopher

Codes :

(A) (i) and (ii) are correct.

(B) (i), (ii) and (iv) are correct.

(C) (iii) and (iv) are correct.

(D) (i), (ii) and (iii) are correct.

18. Which of the following are not the elements of DOI system ?

(i) Policies (ii) Subject

(iii) Description (iv) Resolution

Codes :

(A) (i), (ii) and (iii) are correct.

(B) (i), (iii) and (iv) are correct.

(C) (i), (ii) and (iv) are correct.

(D) (ii), (iii) and (iv) are correct.

19. **Assertion (A) :** Indian libraries are making optimum use of social networking.

Reason (R) : Social networking has wider role in dissemination of information.

Codes :

(A) (A) is true but (R) is false.

(B) (A) is false but (R) is true.

(C) (A) and (R) both are true.

(D) (A) and (R) both are false.

20. Match the following :

List - I	List - II
a. File transfer protocol	i. Data transmission capacity
b. Multimedia	ii. Integration of text, colour sound and animation
c. Bandwidth	iii. Bulletin Board
d. Electronic Notice Board	iv. Internet

Codes :	(a)	(b)	(c)	(d)
(A)	iv	ii	i	iii
(B)	i	iii	ii	iv
(C)	ii	i	iv	iii
(D)	i	iv	ii	i

21. Match the following :

List - I	List - II
a. ISDN	i. Web page
b. URL	ii. Video Conferencing
c. Firewall	iii. Internet Standard for Information Transmission
d. HTTP	iv. Protecting unauthorised access internet

Codes :	(a)	(b)	(c)	(d)
(A)	iii	iv	i	ii
(B)	iv	i	iii	ii
(C)	ii	i	iv	iii
(D)	i	iii	ii	iv

22. National Knowledge Network is tobe implemented by
    (A) National Knowledge Commission
    (B) Information and Library Network

(C) National Information Centre
(D) Department of InformationTechnology

23. ISO 9000 standard denotes the
    (A) consistence confirmance of aproduct or service to a given setof standard or expectations
    (B) Total customer satisfaction
    (C) Representation of stake holders issues.
    (D) Detailed list of measuring techniques

24. The national convention regularly organized by DELNET is known as
    (A) CALIBER (B) ICDL
    (C) NACLIN (D) DELNETCON

25. Which topology of computer network provides faster server access ?
    (i) BUS Network Topology
    (ii) RING Network Topology
    (iii) MULTIPLE RING Network Topology
    (iv) STAR Network Topology

    Codes :
    (A) (i) and (ii) are correct.
    (B) (i) and (iii) are correct.
    (C) (ii) and (iii) are correct.
    (D) (ii) and (iv) are correct.

26. Which of the following are ISDN services ?
    (i) RSS (ii) Teletext
    (iii) Voice mail (iv) Video conference

    Codes :
    (A) (i), (iii) and (iv) are correct.
    (B) (i), (ii) and (iv) are correct.
    (C) (ii), (iii) and (iv) are correct.
    (D) (i), (ii) and (iii) are correct.

27. Planting the virus 'Trojan Horse' in computer network is

    (i) Hacking (ii) Tampering

    (iii) Decryption (iv) Intrusion

    Codes :

    (A) (i), (iii) and (iv) are correct

    (B) (ii), (iii) and (iv) are correct

    (C) (i), (ii) and (iii) are correct

    (D) (i), (ii) and (iv) are correct

28. **Assertion (A) :** RDF supports theuse and exchange of metadataon the web.

    Reason (R) : Bibliographic standards are the means to create and disseminate secondary information.

    Codes :

    (A) (A) is true, (R) is false.

    (B) (A) is false, (R) is true.

    (C) Both (A) & (R) are correct.

    (D) Both (A) & (R) are false.

29. Webform is used in

    (A) Synchronous Virtual Reference Service

    (B) Asynchronous Virtual Reference Service

    (C) Both (A) & (B)

    (D) None of the above

30. What is the process of transferring software programme from secondary storage media to the hard disc called ?

    (A) Download (B) Upload

    (C) Installation (D) Storage

31. Name the storage medium (compatible with speed of CPU) for storing instructions or data temporarily during processing

(A) RAM (B) ROM
(C) Cache (D) EPROM

32. Which set of rules is applicable for exchange of files over Internet ?
(A) FTP/IP (B) HTTP
(C) HTML (D) HYPERLINK

33. What is/are not common feature/s between RFID & Barcode Technology?
(i) Read more than one item at a time
(ii) Able to locate specific items on shelves
(iii) Programmable
(iv) Read while item is moving

Codes :

(A) (i), (ii) are correct.
(B) (iii), (iv) are correct.
(C) (ii), (iv) are correct.
(D) All the above are correct.

34. When a librarian has to show the rationale for the purchase of more e-resources, which of the following/s will help to support his/her stand ?
(i) Collection development policy
(ii) Indent from users
(iii) Book selection tools
(iv) All the above

Codes :

(A) (i) and (ii) are correct.
(B) (i) and (iii) are correct.
(C) (ii) and (iii) are correct.
(D) (iv) is correct.

35. **Assertion (A) :** Machine translation is not a fully dependable service.

Reason (R) : The semantics of languages are not fully encoded in algorithms.

Codes :

(A) (A) is true, but (R) is false.

(B) Both (A) & (R) are true.

(C) (A) is false, but (R) is true.

(D) Both (A) & (R) are false.

36. Match the following :

	List - I	List - II
a.	Internal Fiels	i. .WPD
b.	Universal File Format	ii. .OeB
c.	Corel's Word Perfect	iii. .HTML
d.	Microsoft Reader	iv. .RTF

Codes :	**(a)**	**(b)**	**(c)**	**(d)**
(A)	i	iii	ii	iv
(B)	ii	iv	iii	i
(C)	iv	ii	i	iii
(D)	iii	iv	i	ii

37. Match the following :

List - I	List - II
a. PDFA	i. High colour depth images
b. HTML	ii. Rules for encoding documents electronically
c. TIFF	iii. File format for long term archiving
d. XML	iv. Language for web pages

Codes :	**(a)**	**(b)**	**(c)**	**(d)**
(A)	ii	iii	i	iv
(B)	iii	iv	i	ii
(C)	i	iii	ii	iv
(D)	iv	ii	iii	i

38. Match the following :

	List - I	**List - II**
a.	Resource Description	i. MARC
b.	Resource Discovery	ii. ISO 10160/ 10161
c.	Resource Exchange	iii. Dublin Care
d.	Interlibrary Loan	iv. Z 39.50

Codes :	**(a)**	**(b)**	**(c)**	**(d)**
(A)	ii	i	iv	iii
(B)	iv	ii	i	iii
(C)	iii	iv	ii	i
(D)	iii	iv	i	i

39. **Assertion (A) :** RFID technology is still not widely installed in Indian Library Environment.

Reason (R) : The standardization, application and innovation are constantly changing.

Codes :

(A) Both (A) & (R) are true and (R) is the correct explanation of (A).

(B) Both (A) & (R) are true, but (R) is not the correct explanation of (A).

(C) (A) is true, but (R) is false.

(D) (A) is false, but (R) is true.

40. **Assertion (A) :** Gap device is a non-scientific solution to the problem of growing universe.

Reason (R) : A classificationist cannot forecast the areas/ subjects wherein some new ones may emerge.

Codes :

(A) (A) and (R) are true.

(B) (A) is true and (R) is false.

(C) (A) is false and (R) is true.

(D) (A) and (R) are false.

41. Sector Device is an extension of
    (A) Gap Device
    (B) Empty Device
    (C) Octave Device
    (D) Group Notation Device

42. ZOTERO is a ______.
    (A) Content Management System
    (B) Reference Management System
    (C) Serials Management System
    (D) Bibliographic Rreference Management System

43. A network in which the host computer controls different nodes which further control other nodes, is known as
    (A) Star Network
    (B) Ring Network
    (C) Hierarchical Network
    (D) Multipoint Network

44. In the world wide web, name the acronym that describes the internet address of a file
    (A) ULA (B) RELUR
    (C) URI (D) UR

45. Which of the following is/are related to open access initiatives ?
    (i) Creative Commons
    (ii) DOAJ
    (iii) FOSS
    (iv) GNU

    Codes :
    (A) (i), (iii) and (iv) are correct.
    (B) (i), (ii) and (iii) are correct.

(C) (ii) and (iii) are correct.

(D) (i) and (ii) are correct.

46. User-friendly interface caters to

(i) Human-computer Interaction

(ii) Individual users with customisation

(iii) Simplify execution of operations

(iv) Basis for computer-computer interface

Codes :

(A) (i), (ii) and (iv) are correct.

(B) (i) and (iii) are correct.

(C) (ii) and (iii) are correct.

(D) (i), (iii) and (iv) are correct.

47. Match the following dialogue systems :

List - I	List - II
a. Menu	i. Computer recognizable dialogues
b. Icons	ii. Communicating with computers with everyday language
c. Natural language	iii. List of options available
d. Common language	iv. Pictorial representation of objects

Codes :	(a)	(b)	(c)	(d)
(A)	i	iii	iv	ii
(B)	ii	iv	iii	i
(C)	iii	iv	ii	i
(D)	iv	ii	iii	i

48. Arrange the following in chronological order of their establishment :

(i) ARPANET

(ii) DARPA

(iii) SPUTNIK

(iv) ICCB (Internet Configuration Control Board)

Codes :

(A) iv i iii ii (B) iii ii i iv

(C) ii iii iv i (D) i ii iv i

49. An Application Program Interface (API) language is used for

(A) Network Management

(B) Graphical user Interface

(C) Relational Interface in Data Base Management

(D) Database Management System

50. Which of the following identifies user by a login permission to a licensed site.

(A) Authorization (B) Authentication

(C) Digital signature (D) All of the above

51. The main components of an RFID system include

(A) Handheld Reader, RFID label printer, server and External book return

(B) RFID tags, readers or sensors, Antenna and server

(C) RFID label printer, sensors, antenna and server

(D) RFID tags, server, external book return, sensors

52. Which of the following is not the component of a search engine ?

(A) Spider

(B) Index

(C) Search of retrieval mechanism

(D) Natural language technique

53. 'Communities' is a component of following digital library software

(A) GSDL (B) D space

(C) Fedora (D) i-core

54. The web address that acts as permanent identifier is ______.

(A) URL (B) DOI

(C) PURL (D) U

55. Match the following :

List - I	List - II
a. Algorith	i. Instruction to the computer
b. Flow charts	ii. Debugging
c. Program code	iii. Pictorially represented direction lines
d. Program test	iv. Set of explicit and finite steps

Codes :	**(a)**	**(b)**	**(c)**	**(d)**
(A)	ii	iii	iv	i
(B)	iii	i	iv	ii
(C)	iv	iii	i	ii
(D)	i	ii	iv	iii

56. **Assertion (A) :** Z 39.50 standard protocol enables communication among networked computers through a single search interface.

Reason (R) : Z 39.50 application in library consortia environment can enhance resource sharing.

Codes :

(A) Both (A) and (R) are true.

(B) Both (A) and (R) are false.

(C) (A) is true and (R) is false.

(D) (A) is false and (R) is true.

57. OAISTER is an example of digital libraries architecture based on
    (A) CORBA
    (B) Software Agents Architecture
    (C) Federated Database System
    (D) Metadata Harvesting
58. RSS feed is a tool of
    (A) Web 2.0 (B) Web 1.0
    (C) Web 3.0 (D) Graphic Design
59. Which of the following are the advantages of RFID technology in libraries ?
    (i) Tags can be read inside a case.
    (ii) Hundred of tags can be read ata time.
    (iii) Cheaper than Barcode
    (iv) More security and Privacy

    Codes :
    (A) (i) and (iii) are correct
    (B) (i) and (ii) are correct
    (C) (ii) and (iii) are correct
    (D) (iii) and (iv) are correct
60. Which of the following are limitations of digital libraries ?
    (i) Full text searching
    (ii) Operational costs
    (iii) Rights management
    (iv) Hyper text linking

    Codes :
    (A) (ii), (iii) and (iv) are correct
    (B) (ii) and (iii) are correct
    (C) (i), (ii) and (iv) are correct
    (D) (i) and (iv) are correct

61. Match the following evaluation criteria of print materials :

List - I	**List - II**
a. Authority	i. Typography
b. Scope	ii. Stated purpose
c. Format	iii. Publisher'sreputation
d. Arrangement	iv. Cross references

Codes :	**(a)**	**(b)**	**(c)**	**(d)**
(A)	ii	iii	i	iv
(B)	i	iv	ii	iii
(C)	iii	ii	i	iv
(D)	iii	iv	ii	i

62. **Assertion (A) :** With the introduction of Internet, need for reference librarians has been minimised to fulfil the users reference needs.

Reason (R) : FAQ facility on internet is substituting the need for human interface in libraries.

Codes :

(A) Both (A) and (R) are partially true.

(B) Both (A) and (R) are true.

(C) Both (A) and (R) are false.

(D) (A) is true but (R) is false.

63. **Assertion (A) :** According to the Third Law of Librarianship given by Michael Gorman, we need to use technology intelligently to enhance service.

Reason (R) : Technology is used to solve problems and improve services and achieve costeffectiveness rather than adopted for its own sake.

Codes :

(A) (A) is true, but (R) is false.

(B) Both (A) and (R) are true, but (R) is not correct explanationof (A).

(C) Both (A) and (R) are false.

(D) Both (A) and (R) are true.

64. **Assertion (A) :** Semantic web is an extension of www in which web contents cannot be expressed in natural language.

Reason (R) : Semantic web can be easily associated with spider web.

Codes :

(A) Both (A) and (R) are false.

(B) (A) is true, but (R) is false.

(C) Both (A) and (R) are true.

(D) (A) is false, but (R) is true.

65. **Assertion (A) :** BIOS is a set of programs that handles startup operations in a computer such as power on, self tested and low level control for hardware.

Reason (R) : The graphical display at the beginning of the program prolongs the life of monitor.

Codes :

(A) Both (A) and (R) are true.

(B) (A) is false, but (R) is true.

(C) Both (A) and (R) are false.

(D) (A) is true, but (R) is false.

66. The International Body that coordinates the assignment of unique domain names, protocol address is

(A) IGF (B) IANA

(C) ICANN (D) ISP

67. Which of the following are criteria for Web evaluation ?

(i) Revision (ii) Response time

(iii) Format (iv) Archiving facility

Codes :

(A) (i) and (ii) are correct.

(B) (ii) and (iv) are correct.

(C) (i) and (iii) are correct.

68. Which of the following are the components of Search Engine ?

(i) Spider (ii) TCP/IP

(iii) Search Mechanism (iv) Index

Codes :

(A) (iv), (i) and (ii) (B) (iii), (ii) and (i)

(C) (i), (iii) and (iv) (D) (ii), (iv) and (iii)

69. Which of the following are Library networks ?

(i) Internet (ii) Indonet

(iii) INFLIBNET (iv) OCLC

Codes :

(A) (i) and (ii) are correct.

(B) (ii) and (iv) are correct.

(C) (iii) and (iv) are correct.

(D) (i) and (iv) are correct.

70. The mode of displaying graphic information pixel by pixel with bits in main memory is

(A) Bit handling (B) Bit mapping

(C) Bit pattern (D) Bit matrix

71. An alerting service in the digital environment is offered through :

(i) RSS feeds (ii) E-mail

(iii) Blogs (iv) Bulletin Board

Codes :

(A) (i), (iii) are correct.

(B) (ii), (iii), (iv) are correct.

(C) (i), (ii), (iii) are correct.

(D) (i), (ii), (iv) are correct.

72. **Assertion (A) :** RSS is considered as an alternative to the current awareness service.

Reason (R) : RSS feeds enable us to syndicate data automatically.

Codes :

(A) Both (A) and (R) are true.

(B) Both (A) and (R) are false.

(C) (A) is false, but (R) is true.

(D) (A) is true, but (R) is false.

73. Match the following :

	List - I		**List - II**
a.	Meta search engine	i.	HotBot
b.	Web directory	ii.	Search Engine
c.	Subject gateway	iii.	Galaxy
d.	Archie	iv.	Library Spot

Codes :	**(a)**	**(b)**	**(c)**	**(d)**
(A)	i	iii	iv	ii
(B)	iii	ii	i	iv
(C)	ii	iv	i	iii
(D)	i	iii	ii	iv

74. Which of the following programming language is exclusively used for Artificial Intelligence ?

(A) C (B) J2EE

(C) Prolog (D) JAVA

75. In CDS/ISIS 'delimiters' means
    (A) Field address (B) Field repeatability
    (C) Field format (D) Subfield indicators

76. Joseph W Lippincott Award is presented to the librarians for
    (A) promoting love for books andreading.
    (B) advanced study in the field ofchildren's library.
    (C) achievements in classificationand cataloguing.
    (D) outstanding participation inprofessional library associations.

77. LIS Gateway is maintained by
    (A) ILA (B) IASLIC
    (C) SIS (D) IATLIS

78. Which of the following are not the features of ISDN?
    i. Simultaneous Digital Transmission
    ii. Set of communication standards
    iii. Creates and combines packets
    iv. Program to visit web pages

    Codes :
    (A) i & ii are correct.
    (B) ii & iii are correct.
    (C) iii & iv are correct.
    (D) i & iv are correct.

79. Semantic Web is based on which of the following :
    i. RDF ii. Ontologies
    iii. URL iv. Cloud seeding

    Codes :
    (A) i, ii & iii are correct.
    (B) ii, iii & iv are correct.
    (C) i, iii & iv are correct.
    (D) i, ii & iv are correct.

80. Which of the following are not web 2.0 Tools ?

i. Ontologies ii. Facebook

iii. Intelligent Web iv. RSS Feeds

Codes :

(A) i & ii are correct.

(B) i & iii are correct.

(C) ii & iii are correct.

(D) iii & iv are correct.

81. Arrange the following in the order of development :

i. GML ii. Hypermedia

iii. SGML iv. Memex

Codes :

(A) i, ii, iii, iv (B) iv, ii, i, iii

(C) ii, iii, iv, i (D) iii, ii, i, iv

82. Match the following file formats withthe creators :

	List - I		**List - II**
a.	RTF	i.	Sun Micro System
b.	PDF	ii.	Aldus
c.	TIFF	iii.	Microsoft
d.	AU	iv.	Adobe

Codes :	**(a)**	**(b)**	**(c)**	**(d)**
(A)	iv	iii	ii	i
(B)	iii	iv	ii	i
(C)	ii	iii	iv	i
(D)	i	ii	iv	iii

83. **Assertion (A) :** Social networking tools are very effective for marketing of Library products and services.

Reason (R) : They help to reach out the patrons anywhere and at any time.

Codes :

(A) Both (A) and (R) are true.

(B) Both (A) and (R) are false.

(C) (A) is true, but (R) is false.

(D) (A) is false, but (R) is true.

84. **Assertion (A) :** In the digital environment, the users expect from the library the ability to connect broad range of information resources in a variety of formats with a single point access.

Reason (R) : Libraries already have much of what is required in the digital environment.

Codes :

(A) (A) is true, but (R) is false.

(B) Both (A) and (R) are true.

(C) Both (A) and (R) are false.

(D) (A) is false, but (R) is true.

85. Which of the following makes a network in secured?

(A) Encryption

(B) Network Interface Card (NIC)

(C) Password Capture

(D) Static Keys

86. Which of the following three types of basic languages are used in computer programming ?

(A) Procedural, Non-proceduraland Unconditional

(B) Zero, Low and High levels

(C) Machine, Assembly and Highlevel languages

(D) COBOL, BASIC and C

87. Which of the following are Web-zine ?

(i) Email Magazine (ii) E-Conference

(iii) Online Bulletin (iv) Electronic News Letter

Codes :

(A) (i), (iii) and (iv) (B) (i), (ii) and (iii)

(C) (ii), (iii) and (iv) (D) (i), (ii) and (iv)

88. In reference service, assimilation means :

(i) Recording the retrieved information

(ii) Sharing reference service experience with colleagues

(iii) Furnishing the exact information

(iv) Acquaintance with reference material

Codes :

(A) (i) and (ii) are correct.

(B) (i) and (iv) are correct.

(C) (ii) and (iii) are correct.

(D) (ii) and (iv) are correct.

89. The notation used to increase the capacity of an array are :

(i) Empty digit (ii) Emptying digit

(iii) Indicator digit (iv) Speciator

Codes :

(A) (i) and (ii) are correct.

(B) (iii) and (iv) are correct.

(C) (i), (ii) and (iii) are correct.

(D) (i), (ii) and (iv) are correct.

90. Rich Text Format (RTF) is concerned with

(i) Formatting features like Fonttype, size, etc.

(ii) Transporting text documents across different computers.

(iii) Multimedia formatting.

(iv) Formatting based on binary concept.

Codes :

(A) (ii) and (iii) are correct.

(B) (iii) and (iv) are correct.

(C) (i) and (ii) are correct.

(D) (i) and (iv) are correct.

91. **Assertion (A) :** RSS (Rich Site Summary) is considered as analternate to the SDI Service.

Reason (R) : RSS Feeds enable us to syndicate data automatically.

Codes :

(A) Both (A) and (R) are true.

(B) Both (A) and (R) are false.

(C) (A) is false, but (R) is true.

(D) (A) is true, but (R) is false.

92. **Assertion (A) :** Majority of academic libraries in India are lagging behind in switching over as technology-oriented service institutions.

Reason (R) : The apex academic bodies and library Associations have not taken the lead role to devise standards and policies.

Codes :

(A) (A) is true, (R) is false.

(B) (A) is false, (R) is true.

(C) Both (A) and (R) is true.

(D) Both (A) and (R) are false.

93. LOCKSS (Lots of Copies Keep Stuff Safe) project was launched by :

(A) Mellon Foundation

(B) Stanford University

(C) University of California

(D) OCLC

94. KOHA is written in which of the following language?
(A) C, C++ (B) Java
(C) Karel++ (D) Pearl

95. Which of the following is an example of URN ?
(A) URL (B) URI
(C) DOI (D) ISBN

96. Alerting service is provided
i. Before and after the publication of primary source
ii. For specific search formulation by user
iii. For retrieval of information
iv. For individuals as well as groups

Codes :
(A) i and ii are correct.
(B) i and iv are correct.
(C) ii and iii are correct.
(D) iii and iv are correct.

97. Hierarchical relationship among concepts indicates
i. Genus-species relationship
ii. Equivalance relationship
iii. Whole-part relationship
iv. Associate relationship

Codes :
(A) ii and iv are correct.
(B) iii and ii are correct.
(C) i and iii are correct.
(D) iv and i are correct.

98. Identify the assistive softwares :
i. Cybrarian ii. Dragon
iii. Jaws iv. Librarian

Codes :

(A) i and ii are correct.

(B) i and iii are correct.

(C) ii and iii are correct.

(D) iii and iv are correct.

99. Identify the types of OCR technology

i. Matrix matching

ii. Instructional analysis

iii. Feature extraction

iv. Structural analysis

Codes :

(A) i, ii, iv are true. (B) i, ii, iii are true.

(C) ii, iii, iv are true. (D) i, iii, iv are true.

100. Match the following search techniques with their relevant example :

List - I	List - II
a. Truncation	i. Wom?n
b. Wild cards	ii. Comput*
c. Proximity	iii. edu AND biochemistry AND antibodies
d. Field searching	iv. "content collection"/5

Codes :	(a)	(b)	(c)	(d)
(A)	ii	iii	iv	i
(B)	iv	iii	ii	i
(C)	i	ii	iii	iv
(D)	ii	i	iv	iii

101. Which of the following are features of flash memory?

i. Erasable & Programmable Read Only Memory

ii. Non-volatile memory

iii. Temporary storage unit

iv. Dynamic RAM

Codes :

(A) i, ii, iii are correct. (B) i, ii, iv are correct.

(C) i, ii are correct. (D) ii, iv are correct.

102. SQL is based on which of the following ?

i. Query string ii. Relational algebra

iii. Relational calculus iv. Web search queries

Codes :

(A) i, ii are correct. (B) ii, iii are correct.

(C) iii, iv are correct. (D) ii, iv are correct.

103. Identify the technology of digitization.

i. Bit-depth ii. Resolution

iii. Manipulation iv. Image enhancement

Codes :

(A) ii, iii, iv are correct. (B) i, iii, iv are correct.

(C) i, ii, iv are correct. (D) i, ii, iii are correct.

104. Which are not open source library softwares ?

i. Bibliosys ii. Evergreen

iii. New Genlib iv. Virtua

Codes :

(A) i and ii are correct. (B) i and iii are correct.

(C) i and iv are correct. (D) ii and iv are correct.

105. Identify the compression protocols :

i. TIFF ii. JPEG

iii. ZIFF iv. LZW

Codes :

(A) i, iii, iv are correct. (B) i, ii, iv are correct.

(C) ii, iii, iv are correct. (D) i, ii, iii are correct.

106. **Assertion (A) :** Webliographies are bibliographic tools for print and electronic documents.

Reason (R) : Webliography denotes an enumerative list of hypertext links surrounding a common subject following standard citation styles.

Codes :

(A) (A) is true, but (R) is false.

(B) (A) is false, but (R) is true.

(C) Both (A) and (R) are true.

(D) Both (A) and (R) are false.

107. **Assertion (A) :** An ISO 2709 : 2008 record structure and review format has 'Record Label', 'Directory', 'Data fields' and 'Record Separator'.

Reason (R) : ISO 2709 is a subset of MARC.

Codes :

(A) (A) is true, but (R) is false.

(B) (A) is false, but (R) is true.

(C) Both (A) and (R) are true.

(D) Both (A) and (R) are false.

108. **Assertion (A) :** Precision ratio is a measure of the efficiency of an indexing system.

Reason (R) : Presence of relevant terms increases the precision ratio.

Codes :

(A) (A) is true, but (R) is false.

(B) Both (A) and (R) are true, but (R) is not the correct explanation of (A).

(C) Both (A) and (R) are true and (R) is the correct explanation of (A).

(D) (A) is false, but (R) is true.

109. Match the following publishers with the relevan databases :

	List - I		List - II
a.	Elsevier	i.	Academic search
b.	Thomson Reuters	ii.	Aerospace & high technolog
c.	EBSCO	iii.	Scopus
d.	ProQuest	iv.	Web of knowledge

Codes :	(a)	(b)	(c)	(d)
(A)	ii	i	iv	iii
(B)	i	iii	ii	iv
(C)	iii	iv	i	ii
(D)	iv	ii	iii	i

110. Match the following :

	List - I		List - II
a.	HTML	i.	Intrepretation by web browse
b.	XML	ii.	Describes data
c.	UNICODE	iii.	Display data
d.	VB Script	iv.	Platform independent

Codes :	(a)	(b)	(c)	(d)
(A)	i	iii	ii	iv
(B)	iii	iv	i	ii
(C)	ii	iv	i	iii
(D)	iii	ii	iv	i

111. DOS, UNIX, LINUX, Windows areexamples of :
(A) Application software
(B) System software
(C) Computer language
(D) Operating system

112. Lotka's law is related to :

(A) Word frequency count
(B) Scientific productivity
(C) Distribution of papers in the periodicals
(D) Citation analysis

113. Which of the following evaluation techniques is used in forecasting ?
(A) Market research
(B) Performance evaluation
(C) Cost-benefit analysis
(D) Delphi technique

114. The basic components of network analysis in PERT/CPM are :
(A) Event and performance
(B) Event and activity
(C) Activity and conditions
(D) Conditions and dummy activity

115. SQL stands for :
(A) Structured Query Language
(B) Standard Query Language
(C) Systematic Query Language
(D) Soft Query Language

116. The significant characteristic of ananalogue signal is :
(A) it is discrete (B) it is continuous
(C) it transmits fast (D) it has less noise

117. Identify the entity that belongs to first group of entities in FRBR :
(A) Object (B) Event
(C) Concept (D) Expression

118. LANs are distinguished from other types of

networks by three characteristics ?

(i) Speed

(ii) Size

(iii) Topology

(iv) Transmission technology

Select the correct answer :

Codes :

(A) (ii) (iii) (iv) are correct

(B) (ii) (iii) (i) are correct

(C) (iii) (iv) (i) are correct

(D) (i) (ii) (iv) are correct

119. **Statement (a) :** LISA is an abstracting database which has independent thesaurus for searching abstract.

Statement (b) : LISA abstracting database is available in electronics and print form Select the correct answer :

(A) Statement (a) is wrong but (b) is correct

(B) Both statements (a) and (b) arefalse

(C) Both statements (a) and (b) arecorrect

(D) Statement (b) is wrong but (a)is correct

120. A router :

(A) Receives a signal and retransmits it at a higher level

(B) Helps you interface with another network

(C) Essentially translates protocols

(D) Forwards data packets between tale-communications networks

121. ISO-2709 exchange format specifies which of the following :

(A) The tag to be used
(B) Structure for MARC
(C) Size of RFID tag
(D) Specification for ICT Components

122. Identify the statement that is nottrue about ISDN :
(A) ISDN is not limited to transmission of voice only
(B) ISDN is simply a point-to-pointsolution like a leased line
(C) ISDN is purely digital communication
(D) ISDN can provide simultaneous voice, video and text transmission

123. 'Half Life' relates to :
(A) Rate of Growth (B) Rate of Obsolescence
(C) Degree of Scatter (D) Life of a Journal

124. Which is not applicable to the Digital Library ?
(A) Digital library is a logical extension of the traditional library
(B) Digital library is a system that provides community of users with coherent access to a large repository of knowledge
(C) Digital library is an organisation that does not require the specialised staff
(D) Digital library is used by many at the same time

125. Canon of Sought Heading takes careof :
(A) Permanence of headings
(B) Approaches of users
(C) Arrangement of entries
(D) Consistency in preparation ofentries

126. Which of the following is an example of Associative relationship ?

(A) Vertebrates—Mammals
(B) Photocopies—Xeroxes
(C) Polling—Public Opinion
(D) Polyvinyl Chloride/PVC

127. Which is not applicable to extensible Mark up Language ?
(A) It is compatible with SGML
(B) It is usable over Internet
(C) XML documents are easy tocreate
(D) It has to do with semantics toData

128. ....Search gives more information output :
(A) Boolean 'And' (B) Boolean 'Or'
(C) Boolean 'Not' (D) Phrase Search

129. Identify the MARC tag that is usedfor variable fields containing data related to subject access to the document :
(A) 7 XX (B) 6 XX
(C) 5 XX (D) 2 XX

ANSWERS

1. A	2. A	3. A	4. D	5. A	6. A
7. D	8. B	9. B	10. C	11. A	12. B
13. D	14. C	15. D	16. C	17. D	18. B
19. B	20. A	21. C	22. C	23. A	24. C
25. D	26. C	27. B	28. C	29. B	30. C
31. C	32. B	33. D	34. A	35. B	36. D
37. B	38. D	39. B	40. A	41. C	42. D
43. C	44. D	45. D	46. B	47. C	48. B
49. B	50. B	51. B	52. D	53. B	54. C
55. C	56. A	57. D	58. A	59. A/. D	60. B
61. C	62. A	63. D	64. A	65. D	66. C
67. B	68. C	69. C	70. B	71. D	72. A

73. A	74. C	75. D	76. A	77. A	78. C
79. A	80. B	81. B	82. B	83. A	84. A
85. C	86. C	87. A	88. A	89. A	90. C
91. A	92. C	93. B	94. D	95. D	96. B
97. C	98. C	99. D	100. D	101. C	102. B
103. C	104. C	105. B	106. B	107. A	108. B
109. C	110. D	111. D	112. B	113. D	114. B
115. A	116. B	117. D	118. A	119. C	120. D
121. A	122. B	123. B	124. C	125. B	126. C
127. D	128. B	129. B			

8

General Questions

1. The order of significance of "Thing, Material and Action" among various components of a compound subject was expanded by
   (A) J. Kaiser
   (B) E. J. Coates
   (C) J. R. Sharp
   (D) J. E. L. Farradane
2. Which of the following are Schools of Management thought ?
   (i) Scientific Management School
   (ii) Human Behavioural School
   (iii) Classical School
   (iv) School of Authority

   Codes :

   (A) (ii) and (iv) are correct
   (B) (i), (ii) and (iv) are correct
   (C) (iii) and (iv) are correct
   (D) (i), (ii) and (iii) are correct

3. **Assertion (A) :** If changes cannot be adopted to its framework, the organisational equilibrium will be imbalanced.

   Reason (R) : Organisation works in an environment which is marked by dynamic characteristics.

   Codes :

   (A) (A) is true, but (R) is false

   (B) (A) is false, but (R) is true

   (C) Both (A) and (R) are true

   (D) Both (A) and (R) are false

4. **Assertion (A) :** There is need to continuous evaluation and appreciation of value of libraries.

   Reason (R) : There is economic pressure on public budget.

   Codes :

   (A) Both (A) and (R) are true

   (B) Both (A) and (R) are false

   (C) (A) is true, but (R) is false

   (D) (A) is false, but (R) is true

5. **Assertion (A) :** System analysis identifies the flow of work.

   Reason (R) : System analysis is not necessary if the library is automated.

   Codes :

   (A) (A) is false, but (R) is true

   (B) (A) is true, but (R) is false

   (C) Both (A) and (R) are false

   (D) Both (A) and (R) are true

6. Arrange the following associations according to their year of establishment :

(i) IASLIC (ii) ASLIB
(iii) ALA (iv) SLA

Codes :

(A) (iv), (ii), (iii), (i) (B) (ii), (iii), (iv), (i)
(C) (iii), (iv), (ii), (i) (D) (i), (iv), (ii), (iii)

7. Arrange the following according to their year of origin :

(i) Broad System of Ordering
(ii) Classification in Online Systems
(iii) Automated Keyword Classification
(iv) Classification Research Group

Codes:

(A) (iv), (iii), (i), (ii) (B) (i), (ii), (iv), (iii)
(C) (iii), (i), (ii), (iv) (D) (ii), (iv), (iii), (ii)

8. Jubilee Project is associated with what ?

(A) Evaluation of electronic information services
(B) Public library survey
(C) Strategic management oflibraries
(D) Scale development

9. Scaler chain shows

(A) Authority structure
(B) Scale of performance of staff
(C) Chain for locating racks
(D) A link in the chain

10. When two or more basic subjects having same relational approach form a specific subject, the relation istermed as

(A) Speciater relation (B) Co-ordinate relation
(C) Phase relation (D) Hierarchical relation

11. The concept of 'Stopword' list isrelevant in the context of

    (A) Uniform Indexing (B) Citation Indexing

    (C) Chain Indexing (D) Keyword Indexing

12. 'Segmentation' is associated with

    (A) Reference Service

    (B) Market Survey Report

    (C) Digest Service

    (D) Indexing Service

13. State of the art report generally highlights

    (A) General Aspects

    (B) Technical Aspects

    (C) Administrative Aspects

    (D) All of the above

14. Identify the odd one out.

    (A) ANSI (B) BIS

    (C) BSI (D) ESPN

15. Which of the following is not a part ofword treatment in language dictionaries ?

    (A) Gloss

    (B) Vernacular

    (C) Etymology

    (D) Grammatical information

16. **Assertion (A)** : Netiquette mandates that you do your best to act within the laws of cyber space and society.

    Reason (R) : Failing to respect other people's privacy is bad Netiquette.

    Codes :

    (A) Both (A) and (R) are false.

(B) Both (A) and (R) are true.

(C) (A) is true, but (R) is false.

(D) (A) is false, but (R) is true.

17. **Assertion (A) :** Collection of audiomaterials is less used inAcademic Libraries.

Reason (R) : People consider these materials intellectually less sound and fit only for recreation purpose.

Codes :

(A) (A) is false, but (R) is true.

(B) (A) is true, but (R) is false.

(C) (A) is true and (R) is partiallytrue.

(D) Both (A) and (R) are false.

18. **Assertion (A) :** Introduction of TQM in libraries is not possible.

Reason (R) : It requires open, cooperative culture and employees responsiveness for customer satisfaction.

Codes :

(A) Both (A) and (R) are true.

(B) (A) is true, but (R) is false.

(C) (A) is false, but (R) is true.

(D) Both (A) and (R) are false.

19. Match the following :

List-I	List-II
(a) ibid	(i) see
(b) loc.cit	(ii) previously cited
(c) op.cit	(iii) same reference cited immediately above
(d) vide	(iv) the same place cited

Codes :	**(a)**	**(b)**	**(c)**	**(d)**
(A)	(i)	(ii)	(iii)	(iv)
(B)	(ii)	(i)	(iv)	(iii)
(C)	(iii)	(iv)	(ii)	(i)
(D)	(iv)	(iii)	(i)	(ii)

20. Match the following :

List-I	**List-II**
(a) Small set of dependent activities that form longest path of activity network	(i) PERT
(b) Delighting the customer by fully meeting their needs	(ii) CPM
(c) Inter connecting networks depicting tasks, duration and dependency	(iii) Delphi
(d) Making better forecasts, judgements and advice	(iv) TQM

Codes :	**(a)**	**(b)**	**(c)**	**(d)**
(A)	(i)	(iii)	(ii)	(iv)
(B)	(ii)	(iv)	(i)	(iii)
(C)	(iii)	(iv)	(ii)	(i)
(D)	(iv)	(ii)	(i)	(iii)

21. Match the following :

List-I	**List-II**
(a) Transaction Processing	(i) Lower Level Managers
(b) Operational control	(ii) Clerical Staff
(c) Management control	(iii) Top Level Managers
(d) Strategic Planning	(iv) Middle Level Managers

Codes :	**(a)**	**(b)**	**(c)**	**(d)**
(A)	(iii)	(ii)	(iv)	(i)
(B)	(ii)	(i)	(iv)	(iii)
(C)	(iv)	(ii)	(iii)	(i)
(D)	(i)	(ii)	(iv)	(iii)

22. **Assertion (A) :** Training methods through brain storming stimulate idea generation.

    Reason (R) : Training methods do not provide opportunity to unskilled to become skilled.

    Codes :

    (A) (A) is false but (R) is true.
    (B) Both (A) and (R) are false.
    (C) Both (A) and (R) are true.
    (D) (A) is true but (R) is false.

23. Who categorized the user studies into the following three categories ?

    (i) Behaviour Studies
    (ii) Use studies
    (iii) Information flow studies

    (A) Maurice B Line (B) Menzel
    (C) Cronin (D) Voigt

24. **Assertion (A) :** Qualitative measures must be made quantifiable in order to be convincing.

    Reason (R) : Qualitative measuresare a necessary complement to quantitative measures.

    Codes :

    (A) (A) is true, (R) is false.
    (B) (A) is false, (R) is true.
    (C) Both (A) & (R) are true.
    (D) Both (A) & (R) are false.

25. **Assertion (A) :** Federated search technique is an integral component of an information portal.

    Reason (R) : 'Content Index' contains content that is find by the search server.

    Codes :

    (A) Both (A) and (R) are true.
    (B) Both (A) and (R) are false.
    (C) (A) is true but (R) is false.
    (D) (A) is false but (R) is true.

26. **Assertion (A) :** The array of classes 11, 12, 13 and the array of classes 31, 32, 33 are said to be collateral arrays.

    Reason (R) : They are derived from the original universe 'O'.

    Codes :

    (A) (A) is false, (R) is true.
    (B) (A) is true, (R) is false.
    (C) Both (A) & (R) are true.
    (D) Both (A) & (R) are false.

27. **Assertion (A) :** LIS profession is not considered at par with medical and legal professions.

    Reason (R) : There is no constitutional body for LIS profession like Medical Council of India (MCI) and Bar Council of India (BCI).

    Codes :

    (A) Both (A) and (R) are true.
    (B) Both (A) and (R) are false.
    (C) (A) is true but (R) is false.
    (D) (A) is false but (R) is true.

28. Match the following :

List - I	List - II
a. Means of improving operations and services	i. Preservation
b. Preparation of to-do-list	ii. Standards
c. Performance guidelines	iii. Time management
d. Reinforce the spines of books	iv. Evaluation

Codes :	**(a)**	**(b)**	**(c)**	**(d)**
(A)	iv	iii	ii	i
(B)	iv	ii	iii	i
(C)	ii	iv	iii	i
(D)	iii	ii	i	iv

29. How do we render the name 'Bernardo Augustine De Voto' ?
    (A) Voto, Bernardo, Augustine De
    (B) De Voto, Augustine, Bernardo
    (C) Bernardo Augustine, De Voto
    (D) De Voto, Bernardo Augustine

30. The first printed works are called
    (A) Impensis (B) Incunabula
    (C) Impression (D) Imprimat

31. What are the four entities of FRBR model ?
    (A) Personality, Matter, Energy, Space
    (B) Books, Form, Availability, Type
    (C) Work, Expression, Manifestation, Item
    (D) Discipline, Entity, Action, Personality

32. Which of the following methods are suitable to achieve quality of teaching, learning in LIS ?

(i) Research-led teaching
(ii) State of the art computer lab
(iii) Problem-based learning
(iv) Introducing the course at degree level

Codes :

(A) (ii) and (iv) (B) (i), (iii) and (iv)
(C) (i) and (iii) (D) (iii) and (iv)

33. Poor 'Accessibility' and less 'affordability' of journal subscription in print era led to
(i) High allocation of funds for serials
(ii) Open access movement
(iii) Decrease in subscription of journals
(iv) E-journal consortia subscription

Codes :

(A) (i) & (ii) are correct.
(B) (i), (ii), (iv) are correct.
(C) (ii), (iv) are correct.
(D) (i), (ii), (iii) are correct.

34. Match the following :

List - I	List - II
a. Henri La Fontaine	i. Expansive Classification
b. H.E. Bliss	ii. Bibliographic Classification
c. C.A. Cutter	iii. LC
d. J.C.M. Hansar	iv. UDC

Codes :	(a)	(b)	(c)	(d)
(A)	iv	ii	i	iii
(B)	iii	ii	iv	i
(C)	ii	iv	i	iii
(D)	i	iii	ii	iv

35. Match the following :

	List - I	**List - II**
a.	Papyrus	i. Assyria & Babylonia
b.	Handmade paper	ii. Egypt
c.	Clay tablets	iii. Medieval Europe
d.	Vellum/ Parchment	iv. China

Codes :	**(a)**	**(b)**	**(c)**	**(d)**
(A)	ii	iv	i	iii
(B)	iv	ii	iii	i
(C)	iii	iv	i	ii
(D)	iii	ii	iv	i

36. Match the following :

List - I	**List - II**
a. Icon	i. Character strings
b. Menus	ii. Select objects on the screen
c. Dialogue Bou	iii. Bit mapped region
d. Pointing devices	iv. Obtain information from the end users

Codes :	**(a)**	**(b)**	**(c)**	**(d)**
(A)	i	ii	iii	iv
(B)	iii	iv	ii	i
(C)	ii	iii	iv	i
(D)	iii	i	iv	ii

37. **Assertion (A) :** All the states in India have enacted library legislation.

Reason (R) : NKC recommends for the enactment of library legislation in all the states.

Codes :

(A) Both (A) and (R) are true.

(B) Both (A) and (R) are false.

(C) (A) is true, but (R) is false.

(D) (A) is false, but (R) is true.

38. In the library hierarchy which level of management is responsible for execution of policies ?

(A) Middle level (B) Operational level

(C) Top level (D) Lower level

39. Financial allocation made to a library for purchase of furniture and equipments usually comes under the budget head

(A) Recurring grant

(B) Endowments

(C) Non-recurring grant

(D) Annual grant

40. Major elements of a profession are

(i) Philosophy (ii) Body of knowledge

(iii) Publicity (iv) Status

Codes :

(A) (i), (ii), (iv) are correct.

(B) (i), (ii), (iii) are correct.

(C) (ii), (iii), (iv) are correct.

(D) (i), (iii), (iv) are correct.

41. Which of the following principles are associated with library building planning ?

(i) Principle of Uniformity

(ii) Principle of Comfortability

(iii) Principle of Simplicity

(iv) Principle of Continuity

Codes :

(A) (i), (ii) and (iii) are correct.

(B) (ii), (iii) and (iv) are correct.

(C) (i), (ii) and (iv) are correct.

(D) (iii), (iv) and (i) are correct.

42. The professional ethics help to ____.

(i) Get the right direction

(ii) Enhance image

(iii) Get more salaries

(iv) Resolve day to day issues

Codes :

(A) (ii) and (iii) are correct.

(B) (i) and (iv) are correct.

(C) (i) and (ii) are correct.

(D) (ii) and (iv) are correct.

43. Match the following :

List - I	List - II
a. Douglas McGregor	i. Scientific Management School
b. Abraham Maslow	ii. Theory of Authority Structure
c. F.W. Taylor	iii. Self Actualisation Needs
d. Max Weber	iv. Theory X andTheory Y

Codes :	(a)	(b)	(c)	(d)
(A)	iv	iii	i	ii
(B)	ii	iii	i	iv
(C)	iii	iv	ii	i
(D)	i	iv	ii	iii

44. Match the following DDC numbers :

	List - I		List - II
a.	Education	i.	770
b.	Medicine	ii.	370
c.	Photography	iii.	610
d.	Astronomy	iv.	520

Codes :	**(a)**	**(b)**	**(c)**	**(d)**
(A)	iii	i	iv	ii
(B)	ii	iii	i	iv
(C)	i	iv	iii	ii
(D)	iv	ii	i	iii

45. Match the following :

List - I	**List - II**
a. Unity of command	i. Specialization
b. Unity ofdirection	ii. Strength inunity
c. Esprit decorps	iii. Orders fromonly one person
d. Division ofwork	iv. One boss, oneplan

Codes :	**(a)**	**(b)**	**(c)**	**(d)**
(A)	iv	iii	ii	i
(B)	ii	iv	iii	i
(C)	iii	iv	ii	i
(D)	i	iv	iii	ii

46. **Assertion (A) :** 'Pay and Use' concept has not been accepted in libraries of India.

Reason (R) : Library staff do not possess the essential skills required for product development and promotion.

Codes :

(A) Both (A) and (R) are true.

(B) (A) is true but (R) are false.

(C) (R) is true, but (A) is false.

(D) Both (A) and (R) are false.

47. In C.C. the title 'Medical Jurisprudence' can be classified and sharpened with the help of

(A) Subject Device (B) Alphabetical Device
(C) Classic Device (D) Enumerative Device

48. Template is a
(A) Structured specification
(B) Recursive routine
(C) Assembler program
(D) I/O measure

49. **Assertion (A) :** There is a dismal scene relating to the development of public libraries especially rural libraries in India.
Reason (R) : Majority of the states do not have library legislation.
Codes :
(A) Both (A) and (R) are true.
(B) Both (A) and (R) are false.
(C) (A) is true but (R) is false.
(D) (A) is false but (R) is true.

50. **Assertion (A) :** The use of the symbol 'double colon' (: :) in UDC allows fixed order of component numbers in a compound subject.
Reason (R) : The fixed order facilitates easy access in computer based information retrieval.
Codes :
(A) (A) is true and (R) is false.
(B) (A) is false and (R) is true.
(C) Both (A) and (R) are true.
(D) Both (A) and (R) are false.

51. When a library is planning for a new building project, which of the following technique/(s) is/are applicable to the plan and control the complex, long-term project ?

(i) PERT (ii) TQM

(iii) CPM (iv) MBO

Codes :

(A) (i) and (iii) are correct.

(B) (ii) and (iii) are correct.

(C) (i) and (iv) are correct.

(D) (ii) is correct.

52. Which of the following leadership style(s) are suitable for change management with persuation and inclusiveness ?

(i) Authority

(ii) Systems of Management

(iii) Contingency

(iv) Management

Codes :

(A) (i), (ii) are correct.

(B) (ii), (iii) are correct.

(C) (ii), (iv) are correct.

(D) (ii) is correct.

53. Arrange in sequence, the steps in programming :

(i) Program code

(ii) Program Documentation

(iii) Program test

(iv) Program design

Codes :

(A) iii ii i iv (B) iv i iii ii

(C) iv iii ii i (D) ii iv i iii

54. Arrange in sequence the following committees in order of that year of commencement :

(i) Library Committee
(ii) Committee on national network system for university libraries
(iii) Review committee on Library Science
(iv) Curriculum Development Committee on Library and Information Science

Codes :

(A) i ii iii iv (B) iii iv ii i
(C) iii ii i iv (D) i iii ii iv

55. Match the following :

	List - I		**List - II**
a.	INDEST-AICTE	i.	Centrally funded
b.	CSIR consortia	ii.	Open
c.	UGC Infonet	iii.	Shared Budget
d.	IIM consortia	iv.	Closed group

Codes :	**(a)**	**(b)**	**(c)**	**(d)**
(A)	ii	iv	i	iii
(B)	i	iii	ii	iv
(C)	iii	ii	iv	i
(D)	iv	iii	i	ii

56. Match the following :

	List - I		**List - II**
a.	Coding	i.	Received signal not the one transmitted
b.	Noise	ii.	Measure of closeness of relationship
c.	Entropy	iii.	Message to a signal
d.	Equivocation	iv.	Measure of uncertainty

Codes :	**(a)**	**(b)**	**(c)**	**(d)**
(A)	iv	ii	iii	i
(B)	ii	iii	iv	i
(C)	i	ii	iii	iv
(D)	iii	i	iv	ii

57. **Assertion (A) :** Proliferation of LIS schools in India produced mediocre professionals.

Reason (R) : Curriculum and teaching techniques have not been upgraded at university level.

Codes :

(A) Both (A) and (R) are partially true.

(B) Both (A) and (R) are false.

(C) (A) is true and (R) is false.

(D) (A) is false and (R) is true.

58. **Assertion (A) :** Several Library Science departments in India have shifted to integrated MLIS program.

Reason (R) : MLIS Program (integrated) is a right solution to knowledge explosion in the field.

Codes :

(A) Both (A) and (R) are false.

(B) (A) is true and (R) is false.

(C) Both (A) and (R) are true.

(D) (A) is false and (R) is true.

59. **Assertion (A) :** UGC is financially supporting all academic libraries.

Reason (R) : UGC is primarily responsible for the overall development of libraries of higher education in India.

Codes :

(A) (A) is false and (R) is true.

(B) (A) is true and (R) is false.

(C) Both (A) and (R) are true.

(D) Both (A) and (R) are false.

60. **Assertion (A) :** UDC is used in subject gateways for resource discovery with high recall.

Reason (R) : In online environment, a faceted scheme has a distinct advantage over an enumerative one.

Codes :

(A) (A) is true but (R) is false.

(B) (A) is true, (R) is partially true.

(C) (A) is false, (R) is true.

(D) (A) is partially true, (R) is true.

61. **Assertion (A) :** MARC should never be used outside the context of the cataloguing rules.

Reason (R) : MARC is simply a coding scheme for entering bibliographic information into computer records.

Codes :

(A) Both (A) and (R) are true.

(B) (A) is true but (R) is false.

(C) (A) is false but (R) is true.

(D) Both (A) and (R) are false.

62. **Assertion (A) :** With quick and comprehensive availability of informative through internet resources, need for reference service with a human touch is decreasing.

Reason (R) : Internet resources can satisfy all types of information needs of information seekers.

Codes :

(A) (A) is true and (R) is false.

(B) Both (A) and (R) are false.

(C) (A) is false and (R) is true.

(D) (A) and (R) are true.

63. Which of the following are not Change Management Models ?

(i) Kurtlewin's Model (ii) Beer's Model

(iii) Lasswell's Model (iv) Epidemic Model

Codes :

(A) (i) & (iii) are correct.

(B) (ii) & (iii) are correct.

(C) (iii) & (iv) are correct.

(D) (ii) & (iv) are correct.

64. Which of the following associations have sponsored the Text Encoding Initiatives (TEI) ?

(i) ACL (ii) ACRL

(iii) ALLC (iv) ACH

Codes :

(A) (i), (ii) and (iii) are correct

(B) (ii), (iii) and (iv) are correct

(C) (i), (iv) and (ii) are correct

(D) (i), (iii) and (iv) are correct

65. "Women are more in library profession than men." Identify the variable in the statement.

(i) Men and women are independent variables.

(ii) Men and women are dependent variables.

(iii) Library profession is a dependent variable.

(iv) Library profession is an independent variable.

Codes :

(A) (i) and (iii) are correct

(B) (i) and (iv) are correct

(C) (ii) and (iii) are correct

(D) (ii) and (iv) are correct

66. Which of the following are the Pillars of SCONUL Seven Pillar Model ?

(i) Recognising Information need

(ii) Locating and accessing information

(iii) Using information technology for assessing information need.

(iv) Comparing and evaluating information.

Codes :

(A) (i), (ii) and (iii) are correct

(B) (i), (ii) and (iv) are correct

(C) (ii), (iii) and (iv) are correct

(D) (i) and (iv) are correct

67. Resource Description Framework consists which of the following ?

(i) Subject (ii) Thread

(iii) Predicate (iv) Object

Codes :

(A) (i), (ii) and (iii) (B) (ii), (iii) and (iv)

(C) (iii), (iv) and (i) (D) (iv), (i) and (ii)

68. Arrange the following factors of TQM in the order of their implementation :

i. Development of Human Resource Management

ii. Standardisation of Workprocess

iii. Improvement in Internal Organisation Management

iv. Quality Management Procedures

Codes :

(A) ii iii i iii (B) iii iv ii i

(C) iv iii ii i (D) ii iv iii i

69. Arrange in order the process of stock rectification and stock verification as suggested by S.R. Ranganathan :

i. Checking with charged tray
ii. Shelf Rectification
iii. Shelf checking
iv. Deciding the Quota

Codes :

(A) iii i iv ii (B) iv i ii iii
(C) iv ii iii i (D) ii iv i iii

70. **Assertion (A) :** The hierarchy based classification schemes have a major role in the organization of the web.

Reason (R) : The 'hotlists' retrieved by robots based search engines use the technique of relevance of subject descriptors.

Codes :

(A) (A) is true, but (R) is false.
(B) (A) is false, but (R) is true.
(C) Both (A) and (R) are correct.
(D) Both (A) and (R) are wrong.

71. **Assertion (A) :** Performance Based Budgeting demands that the objectives and goals of agency be clear and performance measures and target to put inplace.

Reason (R) : The key to success firmly rely upon its clear sense of mission and objectives which the funding agencies have proposed to reach them.

Codes :

(A) (A) is true, but (R) is false.
(B) (A) is false, but (R) is true.

(C) Both (A) and (R) are true.

(D) Both (A) and (R) are false.

72. **Assertion (A)** : Majority of University Libraries in India are not fully automated.

Reason (R) : University Libraries in India are meddling with automation of circulation activities.

Codes :

(A) (A) is true but (R) is false.

(B) (A) is false but (R) is true.

(C) Both (A) and (R) are true.

(D) Both (A) and (R) are false.

73. Name the Indian Librarian who was honoured with the title of "Khan Bahadur" in 1935 by the British Government.

(A) S.R. Ranganathan (B) B.S. Kesavan

(C) K.M. Asadullah (D) D.R. Kalia

74. When the permission of copyright owner is not needed ?

(i) Criticism or review (ii) Translation

(iii) Research purpose (iv) Photocopy for sale

Codes :

(A) (i) and (iii) are correct.

(B) (i) and (iv) are correct.

(C) (iii) and (iv) are correct.

(D) (ii) and (iii) are correct.

75. Match the following :

List - I	**List - II**
a. W. Edward Deming	i. Quality Control Circles
b. Joseph M. Juran	ii. TQM
c. Armand V. Feigenbaum	iii. Planning, Control, Improvement
d. Kaoru Ishikava	iv. Plan, Do, Check, Act (PDCA)

Codes :	(a)	(b)	(c)	(d)
(A)	ii	iii	iv	i
(B)	iv	ii	i	iii
(C)	iii	iv	i	ii
(D)	iv	iii	ii	i

76. Match the following :

List - I	List - II
a. Herbert Hicks	i. The Elements of Administration
b. F.W. Taylor	ii. The Management of Organisation
c. Henry Fayol	iii. Scientific Management
d. Colonel L.Urwick	iv. Administrative Management

Codes :	(a)	(b)	(c)	(d)
(A)	i	iv	ii	iii
(B)	iv	ii	iii	i
(C)	ii	iii	iv	i
(D)	iii	iv	i	ii

77. A template is a
    (A) Structured specification
    (B) Recursive routine
    (C) Assembler program
    (D) I/O measure

78. Which of the following concepts are associated with professional ethics ?
    (i) Accountability
    (ii) Unique training
    (iii) High quality service
    (iv) Professional independence

Codes :

(A) (i), (ii), (iii) are correct.

(B) (i), (iii) are correct.

(C) (i), (ii), (iv) are correct.

(D) (iii), (iv) are correct.

79. **Assertion (A) :** Library legislation is not a pre-requisite for providing free library service.

Reason (R) : There are states/union territories that are advanced in public library services without library legislation.

Codes :

(A) (A) is true, but (R) is false.

(B) (A) is false, but (R) is true.

(C) Both (A) and (R) are true.

(D) Both (A) and (R) are false.

80. Assertion (A) : One of the key lessons of the web 2.0 era is that users can add value.

Reason (R) : Web 2.0 serve communities of people and are created and maintained by and for the people.

Codes :

(A) Both (A) and (R) are true.

(B) Both (A) and (R) are false.

(C) (A) is true and (R) is false.

(D) (R) is true and (A) is false.

81. To make a program safe, one should take care of

(A) Strong authentication andaccess controls

(B) Error checking controls

(C) Do risk analysis

(D) Vendor's credibility

82. The three leadership styles identified by Koontz and others are

i. Autocratic	ii. Democratic
iii. Trait approach	iv. Free-reign

Codes :

(A) i, ii and iii are correct.

(B) ii, iii and iv are correct.

(C) iii, iv and i are correct.

(D) i, ii and iv are correct.

83. Arrange in sequence the following committees workshop in order of their year of constitution :

i. UGC Committee for Development of University and College Libraries (S.R.Ranganathan)

ii. UGC Committee on National Network System for University Libraries (Dr. Yashpal)

iii. UGC Review Committee on Library Science (S.R.Ranganathan)

iv. UGC Workshop on Standards for College Libraries

Codes :

(A) iii, iv, i, ii	(B) iii, ii, i, iv
(C) i, iii, iv, ii	(D) i, ii, iv, iii

84. Match the following theories with the respectively profounder :

List - I	**List - II**
a. Cybernetics	i. Charles Osgood (1916)
b. Human information processing	ii. Marshal C.Yovits
c. Psychological approach to message transmission	iii. Nobert Wiener (1894 – 1964)
d. General Information System	iv. R.L. Ackoff

Codes :	**(a)**	**(b)**	**(c)**	**(d)**
(A)	i	iii	ii	iv
(B)	i	ii	iv	iii
(C)	iii	i	iv	ii
(D)	iii	ii	i	iv

85. Match the following :

List - I	**List - II**
a. Referral	i. Support
b. SDI	ii. Reaching out
c. Extension	iii. Directing
d. Reprography	iv. Anticipating

Codes :	**(a)**	**(b)**	**(c)**	**(d)**
(A)	iii	iv	ii	i
(B)	iv	ii	iii	i
(C)	i	iv	ii	iii
(D)	ii	iii	i	iv

86. Match the following :

List - I	**List - II**
a. Similar activities are grouped	i. Bureaucritic System
b. Grouping activities into divisions	ii. Functional System
c. Integration of projects into functional system	iii. Departmentalisation
d. Control and Supervision through hierarchy of positions	iv. Matrix structure

Codes :	**(a)**	**(b)**	**(c)**	**(d)**
(A)	iv	i	ii	iii
(B)	iii	ii	iv	i
(C)	i	ii	iii	iv
(D)	ii	iii	iv	i

87. Match the following :

	List - I		**List - II**
a.	Virtua	i.	Veeru Technologies (KIIKM)
b.	Alice	ii.	Infotech Consultants Pvt. Ltd.
c.	Libsys	iii.	Softlink, Australia
d.	NewGenlib	iv.	VTLS, Virginia

Codes :	**(a)**	**(b)**	**(c)**	**(d)**
(A)	i	iii	ii	iv
(B)	ii	iv	i	iii
(C)	iv	ii	iii	i
(D)	iv	iii	ii	i

88. **Assertion (A) :** There is no need for libraries to invest on reference collection.

Reason (R) : Web is a treasure of all types of information that can replace reference desk.

Codes :

(A) Both (A) and (R) are true.

(B) Both (A) and (R) are false.

(C) (A) is true, but (R) is false.

(D) (A) is false, but (R) is true.

89. **Assertion (A) :** UGC has devised performance indicators for the promotion of faculty and librarians.

Reason (R) : Performance Appraisal is an important tool for merit rating.

Codes :

(A) (A) is true, but (R) is false.

(B) (A) is false, but (R) is true.

(C) Both (A) and (R) are true.

(D) Both (A) and (R) are false.

90. **Assertion (A) :** All unabridged dictionaries provide word meaning, antonyms, synonyms and places, etc.

Reason (R) : All dictionaries provide information on antonyms and homonym, etc.

Codes :

(A) (A) is true, but (R) is false.

(B) Both (A) and (R) are true.

(C) (A) is false, but (R) is true.

(D) Both (A) and (R) are false.

91. **Assertion (A) :** SGML is an international standard that describes the relationship between a document's content and its structure.

Reason (R) : Its primary purpose is to facilitate the sharing of data across different information systems particularly via Internet.

Codes :

(A) Both (A) and (R) are false.

(B) (A) is true, but (R) is false.

(C) Both (A) and (R) are true.

(D) (A) is false, but (R) is true.

92. Match the following :

List - I	List - II
a. Fundamentals of Reference Service	i. A.J. Walford
b. Introduction to Reference works	ii. S.R.Ranganathan

c. Reference service	iii. F.N. Cheneyand W.J.Williams
d. Guide to Reference Books	iv. William A Katz

Codes :	**(a)**	**(b)**	**(c)**	**(d)**
(A)	ii	i	iv	iii
(B)	iii	iv	i	ii
(C)	iv	ii	iii	i
(D)	iii	iv	ii	i

93. Match the following :

	List - I		**List - II**
a.	Check Card	i.	Reader'sTicket
b.	Kardex	ii.	Three Card System
c.	Newark System	iii.	Periodicals
d.	Browne System	iv.	Borrower's Card

Codes :	**(a)**	**(b)**	**(c)**	**(d)**
(A)	ii	iii	iv	i
(B)	iii	iv	i	ii
(C)	ii	iv	iii	i
(D)	iv	i	ii	iii

94. **Assertion (A) :** All classification schemes adopt 'phase relations'.

Reason (R) : Subject formation by loose assemblage leads to complex subjects and isolates.

Codes :

(A) (A) is true, but (R) is false.

(B) Both (A) and (R) are true.

(C) Both (A) and (R) are false.

(D) (A) is false, but (R) is true.

95. **Assertion (A) :** Traditional Management process differ from the 'Quality Management'.

Reason (R) : 'Quality Management' focuses on 'customer' in the management process.

Codes :

(A) (A) is true, but (R) is false.

(B) (A) is false, but (R) is true.

(C) Both (A) and (R) are false.

(D) Both (A) and (R) are true.

96. **Assertion (A) :** UGC notification (2009) mandates submission of electronic theses and dissertations by the researchers in universities to facilitate open access.

Reason (R) : UGC wants to monitor the quality of research through open access.

Codes :

(A) (A) is true, but (R) is false.

(B) (A) is false, but (R) is true.

(C) Both (A) and (R) are true.

(D) Both (A) and (R) are false.

97. Arrange the following according to the year of origin:

i. Encyclopaedia Britannica

ii. World Book Encyclopaedia

iii. Wikipedia

iv. Encyclopaedia Americana

Codes :

(A) iv, i, ii, iii (B) i, iv, ii, iii

(C) ii, iv, i, iii (D) i, ii, iv, iii

98. Arrange the following in correct classified order as per C.C.

i. A ii. 2:5

iii. 2a iv. 234

Codes :

(A) iii, i, iv, ii (B) i, iii, ii, iv

(C) iii, ii, iv, i (D) ii, i, iii, iv

99. Arrange the following according to the procedural steps :

i. Receipt of recommendations

ii. Preparing master card

iii. Checking titles of and bibliographical details

iv. Duplication checking from library catalogue

Codes :

(A) i, ii, iii, iv (B) i, iii, ii, iv

(C) iii, i, iv, ii (D) iv, iii, i, ii

100. Arrange the following according to their publication year :

i. Sears' list of subject headings

ii. Panizzi code

iii. AACR-I

iv. CCC

Codes :

(A) iv, ii, iii, i (B) i, iii, ii, iv

(C) ii, i, iv, iii (D) iii, iv, i, ii

101. Arrange the sequence of the following steps followed in classifying a document according to colon classification :

i. Title with standard facet terms

ii. Analyzed title

iii. Kernel title

iv. Transformed title

Codes :

(A) ii, iv, i, iii (B) i, ii, iii, iv

(C) iii, ii, iv, i (D) iv, iii, ii, i

102. Match the following :

List - I	List - II
a. Infringement	i. Unauthorized use of I.P.
b. Enforcement	ii. Criminal penalties
c. Mis-appropriation	iii. Breach of trade secret
d. Counter feit	iv. Intentional forgery

Codes :	**(a)**	**(b)**	**(c)**	**(d)**
(A)	ii	iii	iv	i
(B)	i	ii	iii	iv
(C)	iii	iv	i	ii
(D)	iv	i	iii	ii

103. In 1990 4P's were translated into 4C's of marketing. Here 'Promotion'(P) represents :

(A) Cost to users

(B) Customer needs and wants

(C) Communication

(D) Convenience

104. The best strategy for a high recall for a user who has one concrete reference with him would be :

(A) Building block

(B) Successive fractions

(C) Citation Pearl Growing

(D) Boolean search

105. Name the author of 'Grammar of Classification' :

(A) S.R. Ranganathan (B) H.E. Bliss

(C) W.C.B. Sayers (D) J. Mills

106. Zero Based Budgeting means :
   (A) A budgeting without funds
   (B) Budgeting afresh
   (C) Budgeting based on previousyear's expenses
   (D) Performance budget
107. In CCF, the equivalent of leader in MARC 21, is called:
   (A) Directory (B) Record Label
   (C) Record Separator (D) Data Fields
108. Which of the following is not a canon for characteristics ?
   (A) Canon of Differentiation
   (B) Canon of Exclusiveness
   (C) Canon of Ascertainability
   (D) Canon of Permanence
109. Which of the following is an example of equivalence relationship ?
   (A) Nervous system—Central nervous system
   (B) Freedom—Liberty
   (C) Hunting—Hunters
   (D) Weaving—Cloth
110. Arrange the following catalogue codes in the chronological sequence of their publication and choose the correct answer by using the codes given below :
   (i) Classified cataloguing code
   (ii) AACR-2
   (iii) ALA Code
   (iv) British Museum Code

Codes :

(A) (iii), (i), (ii), (iv) (B) (iii), (iv), (ii), (i)

(C) (iv), (iii), (i), (ii) (D) (ii), (i), (iii), (iv)

111. The main entry heading according to AACR2 (Revised Edition) for a sound recording of the book by Lewis Carroll titled 'Alice's Adventures in Wonderland; read and sung by Cyril Ritchard; the music composed by Alec Wilder and played by the New York Woodwind Quintet would be :

(A) Carroll, Lewis

(B) Ritchard, Cyril

(C) Wilder, Alec

(D) New York, Woodwind Quintet

112. While formulating a budget for a library, the following factors have tobe considered :

(a) Type of Organisation

(b) Size of the Organisation

(c) Type of Users

(d) Number of books issued to ausers

Select the correct answer :

Codes :

(A) (a), (b) and (c) are correct

(B) (b), (c) and (d) are correct

(C) (c), (d) and (a) are correct

(D) (a), (b) and (d) are correct

113. Match the following List-I and List-II and choose the correct answer by using the codes given below :

List-I	List-II
(i) In AACR-II connecting symbol for size of the document	(a) Colon
(ii) Connecting symbol for statement of responsibility	(b) Plus
(iii) Connecting symbol between place and name of the publisher	(c) Semicolon
(iv) Connecting symbol for accompanying material	(d) Diagonal Slash

Codes :	**(i)**	**(ii)**	**(iii)**	**(iv)**
(A)	(d)	(c)	(b)	(a)
(B)	(c)	(d)	(a)	(b)
(C)	(c)	(a)	(b)	(d)
(D)	(d)	(c)	(b)	(a)

114. Match List-I and List-II and choose the correct answer by using the codes given below :

List-I	List-II
(i) Books in Print	(a) Guardian
(ii) Newspaper	(b) Information Please
(iii) News Digest	(c) R.R. Bowker
(iv) Almanac	(d) Asian Recorder

Codes :	**(i)**	**(ii)**	**(iii)**	**(iv)**
(A)	(c)	(d)	(a)	(b)
(B)	(c)	(d)	(b)	(a)
(C)	(a)	(c)	(d)	(b)
(D)	(c)	(a)	(d)	(b)

115. Match List-I and List-II and choose the correct answer by using the code given below :

List-I	List-II
(i) Papyrus	(a) Skin of Calf
(ii) Parchment	(b) Skin of Sheep
(iii) Vellum	(c) Ancient Paper
(iv) Birch	(d) Bark of a Tree

Codes :	**(i)**	**(ii)**	**(iii)**	**(iv)**
(A)	(c)	(b)	(a)	(d)
(B)	(b)	(c)	(d)	(a)
(C)	(d)	(a)	(b)	(c)
(D)	(a)	(d)	(b)	(c)

116. If selected plays of Vijay Tendulkar have been translated by Yogesh Sharma and compiled with an introduction by S.M. Chari, the main Entry in AACR II Revised Edition would be made under :
   (A) Tendulkar, Vijay
   (B) Sharma, Yogesh
   (C) Chari, S.M.
   (D) Selected Plays of Vijay Tendulkar

117. The term 'Exponential Growth' isreferred to :
   (A) Linear Growth
   (B) Geometrical Progression
   (C) Arithmetical Progression
   (D) Normal Frequency Distribution

118. Canon of Prepotence :
   (A) Decides the position of an entry among the various entries in a catalogue
   (B) Prescribes that the information on the title page of a document and its overflow pages should determine the choice and rendering of headings
   (C) Says that headings of a catalogue entry should be individualised

(D) Prescribes that rules of a catalogue should be revised from time to time

119. **Statement (1) :** The copyright laws prevent unauthorised production of any literary and artistic work.

Statement (2) : The copyright is enfringed even if the copy is made or supplied by or on behalf of a librarian.

In the above statements :

(A) Both (1) and (2) are true

(B) Both (1) and (2) are false

(C) (1) is true but (2) is false

(D) (1) is false but (2) is true

120. Which of the following is a strategy for Knowledge Management ?

(A) Indexing (B) Annotation

(C) Personalisation (D) Abstracting

121. In an Empirical study on impact of internet on reading, 'reading' wouldbe :

(A) An independent variable

(B) The dependent variable

(C) An intervening variable

(D) The continuous variable

122. Match List-I and List-II and choose the correct answer by using the codes given below :

List-I	List-II
(i) CeRA	(a) Education
(ii) FORSA	(b) Agriculture
(iii) INDEST	(c) Astrophysics
(iv) ERIC	(d) Engineering

Codes :	**(i)**	**(ii)**	**(iii)**	**(iv)**
(A)	(a)	(d)	(c)	(b)
(B)	(d)	(a)	(b)	(c)
(C)	(c)	(b)	(d)	(a)
(D)	(b)	(c)	(d)	(a)

123. In Building Block Search Strategy adding an extra facet would result in :
   (A) Higher recall
   (B) Higher precision
   (C) Increase in recall as well as precision
   (D) Lower precision

124. **Statement (1) :** Cross-reference entry of the classification catalogue code is a number entry.
   Statement (2) : It is entered under the dominant class of the document.
   In the above statements :
   (A) Both (1) and (2) are true
   (B) (1) is true but (2) is false
   (C) (1) is false but (2) is true
   (D) Both (1) and (2) are false

125. Arrange the following Public Library Acts according to their year of enactment.
   (i) Mizoram Public Libraries Act
   (ii) Tamil Nadu Public LibrariesAct
   (iii) Haryana Public Libraries Act
   (iv) Orissa Public Libraries Act
   Codes :
   (A) (iv) (iii) (i) (ii) (B) (ii) (iii) (i) (iv)
   (C) (ii) (i) (iv) (iii) (D) (iii) (ii) (i) (iv)

126. **Assertion (A) :** Loose Assemblage is the process of linking together different classes.

Reason (R) : The number ofsubjects are restricted.

In the above statements :

(A) (A) is true but (R) is false

(B) (A) is false but (R) is true

(C) Both (A) and (R) are true

(D) Both (A) and (R) are false

127. Which of the following is not the characteristics of the information society ?

(A) Information used as an economic source

(B) People use information intensively in their activities

(C) Information sector within the economy is developed

(D) Dependence on traditional Knowledge

128. How to write the size of book having height 21.5 cm and width 30 cm ina catalogue entry according to AACR II ?

(A) 21 cm (B) 22 cm

(C) 21 × 30 cm (D) 22 × 30 cm

129. According to ISBD format the GMD is recorded :

(A) Aftèr the statement of responsibility

(B) After the title proper

(C) After the subtitle

(D) After the series statement

130. Match List-I and List-II and choose the correct answer by using the codes given below :

List-I	List-II
(i) Maslow	(a) Hygienic factors
(ii) McGregor	(b) Immaturity/Maturity
(iii) Argyris	(c) Theory Y
(iv) Herzberg	(d) Hierarchy ofneeds

Codes :	**(i)**	**(ii)**	**(iii)**	**(iv)**
(A)	(a)	(b)	(c)	(d)
(B)	(d)	(a)	(b)	(c)
(C)	(d)	(c)	(b)	(a)
(D)	(d)	(c)	(a)	(b)

131. Which one of the following is the function of a library committee ?
   (A) To produce useful reading material
   (B) To lay down general library policy
   (C) To render adequate reference service
   (D) To arrange for resource sharing and inter library loan

132. Arrange the following classification schemes in their chronological order of origin :
   (i) Bibliographic Classification
   (ii) Colon Classification
   (iii) Universal Decimal Classification
   (iv) Dewey Decimal Classification

   Codes :
   (A) (i) (ii) (iii) (iv) (B) (iii) (iv) (ii) (i)
   (C) (iv) (iii) (ii) (i) (D) (i) (iv) (iii) (ii)

133. Which of the following is an indicator of dispersion for a set of observations ?
   (A) Central tendency
   (B) Correlation coefficient

(C) Regression line

(D) Standard Deviation

ANSWERS

1. B	2. D	3. C	4. A	5. B	6. C
7. A	8. A	9. A	10. C	11. D	12. B
13. B	14. D	15. A	16. B	17. C	18. C
19. C	20. B	21. B	22. D	23. B	24. C
25. C	26. B	27. A	28. A	29. D	30. B
31. C	32. C	33. C	34. A	35. A	36. D
37. D	38. A	39. C	40. A	41. B	42. C
43. A	44. B	45. A	46. A	47. A	48. A
49. C	50. A	51. A	52. C	53. B	54. D
55. A	56. D	57. A	58. B	59. A	60. A
61. A	62. A	63. C	64. D	65. A	66. B
67. C	68. D	69. B	70. A	71. C	72. C
73. C	74. A	75. D	76. C	77. A	78. B
79. C	80. C	81. A	82. D	83. C	84. C
85. A	86. D	87. D	88. B	89. C	90. A
91. B	92. D	93. A	94. D	95. D	96. A
97. B	98. C	99. B	100. C	101. C	102. B
103. C	104. C	105. C	106. B	107. B	108. B
109. B	110. C	11. A	112. A	113. B	114. D
115. A	116. A	117. C	118. A	119. C	120. A
121. B	122. D	123. B	124. B	125. B	126. A
127. D	128. D	129. B	130. C	131. B	132. C
133. D					

9

Latest Solved Question Papers

JUNE 2012 NET PAPER-II

1. Who was the Chairman of 'National Policy on Library & Information Systems' (1986) ?
   (A) D. N. Banerjee
   (B) D. P. Chattopadhyay
   (C) Sam Pitroda
   (D) Kalpana Dasgupta
2. The significance of the year 2011 for LIS education in India is
   (A) Golden Jubilee year
   (B) Platinum Jubilee year
   (C) Diamond Jubilee year
   (D) Centenary year
3. Digital Reference Service can be offered through
   (A) FAX (B) OPAC
   (C) Ask your librarian (D) Consortia

4. "Biotechnology" is formed as a result of
   (A) Fusion (B) Lamination
   (C) Fission (D) Agglomeration
5. The order of significance of "Thing, Material and Action" among various components of a compound subject was expanded by
   (A) J. Kaiser (B) E. J. Coates
   (C) J. R. Sharp (D) J. E. L. Farradane
6. Relational Database is
   (A) A work which has some relationship to another work
   (B) A symbol representing relationship between two concepts
   (C) Manipulation commands which relate records in different fields
   (D) All of the above
7. "Shodhganga" is a repository of
   (A) E – Resources (B) E – Thesis
   (C) E – Journals (D) E – Books
8. Which of the following tests can be employed for hypothesis testing ?
   (A) F – test (B) Chi – square test
   (C) t – test (D) All of the above
9. 'RRRLF' falls under the :
   (A) Ministry of Human Resource Development
   (B) Ministry of Information & Broadcasting
   (C) Ministry of Culture
   (D) Ministry of Science & Technology
10. "Internet Public Library" is being maintained by
    (A) MIT, Massachusettes
    (B) University of Michigan

(C) University of Arizona

(D) Drexal University

11. What are the major driving forces behind an 'Information society' ?

(i) R T I (ii) I. C. T.

(iii) Internet (iv) I. T. ACT

Codes :

(A) (ii) & (i) are correct

(B) (ii) & (iv) are correct

(C) (i) & (iv) are correct

(D) (ii) & (iii) are correct

12. Which libraries are functioning as depository libraries ?

(i) Delhi Public Library

(ii) Connemara Public Library

(iii) British Council Library

(iv) Central Reference Library

Codes :

(A) (i), (iii), (iv) are correct

(B) (i) & (iii) are correct

(C) (i) & (ii) are correct

(D) (ii) & (iii) are correct

13. Which of the following are 'Inclusive geographical sources'

(i) Maps (ii) Atlases

(iii) Encyclopaedias (iv) Yearbooks

Codes :

(A) (i) & (ii) are correct

(B) (iii) & (iv) are correct

(C) (ii) & (iii) are correct

(D) (ii) & (iv) are correct

14. Which principles are corollary to Wall picture principle ?
    (i) Cow-calf principle
    (ii) Principle of later-in-time
    (iii) Whole – organ principle
    (iv) All of the above

    Codes :
    (A) (i) and (ii) are correct
    (B) (ii) and (iii) are correct
    (C) (i) and (iii) are correct
    (D) (i) and (iv) are correct

15. The factors that influence computer file organisation are
    (i) Speed of access (ii) Storage space
    (iii) Fixed length fields (iv) File volatility

    Codes :
    (A) (i), (ii) and (iii) are correct
    (B) (i), (ii) and (iv) are correct
    (C) (ii), (iii) and (iv) are correct
    (D) (i), (iii) and (iv) are correct

16. Major problems of 'Information Communication Technology' are
    (i) Information overload
    (ii) Information insecurity
    (iii) Lack of innovative technologies
    (iv) Lack of control overcommunication

    Codes :
    (A) (ii) and (iv) are correct
    (B) (i) and (iv) are correct
    (C) (i), (ii) and (iv) are correct
    (D) (i), (ii) and (iii) are correct

17. Which of the following are 'Open Source Content Management Systems' ?

(i) Drupal (ii) Atex

(iii) Joomla (iv) OpenCms

Codes :

(A) (i), (ii) and (iv) are correct

(B) (i), (ii) and (iii) are correct

(C) (ii), (iii) and (iv) are correct

(D) (i), (iii) and (iv) are correct

18. Which of the following are not styles of citation ?

(i) Anglo American Cataloguing Rules

(ii) MLA Handbook for Writers of Research Papers

(iii) Chicago Manual of Style

(iv) Little Science Big Science

Codes :

(A) (i) and (ii) are correct

(B) (iii) and (iv) are correct

(C) (i) and (iv) are correct

(D) (ii) and (iii) are correct

19. Which of the following are Schools of Management thought ?

(i) Scientific Management School

(ii) Human Behavioural School

(iii) Classical School

(iv) School of Authority

Codes :

(A) (ii) and (iv) are correct

(B) (i), (ii) and (iv) are correct

(C) (iii) and (iv) are correct

(D) (i), (ii) and (iii) are correct

20. Assertion (A) : Users can have access to large number of e-journals.

    Reason (R) : Users are not aware of using e-journals.

    Codes :

    (A) (A) is true, but (R) is false

    (B) Both (A) and (R) are true, but (R) is not the correct explanation of (A)

    (C) (A) is false, (R) is true

    (D) Both (A) and (R) are true and (R) is the correct explanation of (A)

21. **Assertion (A) :** Book selection must be done judiciously.

    Reason (R) : Resource sharing is the need of the hour.

    Codes :

    (A) Both (A) and (R) are true, but (R) is not the correct statement of (A)

    (B) (A) is false, but (R) is true

    (C) (A) is true, but (R) is false

    (D) Both (A) and (R) are false

22. **Assertion (A) :** Primary sources provide most authentic information for research.

    Reason (R) : Primary sources are highly unorganised.

    Codes :

    (A) (A) is false, but (R) is true

    (B) (A) is true, but (R) is false

    (C) Both (A) and (R) are correct and (R) is the correct explanation of (A)

    (D) Both (A) and (R) are correct, but (R) is not the correct explanation of (A)

23. **Assertion (A)** : Abstracting services facilitate literature review.

    Reason (R) : Literature review summarises major findings of various studies.

    Codes :

    (A) (A) is true, but (R) is false
    (B) (A) is false, but (R) is true
    (C) Both (A) and (R) are true
    (D) Both (A) and (R) are false

24. **Assertion (A) :** "Name Authority File" should be used in a library.

    Reason (R) : All works of an author should be collocated.

    Codes :

    (A) (A) is true, but (R) is false
    (B) Both (A) and (R) true and (R) is the correct explanation of (A).
    (C) (A) is false, but (R) is true
    (D) Both (A) and (R) are false

25. **Assertion (A) :** Classification plays asignificant role in online retrieval.

    Reason (R) : Classification played an important role in manual system.

    Codes :

    (A) (A) is true, but (R) is false
    (B) Both (A) and (R) are false
    (C) Both (A) and (R) are true
    (D) (A) is false, but (R) is true

26. **Assertion (A) :** If changes cannot be adopted to its framework, the organisational equilibrium will be imbalanced.

Reason (R) : Organisation works in an environment which is marked by dynamic characteristics.

Codes :

(A) (A) is true, but (R) is false

(B) (A) is false, but (R) is true

(C) Both (A) and (R) are true

(D) Both (A) and (R) are false

27. **Assertion (A)** : There is need to continuous evaluation and appreciation of value of libraries.

Reason (R) : There is economic pressure on public budget.

Codes :

(A) Both (A) and (R) are true

(B) Both (A) and (R) are false

(C) (A) is true, but (R) is false

(D) (A) is false, but (R) is true

28. **Assertion (A)** : System analys is identifies the flow of work.

Reason (R) : System analysis is not necessary if the library is automated.

Codes :

(A) (A) is false, but (R) is true

(B) (A) is true, but (R) is false

(C) Both (A) and (R) are false

(D) Both (A) and (R) are true

29. Arrange the following associations according to their year of establishment :

(i) IASLIC (ii) ASLIB

(iii) ALA (iv) SLA

Codes :

(A) (iv), (ii), (iii), (i) (B) (ii), (iii), (iv), (i)

(C) (iii), (iv), (ii), (i) (D) (i), (iv), (ii), (iii)

30. Arrange the following according to their year of enactment in India :

(i) Freedom of Information Act

(ii) Right to Information Act

(iii) Copyright Act (Revised)

(iv) Information Technology Act

Codes :

(A) (iv), (ii), (i), (iii) (B) (iii), (iv), (i), (ii)

(C) (ii), (iii), (iv), (i) (D) (i), (iv), (ii), (iii)

31. Arrange the following publications according to their year of origin.

(i) Social Science Citation Index

(ii) L I S A

(iii) Library Literature and Information Science

(iv) Library Journal

Codes :

(A) (i), (iii), (iv), (ii) (B) (ii), (i), (iii), (iv)

(C) (iv), (iii), (ii), (i) (D) (iii), (ii), (iv), (i)

32. Arrange the following according to their year of origin :

(i) Broad System of Ordering

(ii) Classification in Online Systems

(iii) Automated Keyword Classification

(iv) Classification Research Group

Codes :

(A) (iv), (iii), (i), (ii) (B) (i), (ii), (iv), (iii)

(C) (iii), (i), (ii), (iv) (D) (ii), (iv), (iii), (ii)

33. Arrange the following according to their year of origin :
    (i) Bradford's Law
    (ii) Lotka's Law
    (iii) Statistical Bibliography
    (iv) Zipf's Law

    Codes :

    (A) (i), (iii), (iv), (ii) (B) (i), (ii), (iv), (iii)
    (C) (iv), (iii), (i), (ii) (D) (iii), (ii), (iv), (i)

34. "Prevention of Cholera in India" generates following index terms according to modified 'Chain Indexing', arrange them in correct order
    (i) India (ii) Cholera
    (iii) Disease (iv) Treatment
    (v) Medicine

    Codes :

    (A) (iii), (iv), (i), (ii), (v) (B) (ii), (i), (iii), (iv), (v)
    (C) (iv), (iii), (ii), (v), (i) (D) (i), (iii), (iv), (v), (ii)

35. Arrange the following according totheir year of first publication :
    (i) Encyclopaedia Britannica
    (ii) Encyclopaedia Americana
    (iii) Encyclopaedia of Library and Information Science
    (iv) McGraw-Hill Encyclopaedia of Science and Technology

    Codes :

    (A) (iv), (iii), (i), (ii) (B) (i), (ii), (iv), (iii)
    (C) (iii), (i), (iv), (ii) (D) (ii), (iv), (i), (iii)

36. Arrange the following according to their year of establishment :

(i) NIC (ii) DESIDOC

(iii) NISCAIR (iv) NASSDOC

Codes :

(A) (i), (iii), (ii), (iv) (B) (iii), (i), (iv), (ii)

(C) (iv), (i), (iii), (ii) (D) (ii), (iv), (i), (iii)

37. Arrange the following Public Library Acts according to their year of enactment :

(i) Uttar Pradesh PL Act

(ii) Arunachal Pradesh PL Act

(iii) Orissa PL Act

(iv) Gujarat PL Act

Codes :

(A) (iv), (iii), (i), (ii) (B) (ii), (iii), (i), (iv)

(C) (ii), (i), (iv), (iii) (D) (iii), (ii), (i), (iv)

38. Match the following :

List - I	**List - II**
(a) Obligation of the State	(i) First Law
(b) Shelf Arrangement & Catalogue	(ii) Second Law
(c) Open Access & Shelf Arrangement	(iii) Third Law
(d) Library location/hours	(iv) Fourth Law

Codes :	**(a)**	**(b)**	**(c)**	**(d)**
(A)	(ii)	(iv)	(iii)	(i)
(B)	(iv)	(iii)	(ii)	(i)
(C)	(i)	(iii)	(iv)	(ii)
(D)	(iii)	(ii)	(i)	(iv)

39. Match the following :

	List - I		List - II
(a)	Asian Recorder	(i)	Location of specific volume of journal
(b)	Union Catalogue of Scientific Serials	(ii)	Articles on Green Revolution
(c)	Books-in-Print	(iii)	Obituary of Dev - Anand
(d)	Social Science Index	(iv)	Availability of books

Codes :	**(a)**	**(b)**	**(c)**	**(d)**
(A)	(iv)	(iii)	(i)	(ii)
(B)	(i)	(iv)	(ii)	(iii)
(C)	(iii)	(i)	(iv)	(ii)
(D)	(ii)	(iv)	(iii)	(i)

40. Match the following :

	List - I		List - II
(a)	User orientation	(i)	Bibliographic service
(b)	Information repackaging	(ii)	Reference service
(c)	Translation	(iii)	Digest series
(d)	Indexing	(iv)	Support service

Codes :	**(a)**	**(b)**	**(c)**	**(d)**
(A)	(i)	(iv)	(iii)	(ii)
(B)	(iii)	(ii)	(i)	(iv)
(C)	(iv)	(i)	(ii)	(iii)
(D)	(ii)	(iii)	(iv)	(i)

41. Match the following :

	List - I		List - II
(a)	Textual representation	(i)	Pascal
(b)	Computer language	(ii)	Gopher
(c)	Network tool	(iii)	Boolean operators
(d)	Searching technique	(iv)	ASCI

Codes :	**(a)**	**(b)**	**(c)**	**(d)**
(A)	(iv)	(i)	(ii)	(iii)
(B)	(i)	(iv)	(iii)	(ii)
(C)	(iii)	(ii)	(iv)	(i)
(D)	(ii)	(iv)	(iii)	(i)

42. Match the following :

	List - I	List - II
(a)	Law of Parsimony	(i) Classification
(b)	Principle of Osmosis	(ii) F. W.Lancaster
(c)	Paperless Society	(iii) Overalleconomy
(d)	APUPA pattern	(iv) Reclassification

Codes :	**(a)**	**(b)**	**(c)**	**(d)**
(A)	(ii)	(i)	(iv)	(iii)
(B)	(iv)	(ii)	(i)	(iii)
(C)	(iii)	(iv)	(ii)	(i)
(D)	(i)	(iii)	(ii)	(iv)

43. Match the following :

	List - I		List - II
(a)	Hubs	(i)	A physical layer device used to interconnect the media segments of an extended network
(b)	Repeater	(ii)	A physical layer device that connects multiple

			computers each via a dedicated cable
(c)	Bus Topology	(iii)	Multiple bridges known for transfer of data between different parts
(d)	Switches	(iv)	A straight line data highway that Carries network information from one Network station to another

Codes :	**(a)**	**(b)**	**(c)**	**(d)**
(A)	(iii)	(iv)	(ii)	(i)
(B)	(ii)	(i)	(iv)	(iii)
(C)	(iv)	(i)	(iii)	(ii)
(D)	(i)	(iii)	(ii)	(iv)

44. Match the following :

	List - I		**List - II**
(a)	RRRLF	(i)	Delhi
(b)	Connemara Public Library	(ii)	Patna
(c)	NISCAIR	(iii)	Kolkata
(d)	Khuda Baksh Oriental Public Library	(iv)	Chennai

Codes :	**(a)**	**(b)**	**(c)**	**(d)**
(A)	(iv)	(iii)	(ii)	(i)
(B)	(ii)	(iii)	(iv)	(i)
(C)	(iii)	(iv)	(i)	(ii)
(D)	(iv)	(i)	(ii)	(iii)

45. Match the following :

	List - I		List - II
(a)	Right man at right library	(i)	Annual financial statement
(b)	Budget	(ii)	Deployment
(c)	Journal	(iii)	TQM
(d)	Identifying user's views and expectations	(iv)	ISSN

Codes :	**(a)**	**(b)**	**(c)**	**(d)**
(A)	(iii)	(i)	(ii)	(iv)
(B)	(ii)	(i)	(iv)	(iii)
(C)	(iv)	(ii)	(iii)	(i)
(D)	(i)	(iii)	(iv)	(ii)

Read the passage given below, and answer the questions based on your understanding of the passage. (Question Nos. 46-50)

The primary concern with the longevity ofdigital documents is the "viewing problem" (Besser, 2000). Unlike analog or physical information, which tends to exist independent of human involvement, digital information needs constant intervention to survive. History has shown that digital documents are problematic by default. Whereas we can actually look at the Sistine Chapel ceiling, painted 500 years ago, it is difficult if not impossible to simply view documents on 8-in. Floppy disks created inthe last 20 years, even if there has been animmediate, proactive role in preserving them. Without concerted effort on the part of archivists and preservationists, digital objects quickly become obsolete or in accessible due to unforeseen, although anticipated, advances in information technology. The variable media art community currently utilizes four digital preservation strategies, all focused on the end product. The first three methods have technical origins and are based on general digital preservation practices. Related to "the viewing problem", they are : *refreshing*, the upgrade of storage mechanisms; *migration*, the premeditated upgrade of file formats; and *emulation*, which focuses on development of operating systems able to run obsolete media. The fourth option, developed by and for the new media art community, is *reinterpretation* (Depocas et al., 2003), where the curators attempt to recreate a work given comprehensive documentation of the original artefact. *Migration* and *emulation* are the two primary methods in managing the problem of obsolete file formats (Waters & Garrett,1996). Migration focuses on the files themselves, periodically updating files in new software formats. The second method of preservation is emulation, which can be either at the system or the software level. System emulation focuses on developing systems that mimic the hardware used to create or run the original artefact.

46. Why digital objects become in accessible quickly ?
    (A) Because of unforeseen advancement of technology
    (B) It is independent of human intervention
    (C) It is independent of any technological advancement
    (D) None of the above

47. Reinterpretation is a digital preservation strategy where curator intends to
    (A) Upgrade file formats
    (B) Upgrade storage mechanism
    (C) Recreate a work
    (D) Upgrade operating system

48. What is the focus of system emulation ?

(A) Developing systems that mimic hardware
(B) Developing systems that mimic software
(C) Developing systems that mimic file formats
(D) None of the above

49. Which of the following is true about migration preservation strategy ?
(A) Migration is not related to theviewing problem
(B) Migration is related to theviewing problem
(C) Migration requires comprehensive documentation
(D) Migration does not have atechnical origin

50. Refreshing preservation strategy focuses on
(A) Comprehensive documentation of original artefact
(B) Development of operating system
(C) Not on viewing problem
(D) Upgradation of storage

ANSWERS

1. B	2. D	3. C	4. A	5. B	6. C
7. B	8. D	9. C	10. D	11. D	12. C
13. B/A	14. C	15. B	16. C	17. D	18. C
19. D	20. B	21. A	22. D	23. D	24. B
25. D	26. C	27. A	28. B	29. C	30. B
31. C	32. A	33. D	34. C	35. B	36. D
37. A	38. A	39. C	40. D	41. A	42. C
43. B	44. C	45. B	46. A	47. C	48. A
49. B	50. D				

JUNE 2012 NET PAPER-III

1. The initiation, selection, exploration, formulation, collection and presentation are two stages of which model of information seeking behaviour
   (A) Ellis Model (B) Krikelas Model
   (C) Kuhlthou Model (D) Wilson Model
2. Jubilee Project is associated with what ?
   (A) Evaluation of electronic information services
   (B) Public library survey
   (C) Strategic management of libraries
   (D) Scale development
3. The publisher of "Information Power : Building Partnership for Learning" is
   (A) AASL (B) AECT
   (C) ALA (D) ILA
4. In 1974, Zurkowski used for the first time which of the following term ?
   (A) Digital Literacy
   (B) Media Literacy
   (C) Computer Literacy
   (D) Information Literacy
5. Inference Engine is a part of which information system ?
   (A) Management information System
   (B) Decision Support System
   (C) Expert System
   (D) Open System
6. Which of the following is not related tocase study approach in a research design ?

(A) Indepth Study
(B) Study of one/limited cases
(C) General study
(D) Little concern about generalisation to a large population

7. "Students' visit to Library is influenced by the availability of Internet". State "Students' visit to library" is which kind of variable ?
(A) Independent Variable
(B) Intervening Variable
(C) Dependent Variable
(D) Intercept Variable

8. Idiographic hypothesis is directed towards predicting the behaviour of
(A) An Individual
(B) Group of People
(C) Masses
(D) People from same school of thought

9. In the process of reasoning when westart with a specific statement, and conclude to a general statement, it iscalled
(A) Deductive Reasoning
(B) Inductive Reasoning
(C) Abnormal Reasoning
(D) Transcendental Reasoning

10. Solomon Four group design is related to
(A) Field studies
(B) Pretest-post test control group design
(C) Data Analysis Model
(D) Statistical Technique

11. The information network that connects Universities and Colleges in United Kingdom :
    (A) JANET (B) SERCNET
    (C) OCLC (D) BONET
12. Internet filtering is
    (A) A form of censorship
    (B) Acceptable user policy
    (C) Access to in appropriate material
    (D) Blocking internet facility
13. Which one of the following is a Bulletin Board Service on Internet ?
    (A) Picaso (B) Google talk
    (C) Blog (D) Oovoo
14. Virus is a software which can
    (A) Manipulate data
    (B) Replicate itself
    (C) Damage computer
    (D) All the above
15. Which one of the following protocol isused in file transfer over internet ?
    (A) FTP (B) SMTP
    (C) POP (D) TCP/IP
16. Scaler chain shows
    (A) Authority structure
    (B) Scale of performance of staff
    (C) Chain for locating racks
    (D) A link in the chain
17. Blair and Maron evaluation study on retrieval effectiveness of full text search is called

(A) SMART Retrieval Experiment
(B) MEDLARS evaluation study
(C) STAIRS project
(D) Cranefield – II Project

18. In cataloguing, the square brackets [ ] are used
(A) to enclose information takenfrom outside
(B) to enclose the details of printed / manufacturer
(C) to enclose series statements
(D) to enclose statement of accompanying material

19. Which Section of AACR – II (R) deals with serial publications ?
(A) Part – A, Section – 3
(B) Part – B, Section – 3
(C) Part – A, Section – 12
(D) Part – B, Section – 12

20. When two or more basic subjects having same relational approach form a specific subject, the relation is termed as
(A) Speciater relation (B) Co-ordinate relation
(C) Phase relation (D) Hierarchical relation

21. The concept of 'Stopword' list is relevant in the context of
(A) Uniform Indexing (B) Citation Indexing
(C) Chain Indexing (D) Keyword Indexing

22. A version of KWIC augmented with author/name is called
(A) WADEX (B) KWOC
(C) KWAC (D) KWIC

23. 'Segmentation' is associated with

(A) Reference Service
(B) Market Survey Report
(C) Digest Service
(D) Indexing Service

24. State of the art report generally highlights
(A) General Aspects
(B) Technical Aspects
(C) Administrative Aspects
(D) All of the above

25. Who propounded "Minimum, Middling and Maximum Theories" of reference service ?
(A) C.M. Winchell (B) James I. Wyer
(C) Samuel Rothstein (D) D.W. Lewis

26. Even though 'Xerography' is a photocopying method, but it is called
(A) Diazographic (B) Thermographic
(C) Electrofax (D) Electrostatic

27. 'CODEN' is connected with
(A) Books (B) Serials
(C) Reports (D) Gray Literature

28. Roget's International Thesaurus is a
(A) Classified List of Words
(B) Book of Synonyms
(C) List of Standard Terms
(D) List of Scientific Terms

29. Information about scale and projection can be found in
(A) Encyclopaedias
(B) Hand books of Manuals
(C) Geographical sources
(D) Directories

30. Who of the following is not the author of any reference book ?
    (A) C.M. Winchell (B) William A Katz
    (C) Louis Shores (D) Maurice B. Line
31. Identify the odd one out.
    (A) ANSI (B) BIS
    (C) BSI (D) ESPN
32. Which of the following is not a part of word treatment in language dictionaries ?
    (A) Gloss
    (B) Vernacular
    (C) Etymology
    (D) Grammatical information
33. Where the first M. Phil programme in Library and Information Science was started in India ?
    (A) University of Madras
    (B) University of Delhi
    (C) University of Mysore
    (D) University of Bombay
34. Corollary for Second Law of Library Science is
    (A) Books for all
    (B) Free Books Service
    (C) Free Library Service
    (D) Books every where
35. Which of the following is not the prerequisite for a National Information Policy ?
    (A) Legislative Frame work
    (B) Production of National Bibliography
    (C) Advisory and Administrative body
    (D) ICT infrastructure facilities

36. World Intellectual Property Organization is related to
    (A) UNESCO
    (B) United Nations
    (C) U.S. Organization
    (D) International Law Organization
37. Redundancy of information is
    (A) Unnecessary and should be eliminated
    (B) Unnecessary but cannot be avoided
    (C) Necessary and some times useful
    (D) Necessary and always desirable
38. Which sources would you consult to know the "Impact Factor" of Journal publications ?
    (i) Web of Science (ii) Science Direct
    (iii) SCOPUS (iv) EBSCO

    Codes :
    (A) (i) and (iv) (B) (ii) and (iii)
    (C) (i) and (iii) (D) (iii) and (iv)
39. Research is conducted to :
    (i) Generate new knowledge
    (ii) Develop a theory
    (iii) Develop communication skills
    (iv) Re-interpret existing knowledge

    Codes :
    (A) (i), (iii) and (ii) are correct
    (B) (iii), (ii) and (i) are correct
    (C) (i), (ii) and (iv) are correct
    (D) (i), (iii) and (iv) are correct
40. Radio Frequency Identification is used in library for:

(i) Circulation of Documents
(ii) Cataloguing of Documents
(iii) Security of Documents
(iv) Acquisition of Documents

Codes :

(A) (i) and (ii) are correct
(B) (ii) and (iv) are correct
(C) (iii) and (ii) are correct
(D) (i) and (iii) are correct

41. BIOS contains :
(i) Operating System Program
(ii) Bootstrap Program
(iii) Application System Program
(iv) Convert Character to Code Program

Codes :

(A) (i) and (ii) are correct
(B) (ii) and (iii) are correct
(C) (iii) and (iv) are correct
(D) (ii) and (iv) are correct

42. Science Citation Index is published by
(A) Thomson Reuters (B) H.W. Wilson
(C) Whitaker (D) R.R. Bowker

43. In the information transfer cycles, internet is acting as
(i) Primary Publisher (ii) Secondary Publisher
(iii) Tertiary Publisher (iv) Primary Distributor

Codes :

(A) (i), (iii) and (iv) are correct.
(B) (i), (ii) and (iv) are correct.

(C) (ii), (iii) and (iv) are correct.

(D) (i), (ii) and (iii) are correct.

44. Methods and Techniques of Human Resource Planning includes

(i) Selection and Recruitment

(ii) Induction and Placement

(iii) Quality Management

(iv) Performance Evaluation

Codes :

(A) (i), (iv) & (ii) are correct.

(B) (iv), (iii) & (i) are correct.

(C) (i), (ii) & (iv) are correct.

(D) (iii) and (i) are correct.

45. **Assertion (A) :** Netiquette mandates that you do your best to act within the laws of cyber space and society.

Reason (R) : Failing to respect other people's privacy is bad Netiquette.

Codes :

(A) Both (A) and (R) are false.

(B) Both (A) and (R) are true.

(C) (A) is true, but (R) is false.

(D) (A) is false, but (R) is true.

46. **Assertion (A) :** Modern Integrated Library Management Softwares offer user friendly Graphical User Interfaces (GUI) on the web.

Reason (R) : Almost every module of modern Integrated Library Management Software is accessible through the internet.

Codes :

(A) Both (A) and (R) are correct.

(B) (A) is correct but (R) is wrong.

(C) Both (A) and (R) are wrong.

(D) (A) is wrong but (R) is correct.

47. **Assertion (A) :** Open Systems Interconnection allows connectivity of ICT components.

Reason (R) : Network Printer goes slow if it is OSI compatible.

Codes :

(A) Both (A) and (R) are true.

(B) Both (A) and (R) are false.

(C) (A) is false, but (R) is true.

(D) (A) is true, but (R) is false.

48. **Assertion (A) :** Many libraries have no written collection development policy and yet have sound collection.

Reason (R) : Demand driven collection plays a strong role in having a sound collection.

Codes :

(A) (A) is true, but (R) is false.

(B) (A) is false, but (R) is true.

(C) Both (A) and (R) are true.

(D) Both (A) and (R) are false.

49. **Assertion (A) :** Browne charging system is simple and less time consuming.

Reason (R) : There is permanent issue record available.

Codes :

(A) (A) is false, but (R) is true.

(B) (A) is true, but (R) is false.

(C) Both (A) and (R) are true.

(D) Both (A) and (R) are false.

50. **Assertion (A) :** Collection of audio materials is less used in Academic Libraries.

Reason (R) : People consider these materials intellectually less sound and fit only for recreation purpose.

Codes :

(A) (A) is false, but (R) is true.

(B) (A) is true, but (R) is false.

(C) (A) is true and (R) is partially true.

(D) Both (A) and (R) are false.

51. **Assertion (A) :** Introduction of TQM in libraries is not possible.

Reason (R) : It requires open, cooperative culture and employees responsiveness for customer satisfaction.

Codes :

(A) Both (A) and (R) are true.

(B) (A) is true, but (R) is false.

(C) (A) is false, but (R) is true.

(D) Both (A) and (R) are false.

52. **Assertion (A) :** An indexing language is an artificial language and it uses controlled vocabulary.

Reason (R) : Controlled vocabulary provides relation between and among terms.

Codes :

(A) Both (A) and (R) are true.

(B) (A) is true, but (R) is false.

(C) (A) is false, but (R) is true.

(D) Both (A) and (R) are false.

53. **Assertion (A) :** Marketing of Information products is the need of the day.

Reason (R) : Information is are source which consumes lot of time and money.

Codes :

(A) (A) is true, but (R) is false.

(B) (A) is false, but (R) is true.

(C) Both (A) and (R) are true.

(D) Both (A) and (R) are false.

54. **Assertion (A) :** Colan classification is an enumerative classification scheme.

Reason (R) : Colan classification has adopted analytico-synthetic approach for the construction of class number

Codes :

(A) (A) is false, but (R) is true.

(B) (A) is true, but (R) is false.

(C) Both (A) and (R) are true.

(D) Both (A) and (R) are false.

55. **Assertion (A) :** INFLIBNET provides document delivery service to all types of libraries in India.

Reason (R) : Modern technologies made it possible for electronic transmission of required documents.

Codes :

(A) Both (A) and (R) are correct.

(B) (A) is wrong, but (R) is correct.

(C) Both (A) and (R) are wrong.

(D) (A) is correct and (R) is wrong.

56. **Assertion (A) :** LIS Education in India achieved a landmark of 100 years but quality is compromised.

Reason (R) : Unplanned proliferation of LIS schools and open learning programmes.

Codes :

(A) Both (A) and (R) are true.

(B) Both (A) are (R) are false.

(C) (A) is false (R) is true.

(D) (A) is true (R) is false.

57. **Assertion (A) :** LIS education is not uniform throughout India.

Reason (R) : Adoption of UGC model syllabus is not mandatory, Local LIS requirements varies.

Codes :

(A) (A) is true, but (R) is false.

(B) (A) is false, but (R) is true.

(C) Both (A) and (R) are true.

(D) Both (A) and (R) are false.

58. **Assertion (A) :** There is need for Library Legislation in all States of India.

Reason (R) : To make Public Library System independent and without political influence.

Codes :

(A) Both (A) and (R) are true.

(B) (A) is true, but (R) is false.

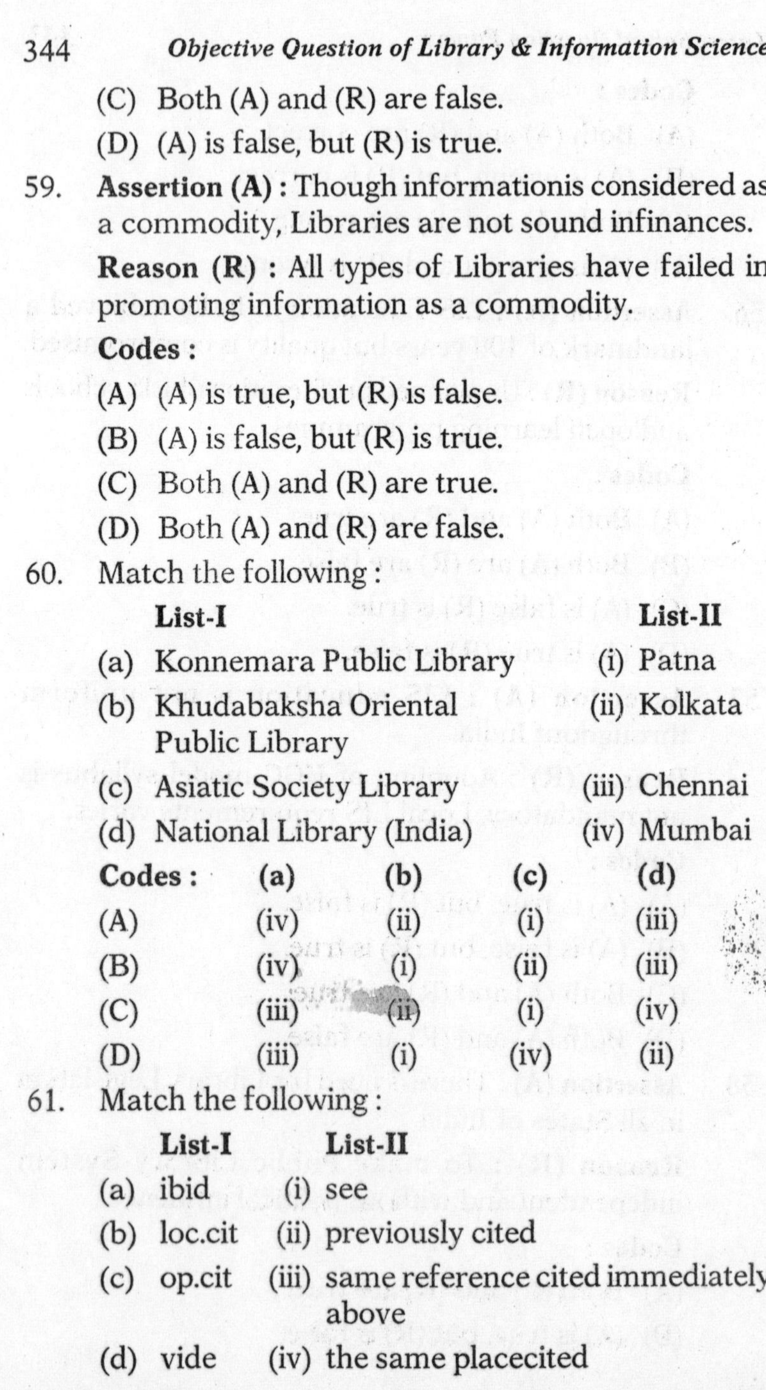

(C) Both (A) and (R) are false.

(D) (A) is false, but (R) is true.

59. **Assertion (A) :** Though informationis considered as a commodity, Libraries are not sound infinances.

Reason (R) : All types of Libraries have failed in promoting information as a commodity.

Codes :

(A) (A) is true, but (R) is false.

(B) (A) is false, but (R) is true.

(C) Both (A) and (R) are true.

(D) Both (A) and (R) are false.

60. Match the following :

	List-I		**List-II**
(a)	Konnemara Public Library	(i)	Patna
(b)	Khudabaksha Oriental Public Library	(ii)	Kolkata
(c)	Asiatic Society Library	(iii)	Chennai
(d)	National Library (India)	(iv)	Mumbai

Codes :	**(a)**	**(b)**	**(c)**	**(d)**
(A)	(iv)	(ii)	(i)	(iii)
(B)	(iv)	(i)	(ii)	(iii)
(C)	(iii)	(ii)	(i)	(iv)
(D)	(iii)	(i)	(iv)	(ii)

61. Match the following :

	List-I		**List-II**
(a)	ibid	(i)	see
(b)	loc.cit	(ii)	previously cited
(c)	op.cit	(iii)	same reference cited immediately above
(d)	vide	(iv)	the same placecited

Codes :	(a)	(b)	(c)	(d)
(A)	(i)	(ii)	(iii)	(iv)
(B)	(ii)	(i)	(iv)	(iii)
(C)	(iii)	(iv)	(ii)	(i)
(D)	(iv)	(iii)	(i)	(ii)

62. Match the following :

	List-I		List-II
(a)	Cole and Eales	(i)	Statistical Bibliography
(b)	Hume	(ii)	Sciento metrics
(c)	Pritchard	(iii)	Statistical Analysis
(d)	T. Braun	(iv)	Bibliometrics

Codes :	(a)	(b)	(c)	(d)
(A)	(iv)	(iii)	(ii)	(i)
(B)	(iii)	(i)	(iv)	(ii)
(C)	(ii)	(iii)	(i)	(iv)
(D)	(i)	(iii)	(iv)	(ii)

63. Match the following :

	List-I		List-II
(a)	Thurst on scale	(i)	Sharing individual preference in a group
(b)	Semantic Differential Scale	(ii)	Group of Judges
(c)	Likert Scale	(iii)	Selection from two opposite position
(d)	Sociometric scale	(iv)	Intensity structure

Codes :	(a)	(b)	(c)	(d)
(A)	(i)	(iv)	(ii)	(iii)
(B)	(ii)	(iii)	(iv)	(i)
(C)	(iv)	(i)	(iii)	(ii)
(D)	(iii)	(ii)	(iv)	(i)

64. Match the following :

List-I		List-II	
(a)	Vidyanidhi	(i)	Institutional Repository
(b)	TKDL	(ii)	Electronic Theses & Dissertations
(c)	DOAJ	(iii)	Digital Library of Journals
(d)	E-Prints @IISc	(iv)	Digital Archive

Codes :	**(a)**	**(b)**	**(c)**	**(d)**
(A)	(ii)	(iv)	(iii)	(i)
(B)	(iii)	(ii)	(i)	(iv)
(C)	(iv)	(iii)	(ii)	(i)
(D)	(i)	(ii)	(iv)	(iii)

65. Match the following :

List-I		List-II	
(a)	HTML File	(i)	Text Format
(b)	PDF File	(ii)	Film Format
(c)	JPG File	(iii)	Web Format
(d)	AVI File	(iv)	Image Format

Codes :	**(a)**	**(b)**	**(c)**	**(d)**
(A)	(i)	(ii)	(iv)	(iii)
(B)	(iii)	(i)	(iv)	(ii)
(C)	(i)	(iv)	(ii)	(iii)
(D)	(iv)	(iii)	(i)	(ii)

66. Match the following :

List-I		List-II	
(a)	DRUPAL	(i)	Integrated Library Management Software
(b)	Moodle	(ii)	Digital Library Software
(c)	D space	(iii)	Content Management Software
(d)	New GenLib	(iv)	Learning Management Software

Codes :	**(a)**	**(b)**	**(c)**	**(d)**
(A)	(iv)	(iii)	(ii)	(i)
(B)	(ii)	(i)	(iv)	(iii)
(C)	(iii)	(iv)	(ii)	(i)
(D)	(i)	(ii)	(iii)	(iv)

67. Match the following :

List-I	**List-II**
(a) FaceBook	(i) Video Networking site
(b) Research Gate	(ii) Social Networking site
(c) Oovoo	(iii) Academic Networking site
(d) Flicker	(iv) Photo Networking site

Codes :	**(a)**	**(b)**	**(c)**	**(d)**
(A)	(i)	(iii)	(ii)	(iv)
(B)	(iv)	(i)	(ii)	(iii)
(C)	(ii)	(iii)	(i)	(iv)
(D)	(iii)	(iv)	(i)	(ii)

68. Match the following :

List-I	**List-II**
(a) Small set of dependent activities that form longest path of activity network	(i) PERT
(b) Delighting the customer by fully meeting their needs	(ii) CPM
(c) Interconnecting networks depicting tasks, duration and dependency	(iii) Delphi
(d) Making better forecasts, judgements and advice	(iv) TQM

Codes :	**(a)**	**(b)**	**(c)**	**(d)**
(A)	(i)	(iii)	(ii)	(iv)
(B)	(ii)	(iv)	(i)	(iii)
(C)	(iii)	(iv)	(ii)	(i)
(D)	(iv)	(ii)	(i)	(iii)

69. Match the following :

List-I	**List-II**
(a) Transaction Processing	(i) Lower Level Managers
(b) Operational control	(ii) Clerical Staff
(c) Management control	(iii) Top Level Managers
(d) Strategic Planning	(iv) Middle Level Managers

Codes :	**(a)**	**(b)**	**(c)**	**(d)**
(A)	(iii)	(ii)	(iv)	(i)
(B)	(ii)	(i)	(iv)	(iii)
(C)	(iv)	(ii)	(iii)	(i)
(D)	(i)	(ii)	(iv)	(iii)

70. Match the following :

List-I	**List-II**
(a) Classical School	(i) John cotton Danna
(b) X & Y Theory	(ii) Henry Fayol
(c) Newark Charging System	(iii) Peter Drucker
(d) MBO	(iv) Douglas McGregor

Codes :	**(a)**	**(b)**	**(c)**	**(d)**
(A)	(i)	(iii)	(iv)	(ii)
(B)	(iii)	(iv)	(i)	(ii)
(C)	(ii)	(iv)	(i)	(iii)
(D)	(iii)	(ii)	(iv)	(i)

71. Match the following :

	List-I		List-II
(a)	C.A. Catter	(i)	Selective Listing
(b)	Kaiser	(ii)	Thing-partmaterial-action
(c)	J.R. Sharp	(iii)	Concrete and process
(d)	D.J. Coates	(iv)	Syndetic cataloguing

Codes :	**(a)**	**(b)**	**(c)**	**(d)**
(A)	(iv)	(i)	(ii)	(iii)
(B)	(iv)	(iii)	(i)	(ii)
(C)	(iii)	(iv)	(ii)	(i)
(D)	(ii)	(iii)	(iv)	(i)

72. Match the following :

	List-I		List-II
(a)	Guidance house RTI Act	(i)	Documentation service
(b)	Orientationin use of multimedia	(ii)	Referral service
(c)	Providinguser with list of information sources	(iii)	Informative Literacy
(d)	Directing the user of INFLIBNET to seek needed information	(iv)	Reference service

Codes :	**(a)**	**(b)**	**(c)**	**(d)**
(A)	(iii)	(ii)	(i)	(iv)
(B)	(iv)	(ii)	(iii)	(i)
(C)	(ii)	(i)	(iv)	(iii)
(D)	(iv)	(iii)	(i)	(ii)

73. Match the following :

List-I	List-II
(a) Whitaker's Almanack	(i) Year of starting 'Publishers Weekly'
(b) Ulrich's International Periodicals Directory	(ii) Availability of V 50 of 'Library Journal'
(c) National Union Catalogue of Scientific Serials in India	(iii) Information on discontinuation of New Encyclopaedia Britannica
(d) Data India	(iv) Astronomical information

Codes :	**(a)**	**(b)**	**(c)**	**(d)**
(A)	(iv)	(i)	(ii)	(iii)
(B)	(ii)	(iv)	(i)	(iii)
(C)	(iii)	(ii)	(i)	(iv)
(D)	(i)	(iv)	(ii)	(iii)

74. Match the following :

List-I	List-II
(a) J. Thompson	(i) Basic Statistics for Libraries
(b) S. Halkett of J Laing	(ii) Planning of Academic and Research Buildings
(c) William A Katz	(iii) Dictionary of anonymous and Pseudonymous literature
(d) K.D. Metcalf	(iv) Introduction to reference work

Codes :	**(a)**	**(b)**	**(c)**	**(d)**
(A)	(i)	(ii)	(iv)	(iii)
(B)	(i)	(iii)	(iv)	(ii)
(C)	(ii)	(iv)	(i)	(iii)
(D)	(iv)	(ii)	(iii)	(i)

75. Match the following :

List-I	**List-II**
(a) Budget prepared using previous period budget	(i) Formula Budget
(b) Budget based on norms and standards	(ii) Zero-based budget
(c) Budget planned integrating number of techniques	(iii) Incremental Budget
(d) Budget prepared identifying current tasks independent of previous year	(iv) Planning programming budgeting system

Codes :	**(a)**	**(b)**	**(c)**	**(d)**
(A)	(iii)	(i)	(iv)	(ii)
(B)	(i)	(iii)	(iv)	(ii)
(C)	(iii)	(ii)	(i)	(iv)
(D)	(i)	(ii)	(iii)	(iv)

ANSWERS

1. C	2. A	3. A	4. B	5. C	6. C
7. C	8. A	9. B	10. B	11. A	12. A
13. C	14. D	15. A	16. A	17. C	18. A
19. C	20. C	21. D	22. A	23. B	24. B
25. C	26. D	27. B	28. A	29. C	30. D
31. D	32. A	33. B	34. A	35. B	36. B

37. A	38. C	39. C	40. D	41. D	42. A
43. D	44. C	45. B	46. A	47. D	48. C
49. B	50. C	51. C	52. A	53. C	54. A
55. B	56. A	57. C	58. B	59. A	60. D
61. C	62. B	63. B	64. A	65. B	66. C
67. C	68. B	69. B	70. C	71. B	72. D
73. A	74. B	75. A			

DEC. 2012 NET PAPER-II

1. According to Machlup the difference between information and knowledge is
   (A) Information increases with use, whereas knowledge is constant.
   (B) Information is stimulatory, whereas knowledge is practical.
   (C) Information is shareable, whereas knowledge is one's property.
   (D) Information is piecemeal, fragmented, particular, whereas knowledge is structured, coherent and universal.
2. "Web of Science" is
   (A) A Citation Index
   (B) A Bibliography
   (C) An Abstracting Service
   (D) All of the above
3. "Facts on File" can be grouped under
   (A) Primary source
   (B) Secondary source
   (C) Tertiary source
   (D) None of the above
4. In MARC 21, subject access fields are
   (A) 3xx (B) 4xx
   (C) 5xx (D) 6xx
5. Transformation of traditional libraries to hybrid / digital libraries is
   (A) Crisis Management
   (B) Re-engineering
   (C) Change Management
   (D) Project Management

6. Which one of the following is not a switching system?
   (A) Packet (B) Circuit
   (C) Router (D) Message
7. Access to back volumes of E-journals is known as ________.
   (A) Random Access (B) Perpetual Access
   (C) Online Access (D) Retrospective Access
8. The chi-square technique is used to compare the observed data with that of
   (A) Collected raw data (B) Expected data
   (C) Analysed data (D) Graphical data
9. 'Parry Committee' (UK) was set up to advise
   (A) School Libraries (B) Public Libraries
   (C) Special Libraries (D) University Libraries
10. FRBR is developed by
   (A) LC (B) UNESCO
   (C) IFLA (D) FID
11. Who were involved in Public Library Movement in India ?
   (i) Sayaji Rao Gaekwad II
   (ii) C.D. Deshmukh
   (iii) S. Radhakrishnan
   (iv) S.R. Ranganathan

   Codes :
   (A) (i) & (iii) are correct
   (B) (ii) & (iv) are correct
   (C) (i) & (iv) are correct
   (D) (ii) & (iii) are correct
12. Which of the following are library networks ?

(i) Internet (ii) DELNET
(iii) NICNET (iv) OCLC

Codes :

(A) (i) and (ii) are correct.
(B) (ii) and (iv) are correct.
(C) (i) and (iii) are correct.
(D) (i) and (iv) are correct.

13. Which of the following are review type services ?
(i) Current Awareness
(ii) Trend Reports
(iii) News Clippings
(iv) State of the Art Report

Codes :

(A) (i), (ii), (iii) are correct.
(B) (i), (iii), (iv) are correct.
(C) (ii) & (iv) are correct.
(D) (ii) & (iii) are correct.

14. The basic characteristics of a system are
(i) Interrelated components
(ii) Independent and can stand alone
(iii) Arranged in hierarchical order
(iv) Inputs, processes, outputs & feed back

Codes :

(A) (i), (ii), (iii) are correct.
(B) (i), (ii), (iv) are correct.
(C) (ii), (iii), (iv) are correct.
(D) (i), (iii), (iv) are correct.

15. The general image file formats are :
(i) TIFF (ii) JPEG
(iii) MPEG (iv) PNG

Codes :

(A) (i), (ii) and (iii) are correct.
(B) (i), (iii) and (iv) are correct.
(C) (i), (ii) and (iv) are correct.
(D) (ii), (iii) and (iv) are correct.

16. Which of the following are common types of protocols ?

(i) HTTP	(ii) FTP
(iii) Telnet	(iv) Gopher

Codes :

(A) (i) and (ii) are correct.
(B) (i), (ii) and (iv) are correct.
(C) (iii) and (iv) are correct.
(D) (i), (ii) and (iii) are correct.

17. Which of the following are not the elements of DOI system ?

(i) Policies	(ii) Subject
(iii) Description	(iv) Resolution

Codes :

(A) (i), (ii) and (iii) are correct.
(B) (i), (iii) and (iv) are correct.
(C) (i), (ii) and (iv) are correct.
(D) (ii), (iii) and (iv) are correct.

18. Which of the following are Trade Bibliographies ?

(i) Books-in-Print
(ii) Indian Books-in-Print
(iii) Indian National Bibliography
(iv) British National Bibliography

Codes :

(A) (i) and (iii) are correct.

(B) (ii) and (iv) are correct.

(C) (i) and (ii) are correct.

(D) (ii) and (iii) are correct.

19. **Assertion (A) :** Distance education for LIS courses is gaining ground in India.

Reason (R) : Majority of people prefer it as an alternative channel of education.

Codes :

(A) (A) is true but (R) is false.

(B) (A) is false but (R) is true.

(C) Both (A) and (R) are correct.

(D) Both (A) and (R) are wrong.

20. **Assertion (A) :** Indian libraries are making optimum use of social networking.

Reason (R) : Social networking has wider role in dissemination of information.

Codes :

(A) (A) is true but (R) is false.

(B) (A) is false but (R) is true.

(C) (A) and (R) both are true.

(D) (A) and (R) both are false.

21. **Assertion (A) :** Knowledge is growing exponentially.

Reason (R) : Number of researchers have increased.

Codes :

(A) Both (A) & (R) are true.

(B) Both (A) and (R) are false.

(C) (A) is false but (R) is true.

(D) (A) is true but (R) is false.

22. **Assertion (A) :** Present decade has accepted E-journals as channels of fast communication.

    Reason (R) : E-publications have added enormous quantity of literature but affected the quality of research.

    Codes :

    (A) (A) is true but (R) is false.

    (B) (A) is false but (R) is true.

    (C) Both (A) and (R) are true and (R) is the correct explanation.

    (D) Both (A) and (R) are true, but (R) is not a correct explanation.

23. **Assertion (A) :** Library & Information centres are knowledge/management centres.

    Reason (R) : Libraries handle tacit knowledge.

    Codes :

    (A) Both (A) and (R) are true.

    (B) (A) is partially true, but (R) is false.

    (C) (A) is false, but (R) is true.

    (D) Both (A) and (R) are false.

24. **Assertion (A) :** Metadata hold much promise for information retrieval and access in the digital age.

    Reason (R) : Metadata can save a number of functions including description, resource discovery and management of resources.

    Codes :

    (A) (A) is true, but (R) is false.

    (B) (A) is false, but (R) is true.

    (C) Both (A) and (R) are true.

    (D) Both (A) and (R) are false.

25. **Assertion (A) :** Training methods through brain storming stimulate idea generation.

    Reason (R) : Training methods do not provide opportunity to unskilled to become skilled.

    Codes :

    (A) (A) is false but (R) is true.

    (B) Both (A) and (R) are false.

    (C) Both (A) and (R) are true.

    (D) (A) is true but (R) is false.

26. **Assertion (A) :** Random samples are not representative of the whole population.

    Reason (R) : Random numbers are used in forming a random sample.

    Codes :

    (A) (A) is true, but (R) is false.

    (B) (A) is false, but (R) is true.

    (C) Both (A) and (R) are true.

    (D) Both (A) and (R) are false.

27. **Assertion (A) :** Information Literacy is a basic skill essential for work environment in 21st century.

    Reason (R) : Information Literacy helps to train the users to make use of ICT.

    Codes :

    (A) Both (A) and (R) are true.

    (B) Both (A) and (R) are false.

    (C) (A) is true, but (R) is false.

    (D) (A) is false, but (R) is true.

28. Arrange the following according to their year of first publication :

    (i) Bliss Classification

    (ii) Dewey Decimal Classification

(iii) Library of Congress Classification

(iv) Universal Decimal Classification.

Codes :

(A) (i), (ii), (iii), (iv) (B) (i), (iii), (ii), (iv)

(C) (iii), (i), (iv), (ii) (D) (ii), (iv), (i), (iii)

29. Arrange the following IFLA programmes according to their year of commencement :

(i) UBC

(ii) UAP

(iii) ISBD

(iv) International MARC Office

Codes :

(A) (i), (iv), (iii), (ii) (B) (ii), (iv), (i), (iii)

(C) (iv), (i), (ii), (iii) (D) (iii), (i), (ii), (iv)

30. Arrange the following according to their year of origin :

(i) Indian National Bibliography

(ii) British National Bibliography

(iii) Cumulative Book Index

(iv) Books in Print

Codes :

(A) (i), (iii), (iv), (ii) (B) (ii), (i), (iii), (iv)

(C) (iv), (iii), (ii), (i) (D) (iii), (iv), (ii), (i)

31. Arrange the following in a chronological order according to their year of establishment :

(i) Library of Congress

(ii) NISCAIR

(iii) Delivery of Books Act

(iv) National Library of India

Codes :

(A) (iii), (iv), (ii), (i) (B) (ii), (iii), (i), (iv)
(C) (i), (iv), (iii), (ii) (D) (iv), (i), (iii), (ii)

32. Arrange the following bibliographical standards according to their year of development :

(i) ISBD (ii) MARC
(iii) Dublin Core (iv) RDF

Codes :

(A) (i), (iii), (ii), (iv) (B) (ii), (i), (iv), (iii)
(C) (iii), (ii), (iv), (i) (D) (iv), (iii), (i), (ii)

33. Arrange the following according to their year of origin :

(i) UNICODE (ii) XML
(iii) HTML (iv) SGML

Codes :

(A) (iv), (iii), (i), (ii) (B) (iii), (iv), (ii), (i)
(C) (ii), (iv), (i), (iii) (D) (i), (ii), (iii), (iv)

34. Arrange the following in order of their year of establishment :

(i) INIS (ii) AGRIS
(iii) MEDLARS (iv) UNESCO

Codes :

(A) (iii), (i), (iv), (ii) (B) (ii), (iv), (i), (iii)
(C) (iv), (iii), (ii), (i) (D) (i), (ii), (iv), (iii)

35. Arrange the following according to their year of enactment :

(i) Tamil Nadu Public Library Act
(ii) Kerala Public Library Act
(iii) Maharashtra Public Library Act
(iv) Orissa Public Library Act

Codes :

(A) (i), (iii), (ii), (iv) (B) (ii), (iii), (iv), (i)

(C) (ii), (iii), (i), (iv) (D) (iv), (iii), (ii), (i)

36. Match the following :

List - I	List - II
a. 'Guide to Use of Books And Libraries'	i. F.W. Lancaster
b. 'If You Want to Evaluate Your Library'	ii. A.C. Foskelt
c. 'Cuneiform to Computer : A History of Reference Sources'	iii. Jean K. Gates
d. 'Subject Approach to Information'	iv. William A. Katz

Codes :	**(a)**	**(b)**	**(c)**	**(d)**
(A)	ii	iii	iv	i
(B)	i	iv	iii	ii
(C)	iii	i	iv	ii
(D)	iv	ii	i	i

37. Match the following :

List - I	List - II
a. Directory	i. Information Please Almanac
b. Annuals	ii. Keesing's Record of World Events
c. Bibliography	iii. Encyclopaedia of Associations
d. News paper Digest	iv. Publishers' Weekly

Codes :	(a)	(b)	(c)	(d)
(A)	iii	i	iv	ii
(B)	i	iii	iv	ii
(C)	iii	ii	iv	i
(D)	iv	i	ii	iii

38. Match the following :

List - I	List - II
a. Guiding users to the place of information	i. Digest
b. Guiding users in the use of information	ii. User orientation
c. Alerting users with the latest arrivals	iii. Referral
d. Providing users with summarised information	iv. Current Awareness

Codes :	(a)	(b)	(c)	(d)
(A)	iii	iv	i	ii
(B)	iii	ii	iv	i
(C)	iv	i	iii	ii
(D)	ii	i	iii	i

39. Match the following :

List - I	List - II
a. B.S. Kesvan	i. School of librarianship
b. Paul Otlet	ii. National Library of India
c. W.C.B. Sayers	iii. UDC
d. M. Taube	iv. Uniterm Indexing

Codes :	(a)	(b)	(c)	(d)
(A)	ii	iii	i	iv
(B)	iii	ii	i	iv
(C)	ii	iii	iv	i
(D)	iv	ii	iii	i

40. Match the following :

List - I	List - II
a. Theory of Motivation	i. Factor of planning
b. Unity of Command	ii. Efficiency and waste prevention
c. MBO	iii. Maslow
d. Forecasting	iv. Peter Drucker

Codes :	**(a)**	**(b)**	**(c)**	**(d)**
(A)	i	ii	iii	iv
(B)	iv	i	ii	iii
(C)	ii	iii	iv	i
(D)	iii	iv	i	ii

41. Match the following :

List - I	List - II
a. Classification	i. LISA
b. Cataloguing	ii. UDC
c. Subject Heading	iii. AACR
d. Library Science Abstracts	iv. LCSH

Codes :	**(a)**	**(b)**	**(c)**	**(d)**
(A)	ii	i	iv	iii
(B)	ii	iii	iv	i
(C)	iv	iii	i	ii
(D)	ii	iv	i	ii

42. Match the following :

List - I (Budgetary technique)	List - II (Limitation of budgetary technique)
a. Line	i. Detailed information required
b. Formula	ii. Time consuming
c. PPBS	iii. Do not permit variation
d. Zero-based	iv. Do not suggest future

Codes :	**(a)**	**(b)**	**(c)**	**(d)**
(A)	ii	i	iv	iii
(B)	iii	ii	i	iv
(C)	iv	iii	i	ii
(D)	i	iv	ii	iii

43. Match the following :

List - I	**List - II**
a. File transfer protocol	i. Data transmission capacity
b. Multimedia	ii. Integration of text, colour sound and animation
c. Bandwidth	iii. Bulletin Board
d. Electronic Notice Board	iv. Internet

Codes :	**(a)**	**(b)**	**(c)**	**(d)**
(A)	iv	ii	i	iii
(B)	i	iii	ii	iv
(C)	ii	i	iv	iii
(D)	i	iv	ii	i

44. Match the following :

List - I	**List - II**
a. ISDN	i. Web page
b. URL	ii. Video Conferencing
c. Firewall	iii. Internet Standard for Information Transmission
d. HTTP	iv. Protecting unauthorised access internet

Codes :	**(a)**	**(b)**	**(c)**	**(d)**
(A)	iii	iv	i	ii
(B)	iv	i	iii	ii
(C)	ii	i	iv	iii
(D)	i	iii	ii	iv

45. Match the following :

	List - I	**List - II**
a.	OCLC	i. Bio-Med
b.	INFLIBNET	ii. Web-Dewey
c.	IISC	iii. N-List
d.	NLM	iv. Digital Library of India

Codes :	**(a)**	**(b)**	**(c)**	**(d)**
(A)	ii	iii	iv	i
(B)	iii	i	ii	iv
(C)	iv	ii	iii	i
(D)	i	iii	iv	ii

Read the passage given below, and answer the questions based on your understanding of the passage. (Question Nos. 46-50)

With the realization across the world that the global economy is going to be increasingly knowledge-based, science and technology have become the subject of discussion not just in classical ministries but also in ministries as diverse as commerce, industry and finance, and in case of United States, even in the State Department. In India, the Prime Minister has made frequent statements about the need to step up scientific research in the country. Several large companies, including multinationals are outsourcing R & D programmes to India. This is partly because scientists are cheaper in India dollar for dollar, but also because India has a large pool of trained scientists. Industry data shows that R & D is now the third-largest segment in India's export of Information Technology (IT) services. Foreign companies have invested over $ 1 billion in research operations in India from 1998 to 2003 and another estimated $ 5 billion are in the pipeline. The United States is the biggest investor followed by Germany, France, Denmark and UK. Japan and China have also begun to invest in research programmes in India. Most foreign investment is being directed to research in computer sciences, pharmaceuticals, molecular chemistry, drug discovery, engineering and automotive design and biotechnology, including plant breeding. Whereas, flow of foreign investments has enthused research institutions that are targeted for collaboration, there is also cause for concern. Although, India now attracts considerable foreign investment in R & D, it has no system in place for assessing how this investment is affecting the country's technological development. Nor is there any mechanism to monitor the impact of such investment on aspects such as skill development, sectoral capacity building etc. Do such foreign – funded research programmes benefit only the scientists and technicians in the form of better salaries and perks or do they also produce benefits for the country as a whole ?

46. Focus on science and technology has increased because
    - (A) Indian commerce and Finance Ministries are giving great importance to it.
    - (B) World economy has become knowledge based.
    - (C) US State Department gives priority on S & T
    - (D) Knowledge Commission has identified it as one of the potential area of development
47. The following group of countries are the biggest investors in research :

(A) U.S., Germany, India, Russia

(B) Britain, France, U.S., India

(C) France, Denmark, U.S.A., U.K.

(D) Japan, China, India, Denmark

48. What is the cause of concern regarding foreign investment in research ?

(A) Scientists and technicians involved in research are not paid well.

(B) There are insufficient institutions that can be targeted for research collaboration.

(C) The benefit of such investments doesn't get transferred to India.

(D) Sufficient methods to assess and evaluate the impact of such investment are not available.

49. Most foreign investment is being made in the area of

(A) Microbiology and life sciences.

(B) Computer science and automotive design.

(C) Physical sciences and planting.

(D) Grafting and biology.

50. Foreign companies are outsourcing R & D programmes to India because

(A) Quality of research is quite high in India.

(B) Outsourcing is cost effective for foreign companies.

(C) There is scarcity of skilled manpower in those countries.

(D) None of the above.

ANSWERS

1. D	2. A	3. B	4. D	5. C	6. C
7. B	8. B	9. D	10. C	11. C	12. B
13. C	14. D	15. C	16. D	17. B	18. C
19. C	20. B	21. A	22. C	23. B	24. C
25. D	26. B	27. C	28. A	29. D	30. D
31. C	32. B	33. A	34. A	35. A	36. C
37. A	38. B	39. A	40. D	41. B	42. C
43. A	44. C	45. A	46. B	47. C	48. D
49. B	50. B				

DEC. 2012 NET PAPER-III

1. Who categorized the user studies into the following three categories ?
   (i) Behaviour Studies
   (ii) Use studies
   (iii) Information flow studies
   (A) Maurice B Line (B) Menzel
   (C) Cronin (D) Voigt
2. Which one of the following is not avirtual library ?
   (A) Without walls.
   (B) With distributed physicallocations.
   (C) Providing integrated andunified remote access togeographically distributed collections.
   (D) Which does not exist in reality.
3. In 1974, Zurkowski used for the firsttime, which of the following term ?
   (A) Digital Literacy (B) Media Literacy
   (C) Computer Literacy (D) Information Literacy
4. Who defined "to be information literate, a person must be able torecognize when information is needed and have the ability to locate, evaluate and use effectively theneeded information." ?
   (A) SLA (B) ALA
   (C) IFLA (D) CILIP
5. Which of the factor is not helping inlimiting the external validity ?
   (A) Reactive effect
   (B) Ecological validity
   (C) Interaction between selection bias of experimental variables
   (D) Ecological effect

6. Semantic differential scale isconcerned with
   (A) Pool of items
   (B) Selection from two opposite positions
   (C) Five point scale
   (D) Selection from a check list
7. In spiral of scientific method, the span of Zenith to descendent is
   (A) Empirical phase (B) Hypothesizing phase
   (C) Deductive phase (D) Verification phase
8. Which of the following variable cannot be expressed in quantitative terms ?
   (A) Socio-Economic status
   (B) Marital status
   (C) Numerical Aptitude
   (D) Professional Attitude
9. National Knowledge Network is tobe implemented by
   (A) National Knowledge Commission
   (B) Information and Library Network
   (C) National Information Centre
   (D) Department of InformationTechnology
10. Metadata Dublin core refers to
   (A) Data elements in database
   (B) Bibliographic elements indatabase
   (C) Field elements in database
   (D) Subject elements in database
11. E-Journal articles can be identified with the help of
   (A) Digital Journal Identifier
   (B) Journal Source Identifier
   (C) Journal Article Identifier
   (D) Digital Object Identifier

12. Z39.50 is a standard for
    (A) Communication formats
    (B) Search and Retrieval services
    (C) Cataloguing Web Resources
    (D) Library Management Services
13. In context to modulation, PCM stands for
    (A) Pulse Code Modulation
    (B) Phase Control Modulation
    (C) Popular Code Modulation
    (D) Penultimate Code Modulation
14. ISO 9000 standard denotes the
    (A) consistence confirmance of a product or service to a given set of standard or expectations
    (B) Total customer satisfaction
    (C) Representation of stakeholders issues.
    (D) Detailed list of measuring techniques
15. The stages in the product life cyclecurve are
    (A) Introduction, Growth, Maturity, Decline
    (B) Introduction, Growth, Maturity, Profit
    (C) Growth, Maturity, Profit, Decline
    (D) Introduction, Growth, Maturity, Saturation
16. The physical and chemical treatment of materials to retard their further deterioration refers to
    (A) Conservation (B) Rescuing
    (C) Prevention (D) Restoration
17. Read the following example and indicate the name of the indexing system used : 'Remuneration of teachers in French universities.'

    The index headings are set as the following two lines:

France

Universities → Teachers →

Remuneration

Universities →France

Teachers → Remuneration

(A) Chain procedure (B) POPSI

(C) PRECIS (D) KWIC

18. Research in automatic classification for information retrieval of term or cluster of terms is called
    (A) Evaluation theory
    (B) Theory of clumps
    (C) Time binding theory
    (D) Dynamic theory
19. As specified by AACR-II (R), the source of information for machine readable data file is
    (A) Internal user label
    (B) Title page
    (C) Colophone
    (D) Title frame
20. NICRYS is information system for
    (A) Machine tools (B) Food science
    (C) Crystallography (D) Drugs
21. The national convention regularly organized by DELNET is known as
    (A) CALIBER (B) ICDL
    (C) NACLIN (D) DELNETCON
22. Report on 'the development of digital libraries of the past decade' is categorized as
    (A) Review Report (B) Trend Report
    (C) Research Report (D) State of the art report

23. Name of the President of Sri Lanka can be found in
    (A) International who's who
    (B) Stateman's Yearbook
    (C) Who's who in the world
    (D) Wilson Biographies
24. Which of the following has stopped publishing in the print from since 2012 ?
    (A) Europa World Yearbook
    (B) Times of India Directory
    (C) New Encyclopedia Britannica
    (D) Keesing's Contemporary Archives
25. Which of the following is not providing encyclopedia type of information ?
    (A) Encyclopedia of Associations
    (B) Compton's Encyclopedia
    (C) Worldbook Encyclopedia
    (D) Encyclopedia Americana
26. Who used the phrase 'control-access directional type sources' ?
    (A) R.E. Bopp (B) B.C. Wynar
    (C) W.A. Katz (D) R. Balay
27. Raja Rammohan Roy Library Foundation (RRRLF) was established by
    (A) Indian Library Association
    (B) Department of Culture, Govt.of India
    (C) Govt. of West Bengal
    (D) Ministry of Home Affairs, Govt. of India
28. Which State Public Library Act has the provision to collect library fund through land tax ?

(A) Tamil Nadu (B) Karnataka
(C) Andhra Pradesh (D) Maharashtra

29. Association of College and Research Libraries (ACRL) (USA) is a
    (A) Division of American Library Association
    (B) Independent Association for Academic & Research Libraries
    (C) Division of Special Libraries Association (USA)
    (D) Division of IFLA

30. Which of the following is not an implication of Fourth Law of Library Science ?
    (A) Classified arrangement
    (B) Stack-room-guides
    (C) Issue Methods
    (D) Rural Library Services

31. Which one of the following is not a recommendation of National Knowledge Commission (India) ?
    (A) Preparation of a National Census of Library
    (B) Encourage greater community participation in library management
    (C) Raja Rammohan Roy library foundation to act as the National co-ordination agency
    (D) Facilitate donation and maintenance of private collection

32. Digital library function incorporate :
    (i) Creating and capturing
    (ii) Storage and management
    (iii) Search and access
    (iv) Abstracting and reviewing

Codes :

(A) (i), (ii) and (iii) are correct.

(B) (i), (iii) and (iv) are correct.

(C) (ii), (iii) and (iv) are correct.

(D) (i), (ii) and (iv) are correct.

33. Which topology of computer network provides faster server access ?

(i) BUS Network Topology

(ii) RING Network Topology

(iii) MULTIPLE RING Network Topology

(iv) STAR Network Topology

Codes :

(A) (i) and (ii) are correct.

(B) (i) and (iii) are correct.

(C) (ii) and (iii) are correct.

(D) (ii) and (iv) are correct.

34. Which of the following are ISDN services ?

(i) RSS (ii) Teletext

(iii) Voice mail (iv) Video conference

Codes :

(A) (i), (iii) and (iv) are correct.

(B) (i), (ii) and (iv) are correct.

(C) (ii), (iii) and (iv) are correct.

(D) (i), (ii) and (iii) are correct.

35. Vocabulary in a database is controlled by :

(i) Thesaurus files (ii) Import files

(iii) Standard files (iv) Authority files

Codes :

(A) (i) and (ii) are correct.

(B) (iii) and (iv) are correct.

(C) (i) and (iii) are correct.

(D) (ii) and (iii) are correct.

36. CCF for bibliographic record refers to

(i) Data transfer

(ii) Data storage

(iii) Standard tags of data identification

(iv) Formatting of records

Codes :

(A) (i) and (iii) are correct.

(B) (i), (ii) and (iv) are correct.

(C) (ii) and (iii) are correct.

(D) (iii), (i) and (ii) are correct.

37. Which of the following are not reference service ?

(i) Preparation of user profile

(ii) Initiation of freshman

(iii) Compilation of documentation list

(iv) Readers Advisory

Codes :

(A) (i) and (ii) (B) (ii) and (iii)

(C) (i) and (iii) (D) (iii) and (iv)

38. Which of the following functions are analysed by ALA as reference service functions ?

(i) Consultation function

(ii) Guidance function

(iii) Instruction function

(iv) Bibliographic function

Codes :

(A) (i), (ii) and (iii) are correct.

(B) (ii), (iii) and (iv) are correct.

(C) (i), (ii) and (iv) are correct.

(D) (i), (iii) and (iv) are correct.

39. Which of the following are the scientists' approach according to Melvin J. Voigt (1961) ?

(i) Current Approach

(ii) Everyday Approach

(iii) Exhaustive Approach

(iv) 'Catching up' or 'brushing up' approach.

Codes :

(A) (ii), (iii) and (iv) (B) (i), (iii) and (iv)

(C) (i), (ii) and (iv) (D) (i), (ii) and (iii)

40. Magazines are suitable for

(i) Leisure and entertainment

(ii) Scholarly information

(iii) Popular information

(iv) Subject information

Codes :

(A) (i), (ii) and (iii) are correct.

(B) (ii), (iii) and (iv) are correct.

(C) (i) and (iii) are correct.

(D) (ii) and (iv) are correct.

41. Planting the virus 'Trojan Horse' in computer network is

(i) Hacking (ii) Tampering

(iii) Decryption (iv) Intrusion

Codes :

(A) (i), (iii) and (iv) are correct

(B) (ii), (iii) and (iv) are correct

(C) (i), (ii) and (iii) are correct

(D) (i), (ii) and (iv) are correct

42. Which of the following are the fundamental conditions for a subject to be protected by IPR ?

(i) The work must be original

(ii) The work must be man made

(iii) The work must be intelligible

(iv) The work must be recorded/fixed

Codes :

(A) (i), (ii) and (iii) are correct.

(B) (i), (iii) and (iv) are correct.

(C) (ii), (iii) and (iv) are correct.

(D) (i), (ii) and (iv) are correct.

43. Which of the following are the problems of present information environment ?

(i) Information indiscipline

(ii) Information literacy

(iii) Information overload

(iv) Information technology

Codes :

(A) (i), (iii) are correct

(B) (i) and (iv) are correct

(C) (ii) and (iv) are correct

(D) (i) and (ii) are correct

44. **Assertion (A) :** Qualitative measures must be made quantifiable in order to be convincing.

Reason (R) : Qualitative measures are a necessary complement to quantitative measures.

Codes :

(A) (A) is true, (R) is false.

(B) (A) is false, (R) is true.

(C) Both (A) & (R) are true.

(D) Both (A) & (R) are false.

45. Which of the following are not partners of National Programme on Technology Enhanced Learning (NPTEL) ?

(i) IIT Madras (ii) IIT Delhi

(iii) IIIT Bangalore (iv) NIT Rourkela

Codes :

(A) (iii) and (iv) (B) (i) and (iv)

(C) (ii) and (iii) (D) (i) and (ii)

46. **Assertion (A) :** Internet can replace libraries.

Reason (R) : Google searches will satisfy the maximum users needs.

Codes :

(A) Both (A) and (R) are true.

(B) Both (A) and (R) are false.

(C) (A) is true but (R) is false.

(D) (A) is false but (R) is true.

47. **Assertion (A) :** Federated search technique is an integral component of an information portal.

Reason (R) : 'Content Index' contains content that is find by the search server.

Codes :

(A) Both (A) and (R) are true.

(B) Both (A) and (R) are false.

(C) (A) is true but (R) is false.

(D) (A) is false but (R) is true.

48. **Assertion (A) :** A combination of hypertext and Hypermedia contains text, images, sounds and other information.

Reason (R) : Hypermedia information is represented in a linear fashion.

Codes :

(A) (A) is true and (R) is false.

(B) Both (A) and (R) are true.

(C) (A) is false and (R) is true.

(D) Both (A) & (R) are false.

49. **Assertion (A) :** Book selection should be done judiciously.

Reason (R) : A library should acquire important and latest book selection tools.

Codes :

(A) (A) is true but (R) is false.

(B) (A) is false but (R) is true.

(C) Both (A) & (R) are true, but (R) is not the correct explanation of (A).

(D) Both (A) & (R) are true and (R)is the correct explanation of (A).

50. Assertion (A) : TQM promotes the way in which a library is organised and perform its ICT functions.

Reason (R) : TQM is seen as a hindrance to library and information services.

Codes :

(A) Both (A) and (R) are true.

(B) Both (A) and (R) are false.

(C) (A) is false and (R) is true.

(D) (A) is true and (R) is false.

51. **Assertion (A) :** The array of classes 11, 12, 13 and the array of classes 31, 32, 33 are said to be collateral arrays.

Reason (R) : They are derived from the original universe 'O'.

Codes :

(A) (A) is false, (R) is true.

(B) (A) is true, (R) is false.

(C) Both (A) & (R) are true.

(D) Both (A) & (R) are false.

52. **Assertion (A) :** RDF supports theuse and exchange of metadataon the web.

Reason (R) : Bibliographic standards are the means to create and disseminate secondary information.

Codes :

(A) (A) is true, (R) is false.

(B) (A) is false, (R) is true.

(C) Both (A) & (R) are correct.

(D) Both (A) & (R) are false.

53. **Assertion (A) :** Informative abstracts provide a concise summary of the subject content of an article.

Reason (R) : These are title oriented than finding-oriented.

Codes :

(A) Both (A) and (R) are true.

(B) (A) is true but (R) is false.

(C) (A) is false but (R) is true.

(D) Both (A) and (R) are false.

54. **Assertion (A) :** E-publications have added enormous quantity of literature but adversely affected the

quality of literature.

Reason (R) : Present decade has accepted E-publication as channels of fast communication.

Codes :

(A) (A) is true (R) is false.

(B) (A) is false, but (R) is correct.

(C) Both (A) & (R) are false.

(D) Both (A) & (R) are true.

55. **Assertion (A) :** Encyclopedias are not relevant for finding geographically information.

Reason (R) : Encyclopedias are the substitute for all categories of reference sources.

Codes :

(A) (A) is false but (R) is true.

(B) Both (A) and (R) are true.

(C) Both (A) and (R) are false.

(D) (A) is true but (R) is false.

56. **Assertion (A) :** LIS profession is not considered at par with medical and legal professions.

Reason (R) : There is no constitutional body for LIS profession like Medical Council of India (MCI) and Bar Council of India (BCI).

Codes :

(A) Both (A) and (R) are true.

(B) Both (A) and (R) are false.

(C) (A) is true but (R) is false.

(D) (A) is false but (R) is true.

57. **Assertion (A) :** Dr. S.R. Ranganathan has been called 'Father of Library and Information Science' in India.

Reason (R) : Library Science education in India was started by Dr. S.R. Ranganathan.

Codes :

(A) (A) is false but (R) is true.

(B) (A) is true but (R) is false.

(C) Both (A) and (R) are true.

(D) Both (A) and (R) are false.

58. **Assertion (A) :** The exclusive rights conferred by Intellectual property rights can generally be transferred / licenced to third parties.

Reason (R) : The creators want to make monetary benefits out of their intellectual product.

Codes :

(A) (A) is true but (R) is false.

(B) (A) is false but (R) is true.

(C) Both (A) & (R) are true.

(D) Both (A) & (R) are false.

59. Which is the correct sequence of the national libraries in the order of their year of establishment?

(i) British Library (formerly British Museum Library)

(ii) Library of Congress (Washington D.C.)

(iii) Lenin Library (Moscow)

(iv) Bibliotheque Nationale (Paris)

Codes :

(A) (i), (ii), (iii), (iv) (B) (ii), (iii), (i), (iv)

(C) (iii), (ii), (iv), (i) (D) (iv), (iii), (ii), (i)

60. What is the correct order of SCONUL's "Seven Pillar Model of Information Skills" ?

(i) Recognise information need

(ii) Construct strategies forlocating

(iii) Compare and evaluate

(iv) Locate and access

Codes :

(A) (i), (ii), (iii), (iv) (B) (ii), (iii), (iv), (i)

(C) (i), (ii), (iv), (iii) (D) (ii), (iii), (i), (iv)

61. Identify the correct order as per increasing data storage capacity :
    (A) CDROM, DVD, Cartridge, Blue Ray Disc
    (B) DVD, Cartridge, Blue Ray Disc, CDROM
    (C) Cartridge, CDROM, DVD, Blue Ray Disc
    (D) Blue Ray Disc, DVD, Cartridge, CDROM

62. Identify the correct order of the LIS Associations as per their year ofestablishment
    (A) CLA, ALA, SLA, IASLIC
    (B) ALA, SLA, CLA, IASLIC
    (C) SLA, IASLIC, ALA, CLA
    (D) CLA, SLA, IASLIC, ALA

63. Arrange the following State Library Acts in chronological order :
    (i) Karnataka Public Library Act
    (ii) Uttar Pradesh Public LibraryAct
    (iii) Goa Public Library Act
    (iv) Bihar Public Library Act

    Codes :

    (A) (i), (iii), (ii), (iv) (B) (i), (ii), (iii), (iv)

    (C) (ii), (iii), (iv), (i) (D) (iii), (i), (iv), (ii)

64. Match the following :

List - I	**List - II**
a. Mean	i. Most frequently occurring value
b. Mode	ii. Average
c. Median	iii. Measure of dispersion
d. Standard Deviation	iv. Middle Value

Codes :	(a)	(b)	(c)	(d)
(A)	iii	iv	i	ii
(B)	ii	i	iv	iii
(C)	iv	iii	i	ii
(D)	ii	iii	iv	i

65. Match the following :

List - I	List - II
a. Bradford	i. Citation indexing
b. Lotka	ii. Distribution of articles published in periodicals
c. Zipf	iii. Scientific productivity of author
d. Garfield	iv. Frequency of word occurrence in a text

Codes :	(a)	(b)	(c)	(d)
(A)	iv	i	iii	ii
(B)	ii	iii	iv	i
(C)	iii	iv	i	ii
(D)	iv	iii	ii	i

66. Match the following :

List - I	List - II
a. Altavista	i. Subject search engine
b. Lycos	ii. Meta search engine
c. Geo index	iii. Regional search engine
d. Savvy search	iv. General search engine

Codes :	(a)	(b)	(c)	(d)
(A)	iii	ii	i	iv
(B)	iii	iv	ii	i
(C)	iv	iii	i	ii
(D)	iv	i	ii	iii

67. Match the following :

	List - I	List - II
a.	Pen drive	i. Communication device
b.	i-Pad	ii. Web server device
c.	WifiModem	iii. Storage device
d.	Cloudcomputing	iv. Computing device

Codes :	**(a)**	**(b)**	**(c)**	**(d)**
(A)	i	iii	ii	iv
(B)	iii	iv	i	ii
(C)	iv	iii	ii	i
(D)	iii	ii	i	iv

68. Match the following :

	List - I	List - II
a.	Informix	i. Image software
b.	OmniPage	ii. Remote login software
c.	TIFFviewer	iii. DBMS software
d.	TeamViewer	iv. OCR software

Codes :	**(a)**	**(b)**	**(c)**	**(d)**
(A)	ii	i	iii	iv
(B)	iii	iv	i	ii
(C)	i	ii	iii	iv
(D)	iv	iii	ii	i

69. Match the following :

	List - I	List - II
a.	Means of improving operations and services	i. Preservation
b.	Preparation of to-do-list	ii. Standards
c.	Performance guidelines	iii. Time management
d.	Reinforce the spines of books	iv. Evaluation

Codes :	(a)	(b)	(c)	(d)
(A)	iv	iii	ii	i
(B)	iv	ii	iii	i
(C)	ii	iv	iii	i
(D)	iii	ii	i	iv

70. Match the following :

	List - I		List - II
a.	Chain indexing	i.	Derek Austin
b.	Relational indexing	ii.	S.R.Ranganathan
c.	Subject Indexing	iii.	J.E.L.Farradane
d.	PRECIS	iv.	E.J. Coats

Codes :	(a)	(b)	(c)	(d)
(A)	i	ii	iv	iii
(B)	ii	iii	iv	i
(C)	i	ii	iii	iv
(D)	ii	iv	i	iii

71. Match the following :

	List - I		List - II
a.	Collateral classes	i.	Class comprising two or more entities
b.	Multiple classes	ii.	Classes of the same order but not belonging toone in the same order
c.	Chain of classes	iii.	A subject fixed with others in the universal of subject
d.	Co-ordinate classes	iv.	A sequence of classes made up of any given class and itsuniverse

Codes :	(a)	(b)	(c)	(d)
(A)	ii	iv	i	iii
(B)	i	iii	ii	iv
(C)	ii	i	iv	iii
(D)	i	iv	ii	iii

72. Match the following :

	List - I		**List - II**
a.	William Martin	i.	Little Science Big Science
b.	Alvin Toffler	ii.	Information society
c.	Eric J deSolla Price	iii.	Documentation
d.	S. C. Bradford	iv.	The Third Wave

Codes :	(a)	(b)	(c)	(d)
(A)	ii	iv	iii	i
(B)	iv	ii	iii	i
(C)	ii	iv	i	iii
(D)	i	iv	ii	iii

73. Match the following :

	List - I		**List - II**
a.	Communication Barrier	i.	Radio
b.	Communication Medium	ii.	Shanon & Weaver
c.	Communication Model	iii.	Video conferencing
d.	Interactive Communication	iv.	Noise

Codes :	(a)	(b)	(c)	(d)
(A)	i	ii	iii	iv
(B)	iv	i	ii	iii
(C)	ii	iii	iv	i
(D)	iii	ii	i	iv

74. Match the following :

List - I	List - II
a. Osgood and Schramm	i. General Model
b. Berlo	ii. Mathematical Model
c. Shannon and Weaver	iii. Circular Model
d. George Gerbner	iv. S-M-C-R Model

Codes :	**(a)**	**(b)**	**(c)**	**(d)**
(A)	i	ii	iii	iv
(B)	ii	iii	iv	i
(C)	iii	iv	ii	i
(D)	iv	i	ii	iii

75. Match the following :

List - I	List - II
a. Information contribution to the GNP of anation	i. Social information
b. Information that changes human activity	ii. Technological information
c. Information that establishes interaction between government and people	iii. Economic information
d. Information that forms a modern society	iv. Political information

Codes :	**(a)**	**(b)**	**(c)**	**(d)**
(A)	iii	i	iv	ii
(B)	i	iii	iv	ii
(C)	iv	ii	i	iii
(D)	ii	iii	iv	i

ANSWERS

1. B	2. B	3. D	4. B	5. D	6. B
7. C	8. D	9. C	10. A	11. D	12. B
13. A	14. A	15. A	16. A	17. C	18. B
19. A	20. C	21. C	22. B	23. B	24. C
25. A	26. C	27. B	28. B	29. A	30. D
31. C	32. A	33. D	34. C	35. B	36. A
37. C	38. B	39. D	40. C	41. B	42. D
43. A	44. C	45. A	46. B	47. C	48. A
49. C	50. D	51. B	52. C	53. B	54. D
55. B	56. A	57. B	58. C	59. A	60. C
61. C	62. B	63. A	64. B	65. B	66. C
67. B	68. B	69. A	70. B	71. C	72. C
73. B	74. C	75. A			

JUNE 2013 NET PAPER-III

1. "Poole's Index to Periodical Literature" was brought out by
   (A) William Frederick (B) F.W. Lancaster
   (C) Van Rijsbergen (D) H.P. Luhn
2. Walford's Guide to Reference Material is published by
   (A) American Library Association, Chicago
   (B) R.R. Bowkar, London
   (C) Library Association Publishing, London
   (D) Learned Information Ltd., New Jersey
3. Starting, Chaining, Browsing, Differentiating, Monitoring, Extracting, Verification and Ending are important stages of which information seeking behaviour model ?
   (A) Dervin's Model
   (B) Ellis Model
   (C) Marchionnini Model
   (D) Kuhlthan Model
4. What kind of arrangement is followed in LISA ?
   (A) Alphabetical (B) Chronological
   (C) Classified (D) Geographical
5. Webform is used in
   (A) Synchronous Virtual Reference Service
   (B) Asynchronous Virtual Reference Service
   (C) Both (A) & (B)
   (D) None of the above
6. An online search in which all aspects of the records in natural language may be used as sought terms is

(A) Alphabetical collateral search
(B) Multi-aspect search
(C) Free text searching
(D) Streaming search

7. Science Abstracts published by
(A) INSPEC (Institute of Electrical Engineering)
(B) Institute of Physics, London
(C) American Institute of Physics
(D) PSOJ (Physical Society of Japan)

8. Work study, standardised tools, selecting and training of workers are the contributions of
(A) Louis Brndeis (B) F.W. Taylor
(C) Henry Fayol (D) Lyndall Urwick

9. When the population is heterogenous, which of the following methods give better results ?
(A) Purposive Sampling
(B) Quota Sampling
(C) Random Sampling
(D) Stratified Random Sampling

10. Which of the following is/are not database object(s)?
(A) Tables (B) Queries
(C) Relationships (D) Report

11. What is the process of transferring software programme from secondary storage media to the hard disc called ?
(A) Download (B) Upload
(C) Installation (D) Storage

12. Name a technique used for searching sorted data in a database
(A) Boolean operator (B) Inverting file
(C) Indexing (D) Binary

13. Information about Government of India's stand on 'FDI' can be foundin
    (A) Gazetteer of India
    (B) Britanniea Book of the Year
    (C) Statesman's Yearbook
    (D) Asian Recorder
14. "Anomalous State of Knowledge (ASK) Model", one of the user centered models of information retrieval was proposed by
    (A) P. Ingwersen (B) T. Saracevic
    (C) J.N. Belkin (D) D. Ellis
15. The 'Cranefield Test', associated with evaluation of information retrieval system was carried under the direction of ______.
    (A) C.W. Cleverdon
    (B) G. Salton
    (C) D.C. Blair & M.E. Maron
    (D) E. Voorhees
16. LAMP stands for
    (A) Library Archives Management Programme
    (B) Laser Analysis and Multi-media Performance
    (C) Linux Apache.MySQL Perl
    (D) Library Automation Managem Protocol
17. "Information Literacy Competency Standards for Higher Education" is prepared by
    (A) AASL (B) IFLA
    (C) SCONUL (D) ACRL
18. Name the storage medium (compatible with speed of CPU) for storing instructions or data temporarily during processing

(A) RAM (B) ROM

(C) Cache (D) EPROM

19. "Scitation" is the online host service of
    (A) American Institute of Physics
    (B) University of Maryland
    (C) Society for Industrial Research
    (D) Oxford University
20. The process of surrogation, repackaging and compaction of the primary literature that results in creation of secondary journals, is
    (A) Newsletter
    (B) Abstracting and Indexing Periodical
    (C) House Journals
    (D) Electronic Journal
21. Which of the following is not a language of DBMS ?
    (A) DDL (B) DML
    (C) PASCAL (D) PLI
22. How do we render the name 'Bernardo Augustine De Voto' ?
    (A) Voto, Bernardo, Augustine De
    (B) De Voto, Augustine, Bernardo
    (C) Bernardo Augustine, De Voto
    (D) De Voto, Bernardo Augustine
23. Which reference tool defines Reference service as ".... that phase of work which is directly concerned with assistance to readers in securing information and in using the resources of the library in study and research" ?
    (A) Encyclopaedia of Librarianship
    (B) Encyclopaedia of Library and Information Science

(C) ALA Glossary of Library Terms

(D) ALA World Encyclopaedia of Library & Information Services

24. Indian National Advisory Board for Libraries was setup in 1966 by

(A) Association of Indian Universities

(B) Ministry of Education

(C) Planning Commission

(D) University Grants Commission

25. The process of establishing headings and providing 'Cross references' is called

(A) Access points

(B) Headings

(C) Authority control

(D) Bibliographic Records

26. Which set of rules is applicable for exchange of files over Internet ?

(A) FTP/IP (B) HTTP

(C) HTML (D) HYPERLINK

27. The first printed works are called

(A) Impensis (B) Incunabula

(C) Impression (D) Imprimat

28. Which Law of Library Science, restated with emphasis on information as a dynamic, continuum and never ending phenomenon ?

(A) Fifth Law (B) Fourth Law

(C) Third Law (D) Second Law

29. Andrew Carnegie donated two million pounds for development of ______.

(A) Library Collection (B) Library Building

(C) Library Furniture (D) Library Staff

30. Whose model of communication of knowledge suggests that communication as an open system may be regarded as subjective, selective, variable and yet unpredictable ?
    (A) G. Gerbner
    (B) Juger Hebermans
    (C) E Shanon & Weaver
    (D) M. Foucault
31. Which Committee/Commission recommended that Imperial Library be designated as Copyright Library?
    (A) Fayzee Commission, 1939
    (B) Riche Committee, 1926
    (C) Statham Committee, 1932
    (D) Sadler Committee, 1916
32. What are the four entities of FRBR model ?
    (A) Personality, Matter, Energy, Space
    (B) Books, Form, Availability, Type
    (C) Work, Expression, Manifestation, Item
    (D) Discipline, Entity, Action, Personality
33. Who said that information is both a product and process ?
    (A) S.R. Ranganathan (B) J. Martin
    (C) D.J. Foskett (D) S.C. Bradford
34. The process of planning, allocating, organizing and evaluating library tasks and activities within the framework of major objectives, mission and policy refers to
    (A) Functional control
    (B) Functional Classification
    (C) Functional Approach
    (D) Functional Authority

35. One of the authorized user makes bulk downloading of a Journal using robots and consequently licensor blocks access of the journal. What may be the most appropriate action(s) that librarian should initiate ?
   (i) Cancellation of authentication of the said user.
   (ii) Asking the licensor for blocking up the access without prior information.
   (iii) Investigate and take corrective measures.
   (iv) Notify user community of user restrictions.

   Codes :
   (A) (ii), (iv) are correct. (B) (ii), (iii) are correct.
   (C) (i), (iii) are correct. (D) (i), (ii) are correct.

36. The purposes of Metadata are
   (i) Unique identification
   (ii) Authentication of records
   (iii) Shelf arrangement
   (iv) Shows the collection of a library

   Codes :
   (A) (i), (ii) are correct. (B) (ii), (iii) are correct.
   (C) (iii), (iv) are correct. (D) (iv), (i) are correct.

37. The primary difference between knowledge classification and library classification are
   (i) Knowledge classification arranges knowledge itself.
   (ii) Library classification arranges the expression of knowledge in the form of documents.
   (iii) Knowledge classification is the basis of Library Classification.
   (iv) Knowledge classification follows system of numbers, called notation.

Codes :

(A) (i) and (ii) are correct.

(B) (ii) and (iii) are correct.

(C) (i), (ii) and (iv) are correct.

(D) (i), (ii) and (iii) are correct.

38. Which of the following activities are supported by UGC ?

(i) Facilitating increased access to information.

(ii) Monitoring the implementation of revised curriculum.

(iii) Making policies for human resource development.

(iv) Funding all academic libraries.

Codes :

(A) (i) and (ii) are correct.

(B) (i) and (iii) are correct.

(C) (ii) and (iii) are correct.

(D) (i) and (iv) are correct.

39. Which of the following methods are suitable to achieve quality of teaching, learning in LIS ?

(i) Research-led teaching

(ii) State of the art computer lab

(iii) Problem-based learning

(iv) Introducing the course at degree level

Codes :

(A) (ii) and (iv) (B) (i), (iii) and (iv)

(C) (i) and (iii) (D) (iii) and (iv)

40. Poor 'Accessibility' and less 'affordability' of journal subscription in print era led to

(i) High allocation of funds for serials

(ii) Open access movement

(iii) Decrease in subscription of journals

(iv) E-journal consortia subscription

Codes :

(A) (i) & (ii) are correct.

(B) (i), (ii), (iv) are correct.

(C) (ii), (iv) are correct.

(D) (i), (ii), (iii) are correct.

41. The alternatives and modifications to H-Index are

(i) I-index

(ii) Pure-h Index

(iii) Scimgo Journal Rank

(iv) European Impact Factor

Codes :

(A) (i) & (iii) are correct.

(B) (i) & (ii) are correct.

(C) (i) and (iv) are correct.

(D) (ii) & (iii) are correct.

42. Digitization of various cultural resources is possible through

(i) Scanners (ii) Digital cameras

(iii) Video cameras (iv) Smart & Mobile phones

Codes :

(A) (i), (ii) are correct.

(B) (iv), (iii) are correct.

(C) (iii), (iv) are correct.

(D) (i), (ii), (iii) & (iv) are correct.

43. What is/are not common feature/s between RFID & Barcode Technology?

(i) Read more than one item at a time

(ii) Able to locate specific items on shelves

(iii) Programmable

(iv) Read while item is moving

Codes :

(A) (i), (ii) are correct.

(B) (iii), (iv) are correct.

(C) (ii), (iv) are correct.

(D) All the above are correct.

44. When a librarian has to show the rationale for the purchase of more e-resources, which of the following/s will help to support his/her stand ?

(i) Collection development policy

(ii) Indent from users

(iii) Book selection tools

(iv) All the above

Codes :

(A) (i) and (ii) are correct.

(B) (i) and (iii) are correct.

(C) (ii) and (iii) are correct.

(D) (iv) is correct.

45. **Assertion (A) :** Machine translation is not a fully dependable service.

Reason (R) : The semantics of languages are not fully encoded in algorithms.

Codes :

(A) (A) is true, but (R) is false.

(B) Both (A) & (R) are true.

(C) (A) is false, but (R) is true.

(D) Both (A) & (R) are false.

46. Match the following :

	List - I		**List - II**
a.	INFLIBNET	i.	Digital Library
b.	INDEST-AICTE	ii.	Resource aggregator
c.	DELNET	iii.	E-consortia
d.	e-Gyankosh	iv.	Organisation

Codes :	**(a)**	**(b)**	**(c)**	**(d)**
(A)	i	ii	iii	iv
(B)	iv	iii	ii	i
(C)	iii	ii	i	iv
(D)	ii	iii	iv	i

47. Match the following :

	List - I		**List - II**
a.	Amenable to further algebraic treatment	i.	Mean deviation
b.	Estimated without knowing values of extreme items	ii.	Median
c.	Mathematie-ally and logically incorrect	iii.	Inter-quartile deviation
d.	The dispersion does not cover all items of a series	iv.	Arithmetic means

Codes :	**(a)**	**(b)**	**(c)**	**(d)**
(A)	iv	ii	i	iii
(B)	iii	ii	i	iv
(C)	ii	iv	iii	i
(D)	i	iii	iv	i

48. Match the following :

	List - I		**List - II**
a.	Trade Publisher	i.	UNESCO
b.	Subject book publisher	ii.	American Psychological Society
c.	Government Press	iii.	Harper Collins
d.	Scholarly Publisher	iv.	W.B. Saunders

Codes :	**(a)**	**(b)**	**(c)**	**(d)**
(A)	ii	iv	iii	i
(B)	iv	iii	i	ii
(C)	i	iv	iii	ii
(D)	iii	iv	i	ii

49. Match the following :

	List - I		**List - II**
a.	Statistical Quality/ Process Control (SQC/SPC)	i.	Identify the intensity of each problem in the production process
b.	Check Sheets	ii.	Selected variables checked
c.	Pareto Chart	iii.	Identify the relationship between problems and causes
d.	Fish Bone Diagram	iv.	Record variables in the production process

Codes :	**(a)**	**(b)**	**(c)**	**(d)**
(A)	ii	iv	i	iii
(B)	iv	ii	iii	i
(C)	iii	iv	i	ii
(D)	i	ii	iv	ii

50. Match the following :

List - I	List - II
a. Sinha Committee	i. Library staff strength
b. Dr. S.R. Ranganathan Committee	ii. Central Medical Library
c. Report of Dr. Shaw and Dr. D.B. Krishna Rao	iii. Libraries at Panchayat, Block, District and State level
d. Dr. J. Bhore Committee	iv. National Agricultural System of Agriculture Libraries

Codes :	**(a)**	**(b)**	**(c)**	**(d)**
(A)	iii	i	ii	iv
(B)	iv	iii	ii	i
(C)	iii	i	iv	ii
(D)	i	iii	ii	iv

51. Match the following :

List - I	List - II
a. Finding solution to the problem of pilferage in libraries	i. Historical Research
b. Implementation of cloud computing services in special libraries	ii. Action Research
c. A study of mathematician turned librarian	iii. Experimental Research
d. Use of web resources in Central Universities of India	iv. Survey Research

Codes :	**(a)**	**(b)**	**(c)**	**(d)**
(A)	ii	iii	i	iv
(B)	iii	ii	iv	i
(C)	iv	i	ii	iii
(D)	i	iv	iii	ii

52. Match the following :

	List - I	**List - II**
a.	Internal Fiels	i. .WPD
b.	Universal File Format	ii. .OeB
c.	Corel's Word Perfect	iii. .HTML
d.	Microsoft Reader	iv. .RTF

Codes :	**(a)**	**(b)**	**(c)**	**(d)**
(A)	i	iii	ii	iv
(B)	ii	iv	iii	i
(C)	iv	ii	i	iii
(D)	iii	iv	i	ii

53. Match the following :

List - I	**List - II**
a. Classical Models	i. Ruesch and Bateson's Functional Model
b. Linear Model	ii. Aristotle
c. Non-linear Model	iii. Lasswell
d. Multi-dimensional	iv. Westley and Mackan's Conceptual Model

Codes :	**(a)**	**(b)**	**(c)**	**(d)**
(A)	ii	iii	iv	i
(B)	ii	iv	i	iii
(C)	i	ii	iii	iv
(D)	iii	ii	iv	i

54. Match the following :

	List - I		List - II
a.	Henri La Fontaine	i.	Expansive Classification
b.	H.E. Bliss	ii.	Bibliographic Classification
c.	C.A. Cutter	iii.	LC
d.	J.C.M. Hansar	iv.	UDC

Codes :	**(a)**	**(b)**	**(c)**	**(d)**
(A)	iv	ii	i	iii
(B)	iii	ii	iv	i
(C)	ii	iv	i	iii
(D)	i	iii	ii	iv

55. Match the following :

	List - I		List - II
a.	PDFA	i.	High colour depth images
b.	HTML	ii.	Rules for encoding documents electronically
c.	TIFF	iii.	File format for long term archiving
d.	XML	iv.	Language for web pages

Codes :	**(a)**	**(b)**	**(c)**	**(d)**
(A)	ii	iii	i	iv
(B)	iii	iv	i	ii
(C)	i	iii	ii	iv
(D)	iv	ii	iii	i

56. Match the booksagainst their authors :

	List - I		List - II
a.	Introduction to Modern Information Retrieval (McGraw Hill)	i.	H. Borko & C. Bernier
b.	Indexing Concepts and Methods (Academic Press)	ii.	G. Salton & M.J. McGill

c.	Thesaurus Construction : A Practical Manual (Aslib)	iii.	J.E. Rowley & R. Hartley
d.	Organising Knowledge : An Introduction to Managing Access to Information (Ashgate)	iv.	J. Aitchison & A. Gilchrist

Codes :	**(a)**	**(b)**	**(c)**	**(d)**
(A)	i	ii	iii	iv
(B)	ii	i	iv	iii
(C)	iv	i	ii	iii
(D)	iii	i	iv	ii

57. Match the following :

	List - I		**List - II**
a.	Papyrus	i.	Assyria & Babylonia
b.	Handmade paper	ii.	Egypt
c.	Clay tablets	iii.	Medieval Europe
d.	Vellum/ Parchment	iv.	China

Codes :	**(a)**	**(b)**	**(c)**	**(d)**
(A)	ii	iv	i	iii
(B)	iv	ii	iii	i
(C)	iii	iv	i	ii
(D)	iii	ii	iv	i

58. Match the following :

List - I	**List - II**
a. Icon	i. Character strings
b. Menus	ii. Select objects on the screen
c. Dialogue Bou	iii. Bit mapped region
d. Pointing devices	iv. Obtain information from the end users

Codes :	(a)	(b)	(c)	(d)
(A)	i	ii	iii	iv
(B)	iii	iv	ii	i
(C)	ii	iii	iv	i
(D)	iii	i	iv	ii

59. Match the following :

List - I	List - II
a. Resource Description	i. MARC
b. Resource Discovery	ii. ISO 10160/ 10161
c. Resource Exchange	iii. Dublin Care
d. Interlibrary Loan	iv. Z 39.50

Codes :	(a)	(b)	(c)	(d)
(A)	ii	i	iv	iii
(B)	iv	ii	i	iii
(C)	iii	iv	ii	i
(D)	iii	iv	i	i

60. Match the following :

List - I	List - II
a. Public Library Extension	i. KD Metcalf
b. Academic Library Management	ii. M A Gelfand
c. University Libraries for Developing Countries	iii. L R McColvin
d. Planning Academic and Research Library Buildings	iv. M B Line

Codes :	(a)	(b)	(c)	(d)
(A)	iii	iv	ii	i
(B)	iv	ii	i	iii
(C)	iii	i	iv	ii
(D)	ii	iii	i	iv

61. Match the following :

	List - I		List - II
a.	Indian Cultural Heritage	i.	TKDL
b.	Race & Brittle documents	ii.	IGNCA
c.	Traditional Knowledge	iii.	C-DAC
d.	Mobile Digital Library	iv.	National Library

Codes :	**(a)**	**(b)**	**(c)**	**(d)**
(A)	i	iv	iii	ii
(B)	iv	iii	ii	i
(C)	ii	iv	i	iii
(D)	iii	ii	iv	i

62. Match the following :

	List - I		List - II
a.	Carol Kuhlthau	i.	8 stages
b.	David Ellis	ii.	ISB is a 6 stage process
c.	M.J. Belkin	iii.	ISB is of 8 key activities
d.	Marchionnini	iv.	ISB is 4 dimension characteristic

Codes :	**(a)**	**(b)**	**(c)**	**(d)**
(A)	ii	iii	iv	i
(B)	ii	iii	i	iv
(C)	iii	i	iv	ii
(D)	iv	ii	i	ii

63. **Assertion (A) :** Colon classification is popular in online catalogues.

Reason (R) : Traditional classification systems are used in online searching advantageously.

Codes :

(A) (A) is true, but (R) is false.

(B) Both (A) & (R) are true, but (R) is not the correct explanation of (A).

(C) (A) is false, but (R) is true.

(D) Both (A) & (R) are true.

64. **Assertion (A) :** Technical writing standards, style manuals and citation standards are very essential in structuring the research report.

Reason (R) : Value will get enhanced by standardising the structure of research report.

Codes :

(A) (A) is true and (R) is partially true.

(B) Both (A) and (R) are true.

(C) Both (A) and (R) are false.

(D) (A) is true and (R) is false.

65. **Assertion (A) :** The encouraging environment of all time, full reading halls with the students in the libraries is diminishing day by day.

Reason (R) : All the reading material is easily available and accessible on Internet to all the students.

Codes :

(A) Both (A) and (R) are true.

(B) Both (A) and (R) are false.

(C) (A) is true, but (R) is false.

(D) (A) is false, but (R) is true.

66. **Assertion (A) :** There is a tremendous increase in number of doctoral degrees being awarded in library and information science.

Reason (R) : Any academieian in LIS holding a Ph.D

degree is entitled to supervise research programme.

Codes :

(A) (A) is true and (R) is partially true.

(B) Both (A) and (R) are true.

(C) Both (A) and (R) are false.

(D) (A) is false and (R) is true.

67. **Assertion (A) :** The information seeking behaviour research at the current times is on the social and cultural context of human interaction with information.

Reason (R) : Attempt is being made to interpret social and cultural experiences of individuals with respect to their information seeking and searching experiences.

Codes :

(A) (A) is true and (R) is false.

(B) Both (A) and (R) are false.

(C) (A) is false and (R) is true.

(D) Both (A) and (R) are true.

68. **Assertion (A) :** With the emergence of Internet, there is no need for reference service in this technology-based era.

Reason (R) : Internet has allowed access to every one to seek his/her information from anywhere, any time.

Codes :

(A) Both (A) and (R) are true.

(B) Both (A) and (R) are false.

(C) (A) is false but (R) is partially true.

(D) (A) is true, but (R) is false.

69. **Assertion (A) :** Micrographic services have lost acceptance for preservation and dissemination of archival material.

Reason (R) : ICT has brought in cost effective alternatives and replaced micrographic services.

Codes :

(A) (A) is true and (R) is partially true.

(B) Both (A) & (R) are false.

(C) (A) is true, (R) is false.

(D) (A) is false, (R) is true.

70. **Assertion (A) :** Institutions generate information through research and development activities.

Reason (R) : All such generated information forms the grey literature.

Codes :

(A) Both (A) and (R) are true.

(B) Both (A) and (R) are false.

(C) (A) is true, (R) is partially true.

(D) (A) is false, (R) is true.

71. **Assertion (A) :** Maximizing the access to information in higher education is the motto of UGC-INFONET Project.

Reason (R) : The financial grants of UGC-INFONET are not being fully utilized by all University Libraries for the assigned purpose.

Codes :

(A) Both (A) and (R) are false.

(B) (A) is true and (R) is partially true.

(C) (A) is true and (R) is false.

(D) (A) is false and (R) is true.

72. **Assertion (A) :** The effective reprographic service in libraries indirectly demotivates the user for tearing/theft of reading material.

    Reason (R) : The user gets the photocopy of reading materials free of cost.

    Codes :

    (A) (A) is false and (R) is true.

    (B) Both (A) and (R) are true.

    (C) (A) is true and (R) is false.

    (D) Both (A) and (R) are false.

73. **Assertion (A) :** RFID technology is still not widely installed in Indian Library Environment.

    Reason (R) : The standardization, application and innovation are constantly changing.

    Codes :

    (A) Both (A) & (R) are true and (R) is the correct explanation of (A).

    (B) Both (A) & (R) are true, but (R) is not the correct explanation of (A).

    (C) (A) is true, but (R) is false.

    (D) (A) is false, but (R) is true.

74. **Assertion (A) :** Gap device is a non-scientific solution to the problem of growing universe.

    Reason (R) : A classificationist cannot forecast the areas/ subjects wherein some new ones may emerge.

    Codes :

    (A) (A) and (R) are true.

    (B) (A) is true and (R) is false.

    (C) (A) is false and (R) is true.

    (D) (A) and (R) are false.

75. **Assertion (A) :** All the states in India have enacted library legislation.

Reason (R) : NKC recommends for the enactment of library legislation in all the states.

Codes :

(A) Both (A) and (R) are true.

(B) Both (A) and (R) are false.

(C) (A) is true, but (R) is false.

(D) (A) is false, but (R) is true.

ANSWERS

1. A	2. C	3. B	4. C	5. B	6. C
7. A	8. B	9. D	10. C	11. C	12. D
13. D	14. C	15. A	16. C	17. D	18. C
19. A	20. B	21. A	22. D	23. C	24. B
25. C	26. B	27. B	28. A	29. B	30. A
31. B	32. C	33. B	34. C	35. D	36. A
37. D	38. B	39. C	40. C	41. B	42. D
43. D	44. A	45. B	46. B	47. A	48. D
49. A	50. C	51. A	52. D	53. A	54. A
55. B	56. B	57. A	58. D	59. D	60. A
61. C	62. A	63. C	64. A	65. C	66. A
67. D	68. C	69. A	70. C	71. B	72. C
73. B	74. A	75. D			

JUNE 2013 NET PAPER-II

1. The distinct characteristic(s) of digital objects are
   (A) Physical Medium
   (B) Logical process
   (C) Conceptual recognition and transaction
   (D) All the above
2. 'Who's who in India', an irregular publication is published by
   (A) Business Press, Bombay
   (B) Sterling, New Delhi
   (C) Tradesman & Men Asia, Delhi
   (D) Sahitya Samsad, Calcutta
3. Which department of the Government of India deals with Public Libraries ?
   (A) Department of Archaeology
   (B) Department of Culture
   (C) Department of PrimaryEducation
   (D) Department of Science andTechnology
4. Information on Prime Minister of Bangladesh can be found in
   (A) International Who's Who
   (B) Who's Who in Bangladesh
   (C) Current Biography
   (D) Statesman's Yearbook
5. 'Eradication of Malaria in India1990-1999' – a report can becategorised under
   (A) Trend Report
   (B) Review Report
   (C) State of the Art Report
   (D) Research Report

6. Which is not a reprographic service ?
   (A) Micro Copying (B) Blue Printing
   (C) Paper Printing (D) Thermo Copying
7. ERIC is sponsored by
   (A) US National Health Institute
   (B) Health and Rehabilitation Services Division, A LA
   (C) Department of Health Education & Welfare, Government of USA
   (D) Health Science Information Centre, USA
8. In the library hierarchy which level of management is responsible for execution of policies ?
   (A) Middle level (B) Operational level
   (C) Top level (D) Lower level
9. METS stands for
   (A) Machine Encoded Transmission System
   (B) Metadata Encoded for Textual Sources
   (C) Machine Encoded Textual Standard
   (D) Metadata Encoding Transmission Standard
10. Sector Device is an extension of
   (A) Gap Device
   (B) Empty Device
   (C) Octave Device
   (D) Group Notation Device
11. "Control, Disease, Malaria, Brain" indicates that it is
   (A) Raw Title (B) Expressive Title
   (C) Kernel Title (D) Transformed Title
12. A graphical representation using symbols to represent operations, data, flow, etc. is

(A) Logical Chart (B) Flow Chart
(C) System Flow Chart (D) Network Chart

13. The 12 rules for relational database were given by
(A) E.F. Codd (B) Charles Babbage
(C) James Weyer (D) Tim Berners Lee

14. A technique displaying graphic information on screen, pixel by pixel with bits held in main memory is
(A) Bit handling (B) Bit mapping
(C) Bit pattern (D) Bit matrix

15. ZOTERO is a ______.
(A) Content Management System
(B) Reference Management System
(C) Serials Management System
(D) Bibliographic Rreference Management System

16. A network in which the host computer controls different nodes which further control other nodes, is known as
(A) Star Network
(B) Ring Network
(C) Hierarchical Network
(D) Multipoint Network

17. Impact factor is devised by
(A) Eugene Garfield (B) Alan Pritchard
(C) David Hume (D) Louis Brandeis

18. A skilful method of providing means, mechanism and structural elements to streamline organizational work is known as
(A) Role Analysis (B) Strategic Planning
(C) Work Culture (D) Autonomous Planning

19. Financial allocation made to a library for purchase of furniture and equipments usually comes under the budget head
    (A) Recurring grant
    (B) Endowments
    (C) Non-recurring grant
    (D) Annual grant
20. Historical/Government records related to an organisation are maintained in
    (i) Archieves
    (ii) Museums
    (iii) Repositories
    (iv) Government libraries
    Codes :
    (A) (i) and (ii) are correct.
    (B) (ii) and (iii) are correct.
    (C) (i) and (iii) are correct.
    (D) (ii) and (iv) are correct.
21. Major elements of a profession are
    (i) Philosophy (ii) Body of knowledge
    (iii) Publicity (iv) Status
    Codes :
    (A) (i), (ii), (iv) are correct.
    (B) (i), (ii), (iii) are correct.
    (C) (ii), (iii), (iv) are correct.
    (D) (i), (iii), (iv) are correct.
22. Which of the following states don'thave library legislation ?
    (i) Haryana (ii) Delhi
    (iii) J & K (iv) Manipur

Codes :

(A) (i) and (ii) are correct.

(B) (ii) and (iii) are correct.

(C) (i) and (iv) are correct.

(D) (ii) and (iii) are correct.

23. Which of the following principles are associated with library building planning ?

(i) Principle of Uniformity

(ii) Principle of Comfortability

(iii) Principle of Simplicity

(iv) Principle of Continuity

Codes :

(A) (i), (ii) and (iii) are correct.

(B) (ii), (iii) and (iv) are correct.

(C) (i), (ii) and (iv) are correct.

(D) (iii), (iv) and (i) are correct.

24. ETD database in India is maintained by

(i) Shodhgangotri

(ii) Vidyanidhi

(iii) Shodhganga

(iv) INDEST-AICTE consortium

Codes :

(A) (i) and (iii) are correct.

(B) (ii), (iii) and (iv) are correct.

(C) (ii) and (iii) are correct.

(D) (iii) and (iv) are correct.

25. Vocabulary in a database iscontrolled by

(i) Thesaurus files (ii) Dictionary files

(iii) Standard files (iv) Authority files

Codes :

(A) (i) and (ii) are correct.

(B) (iii) and (iv) are correct.

(C) (i) and (iii) are correct.

(D) (i) and (iv) are correct.

26. Limitations of Bibliometrics is/are

(i) Analysing research anddevelopment trends

(ii) Describing text, not necessarilymeaning and context

(iii) Identifying the active areas ofresearch

(iv) Citation bias

Codes :

(A) (ii) and (iv) are correct.

(B) (i) and (iii) are correct.

(C) (i), (ii) and (iv) are correct.

(D) (ii) and (iii) are correct.

27. Identify the technique(s) to collect the data regarding the number of persons visited the periodical sectionof the library at different hours of the day.

(i) Questionnaire (ii) Interview

(iii) Observation (iv) Library records

Codes :

(A) (i) and (ii) are correct.

(B) (ii) and (iii) are correct.

(C) (iii) and (iv) are correct.

(D) (ii) and (iv) are correct.

28. Which of the following are prohibited under copyright ?

(i) Downloading a document, printing multiple copies

(ii) Placing a copyright protected document on web-server

(iii) Downloading a document and save it in folder

(iv) Downloading a document with license to use and E-mailing it

Codes :

(A) (i), (iii) and (iv) are correct.

(B) (i), (ii) and (iii) are correct.

(C) (iii), (iv) and (ii) are correct.

(D) (i), (ii) and (iv) are correct.

29. The professional ethics help to ____.

(i) Get the right direction

(ii) Enhance image

(iii) Get more salaries

(iv) Resolve day to day issues

Codes :

(A) (ii) and (iii) are correct.

(B) (i) and (iv) are correct.

(C) (i) and (ii) are correct.

(D) (ii) and (iv) are correct.

30. Match the following :

List - I	**List - II**
a. Systematic Bibliography	i. List of macro/micro ideas of articles
b. Analytical or Critical Bibliography	ii. Investigation of physical nature of books

c. Historical Bibliography	iii. Listing of items with minimum details
d. Documentary Bibliography	iv. Concerned with art of writing, printing and binding

Codes :	**(a)**	**(b)**	**(c)**	**(d)**
(A)	i	iv	iii	ii
(B)	ii	i	iv	iii
(C)	iii	ii	iv	i
(D)	ii	iv	iii	i

31. Match the following queries with their appropriate category of reference source :

	List - I	**List - II**
a.	Enrolment of students in a university	i. Year book
b.	Weather of Denmark	ii. Statistical source
c.	No. Offor eigners visited World Book Fair in 2011	iii. Directory
d.	No. of hospitals in China	iv. Geographical Source

Codes :	**(a)**	**(b)**	**(c)**	**(d)**
(A)	iv	iii	i	ii
(B)	i	iii	ii	iv
(C)	ii	iv	i	iii
(D)	iii	iv	i	ii

32. Match the following :

List - I	List - II
a. 1st Law of Library Science	i. Real time access
b. 2nd Law of Library Science	ii. Search engine & subject gateways
c. 3rd Law of Library Science	iii. Web access to resources
d. 4th Law of Library Science	iv. Open access initiatives

Codes :	(a)	(b)	(c)	(d)
(A)	iii	iv	ii	i
(B)	iv	i	ii	iii
(C)	i	iii	ii	iv
(D)	ii	iv	i	iii

33. Match the following :

List - I	List - II
a. Douglas McGregor	i. Scientific Management School
b. Abraham Maslow	ii. Theory of Authority Structure
c. F.W. Taylor	iii. Self Actualisation Needs
d. Max Weber	iv. Theory X and Theory Y

Codes :	(a)	(b)	(c)	(d)
(A)	iv	iii	i	ii
(B)	ii	iii	i	iv
(C)	iii	iv	ii	i
(D)	i	iv	ii	iii

34. Match the following DDC numbers :

	List - I		List - II
a.	Education	i.	770
b.	Medicine	ii.	370
c.	Photography	iii.	610
d.	Astronomy	iv.	520

Codes :	**(a)**	**(b)**	**(c)**	**(d)**
(A)	iii	i	iv	ii
(B)	ii	iii	i	iv
(C)	i	iv	iii	ii
(D)	iv	ii	i	iii

35. Match the following :

List - I	List - II
a. Key to a given collection	i. Abstract
b. Key to literary sources on a subject	ii. Index
c. Representation of subject concept	iii. Catalogue
d. Condensation of a document	iv. Bibliography

Codes :	**(a)**	**(b)**	**(c)**	**(d)**
(A)	iii	iv	ii	i
(B)	ii	iii	iv	i
(C)	i	ii	iii	iv
(D)	iv	i	ii	iii

36. Match the following :

	List - I		List - II
a.	Unity of command	i.	Specialization
b.	Unity ofdirection	ii.	Strength inunity
c.	Esprit decorps	iii.	Orders fromonly one person
d.	Division of work	iv.	One boss, one plan

Codes :	(a)	(b)	(c)	(d)
(A)	iv	iii	ii	i
(B)	ii	iv	iii	i
(C)	iii	iv	ii	i
(D)	i	iv	iii	ii

37. Give in sequence, the following in order of their origin :
    i. National Library
    ii. Calcutta Public Library
    iii. Imperial Library Act
    iv. Imperial Library

    Codes :

    (A) ii iii iv i　　(B) i ii iii iv
    (C) iii i iv ii　　(D) ii iv iii i

38. Arrange the following according to year of publication :
    i. Colon Classification
    ii. Prolegomena to Classification
    iii. Five Laws of Library Science
    iv. Classified Catalogue Code

    Codes :

    (A) iii iv i ii　　(B) iv ii i iii
    (C) iii i iv ii　　(D) i ii iv iii

39. **Assertion (A) :** Digitization has proved to be possible for every format and medium held by library.

    Reason (R) : All libraries are making their text and visual collections digitized.

    Codes :

    (A) (A) is true, but (R) is false.
    (B) (A) is false, but (R) is true.

(C) Both (A) and (R) are true.

(D) Both (A) and (R) are false.

40. **Assertion (A) :** In spite of political, economic and technological support, the growth of Public Library System is lopsided.

    Reason (R) : The public libraries are totally depending on cess/taxamounts.

    Codes :

    (A) Both (A) and (R) are true.

    (B) Both (A) and (R) are false.

    (C) (A) is true, but (R) is false.

    (D) (A) is false, but (R) is true.

41. Assertion (A) : 'Pay and Use' concept has not been accepted in libraries of India.

    Reason (R) : Library staff do not possess the essential skills required for product development and promotion.

    Codes :

    (A) Both (A) and (R) are true.

    (B) (A) is true but (R) are false.

    (C) (R) is true but (A) is false.

    (D) Both (A) and (R) are false.

42. Assertion (A) : Library Science profession in India enjoys the status at par with medical, legal and management professions.

    Reason (R) : S.R. Ranganathan's contributions and teachings for Indian librarianship secured a status to the profession.

    Codes :

    (A) (A) is true, but (R) is false.

    (B) (A) is false, but (R) is true.

(C) Both (A) and (R) are true.

(D) Both (A) and (R) are false.

43. **Assertion (A) :** In conducting research, Social Sciences are not considered at par with natural sciences.

Reason (R) : Research in Social Sciences can't be performed sorigorously as can be in Natural Sciences.

Codes :

(A) Both (A) and (R) are true.

(B) Both (A) and (R) are false.

(C) (A) is true, but (R) is false.

(D) (A) is false, but (R) is true.

44. **Assertion (A) :** Research starts in mind first and then in laboratories.

Reason (R) : Systematically conducted research leads to generalization.

Codes :

(A) (A) is true, but (R) is false.

(B) (A) is false, but (R) is true.

(C) Both (A) and (R) are true.

(D) Both (A) and (R) are false.

45. **Assertion (A) :** Systematic and efficient use of statistical tools in research helps in precise interpretation of research results.

Reason (R) : Statistical tools cannot give specific explanations ofthe data.

Codes :

(A) Both (A) and (R) are true.

(B) (A) is true and (R) is false.

(C) Both (A) and (R) are false.

(D) (A) is false and (R) is true.

Read the following passage and answer the questions 46 - 50 :

While Boyd allows that some people consider email or discussion lists to be Social Software, he makes an important distinction between traditional communication software and Social Software. He explains that traditional software places people into groups with atop-down approach; in other words, it assigns membership. However, Social Software takes a bottom-up approach, which enables people to organize themselves into a network based on their preferences. Therefore, with a bottom-up approach, people can sign up for a system and build communities using their personal preferences (Marenzi *et al.*, 2008). Incontrast, traditional communication software uses a top-down approach where people are assigned into a specific organization or groups. Social Software is based on supporting individuals who interact socially with people who have similar interests (Marenzi *et al.*, 2008). Inaddition, users typically enjoy Social Software itself and work with various Social Software applications voluntarily. For example, the authors of social media enjoy content that they have created themselves, content that is copied from other media, and mash-ups that contain a mix of content that could possibly be from several authors (Ahonen and Lietsala, 2007). The popularity of social technologies is attributed to the increase in low-cost tools and the critical mass of millions of people who are now connected to the Internet and to the people's need to feel like part of a community (Avram, 2006). These users tend to rely more on their own personal social networks than on traditional business structures. (Vinson 2005) describes additional features of Social Software tools: they allow people to easily participate (by both contributing and reading) in the activities; they provide the opportunity for networking and allow for the self-forming of networks since people are usually both consumers and producers; and each individual can be a member onseveral networks simultaneously (Avram, 2006).

46. People are assigned into specific organization or groups in _______ approach.
   (A) Top-down approach
   (B) Down-top approach
   (C) Top-bottom system approach
   (D) Down-top system approach
47. The basic feature(s) of social software is/are :
   (A) Social interaction
   (B) Personal interaction
   (C) Enjoying social software
   (D) (A) and (C) are correct.
48. Authors of social media enjoy_______ of contents.
   (A) Self created contents
   (B) Contents from magazines
   (C) Contents from many formats
   (D) Contents from many languages
49. The reason/s attributed to the popularity of social networking is/are :
   (A) Masses have started using internet.
   (B) All have free access to internet.
   (C) All are technology literates.
   (D) Stimulation of on-line communities over the traditional communities.
50. The social software tools allow.
   (A) Easy participation
   (B) Quick networking
   (C) Consumer networking
   (D) Both (A) & (B)

ANSWERS

1. D	2. A	3. B	4. D	5. A	6. C
7. D	8. A	9. D	10. C	11. C	12. B
13. A	14. B	15. D	16. C	17. A	18. B
19. C	20. C	21. A	22. B	23. B	24. C
25. B	26. A	27. C	28. D	29. C	30. C
31. D	32. A	33. A	34. B	35. A	36. A
37. D	38. C	39. A	40. C	41. A	42. B
43. A	44. C	45. A	46. A	47. D	48. A
49. A	50. D				

JUNE 2013 NET II RECONDUCTED
08/09/2013 DELHI & RANCHI

1. WIPO is located at
   (A) New York (B) London
   (C) Geneva (D) Paris
2. The National Mission on Libraries, India was established in which year ?
   (A) 2009 (B) 2010
   (C) 2011 (D) 2012
3. The production of mental reflection and imagination is known as
   (A) Information (B) Idea
   (C) Data (D) Knowledge
4. Who is the propounder of the term 'Information Transfer' ?
   (A) Ranganathan (B) J. Martin
   (C) Calvin Moores (D) Beesman
5. Which organisation was joined with 'Library Association' to form CILIP in 2007 ?
   (A) Institute of Bibliography
   (B) Institute of Information Scientists
   (C) Institute of Documentation
   (D) Institute of Librarianship
6. Dictionary of National Biography (DNB) contains biography of prominent people of
   (A) All nations (B) Europeans
   (C) Americans (D) Britishers
7. The "citation indexes" are now available online as
   (A) Web of Science (B) JCCC
   (C) Scopus (D) EBSC

8. Which among the following is free Audio book site?
   (A) Ebrary (B) Virtua
   (C) Librivox (D) Google Books
9. The online version of 'McGraw Hill Encyclopaedia of Science and Technology' is
   (A) Access Science
   (B) McGraw Hill Online
   (C) Online Encyclopaedia of Science and Technology
   (D) Science online
10. 'Indian National Bibliography' is arranged under two parts, General Publication and _____ Publications.
   (A) Private (B) Electronic
   (C) Governmental (D) Non-book
11. The concept of 'Reference Service' is given by
   (A) J.H. Shera (B) A. Strauss
   (C) S.R. Ranganathan (D) Samuel Green
12. Which of the following is not an alerting service ?
   (A) CAS
   (B) SDI
   (C) Document Delivery Service
   (D) Electronic Clipping Service
13. The concept of 'Ask Library Anything' was originally initiated by
   (A) Indian Library Association
   (B) ASLIB
   (C) Special Library Association
   (D) American Library Association
14. In C.C. the title 'Medical Jurisprudence' can be classified and sharpened with the help of

(A) Subject Device (B) Alphabetical Device
(C) Classic Device (D) Enumerative Device

15. Template is a
    (A) Structured specification
    (B) Recursive routine
    (C) Assembler program
    (D) I/O measure

16. 'Research-in-progress' database in India is________.
    (A) Vidyanidhi
    (B) Shodhganga
    (C) Shodhgangotri
    (D) Indian National Depository Library

17. 'Open Journal Access System' in India is mainly managed by
    (A) NIC (B) CSIR
    (C) ICSSR (D) INFLIBNET

18. In the world wide web, name the acronym that describes the internet address of a file
    (A) ULA (B) RELUR
    (C) URI (D) UR

19. TKDL is developed and managed by
    (A) National Library and RRRLF
    (B) CSIR and RRRLF
    (C) CSIR and AYUSH
    (D) AYUSH and National Library

20. Web impact factor is developed by
    (A) P. Ingwersen (B) L. Bornebora
    (C) M. Thelwall (D) R. Rousseau

21. Which of the following guides are used in maintenance section of the library ?

(i) Gangway guides (ii) Shelf guides
(iii) Tier guides (iv) User guides

Codes :

(A) (i), (ii) and (iv) are correct.
(B) (i), (ii) and (iii) are correct.
(C) (ii), (iii) and (iv) are correct.
(D) (i), (iii) and (iv) are correct.

22. Which of the following are 'TQM' tools ?

(i) Fishbone Diagram (ii) Histogram
(iii) Pie Chart (iv) Run Charts

Codes :

(A) (i), (iii) and (iv) are correct.
(B) (i), (ii), (iii) and (iv) are correct.
(C) (ii), (iii) and (iv) are correct.
(D) (i), (ii) and (iv) are correct.

23. Library Ethics is a combination of what ?

(i) Responsibility (ii) Accountability
(iii) Commitment (iv) Decision Making

Codes :

(A) (i), (ii) and (iii) are correct.
(B) (ii), (iii) and (iv) are correct.
(C) (i), (iii) and (iv) are correct.
(D) (i), (ii) and (iv) are correct.

24. Which of the following is/are related to open access initiatives ?

(i) Creative Commons (ii) DOAJ
(iii) FOSS (iv) GNU

Codes :

(A) (i), (iii) and (iv) are correct.
(B) (i), (ii) and (iii) are correct.

(C) (ii) and (iii) are correct.

(D) (i) and (ii) are correct.

25. User-friendly interface caters to

(i) Human-computer Interaction

(ii) Individual users with customisation

(iii) Simplify execution of operations

(iv) Basis for computer-computer interface

Codes :

(A) (i), (ii) and (iv) are correct.

(B) (i) and (iii) are correct.

(C) (ii) and (iii) are correct.

(D) (i), (iii) and (iv) are correct.

26. As per Voigt's study, which are the approaches of the scientists towards information ?

(i) Current (ii) Everybody

(iii) Exhaustive (iv) Browsing

Codes :

(A) (ii), (iii) and (iv) are correct.

(B) (i), (iii) and (iv) are correct.

(C) (i), (ii) and (iii) are correct.

(D) (i), (ii) and (iv) are correct.

27. Why to cite ?

(i) Acknowledging the source

(ii) Crediting the original ideas

(iii) Substantiate findings

(iv) For popularising cited sources

Codes :

(A) (i), (ii) and (iv) are correct.

(B) (i), (ii) and (iii) are correct.

(C) (ii), (iii) and (iv) are correct.

(D) All are correct.

28. Match the following :

List - I	List - II
a. DCMES	i. Defined Functional Requirements of Records
b. MARC	ii. Rules for Bibliographic Records
c. RDA	iii. Retrieval and Data Exchange
d. FRBR	iv. Coding Scheme for computerised Bibliographic Records

Codes :	(a)	(b)	(c)	(d)
(A)	iii	iv	ii	i
(B)	iv	ii	iii	i
(C)	i	ii	iii	iv
(D)	ii	iv	i	ii

29. Match the following dialogue systems :

List - I	List - II
a. Menu	i. Computer recognizable dialogues
b. Icons	ii. Communicating with computers with everyday language
c. Natural language	iii. List of options available
d. Common language	iv. Pictorial representation of objects

Codes :	(a)	(b)	(c)	(d)
(A)	i	iii	iv	ii
(B)	ii	iv	iii	i
(C)	iii	iv	ii	i
(D)	iv	ii	iii	i

30. Match the following :

	List - I		List - II
a.	POSDCORB	i.	Robert McNamara
b.	TQM	ii.	Peter Phyrr
c.	ZBB	iii.	Gulick F. Urwick
d.	PPBS	iv.	Edward Deming

Codes :	(a)	(b)	(c)	(d)
(A)	iv	iii	i	ii
(B)	iii	iv	ii	i
(C)	iii	i	ii	iv
(D)	ii	i	iii	i

31. Match the following :

List - I	List - II
a. Remote resource sensing satellite	i. Processing data
b. Memory chips	ii. Transportation of data
c. VLSI chips	iii. Capture data
d. Optical fibre	iv. Storage data

Codes :	(a)	(b)	(c)	(d)
(A)	i	ii	iii	iv
(B)	iv	iii	ii	i
(C)	ii	iii	iv	i
(D)	iii	iv	i	ii

32. Match the following :

	List - I		List - II
a.	$f(r) = K/r$	i.	Bradford
b.	$xny = C$	ii.	Zipf's
c.	$L : n : n2$	iii.	Pareto
d.	80 – 20	iv.	Lotka

Codes :	(a)	(b)	(c)	(d)
(A)	iv	ii	iii	i
(B)	ii	iii	iv	i
(C)	ii	iv	i	iii
(D)	i	iii	ii	iv

33. Match the following :

List - I	List - II
a. Scientific Management	i. Max Weber
b. System School	ii. Mary Follett
c. Human Behaviour School	iii. Henry Fayol
d. Classical School	iv. Louis Brandeis

Codes :	(a)	(b)	(c)	(d)
(A)	iv	i	ii	iii
(B)	iv	ii	i	iii
(C)	ii	i	iii	iv
(D)	i	iv	ii	i

34. Match the following as per Ranganathan's Staff formula recommended for a university library :

List - I	List - II
a. Acquisition Section	i. 1 person for 1500 readers
b. Reference Section	ii. 1 person for 500 titles
c. Periodical Section	iii. 1 person for 6000 titles
d. Circulation Section	iv. 1 person for 50 readers

Codes :	(a)	(b)	(c)	(d)
(A)	i	iv	iii	ii
(B)	iii	iv	ii	i
(C)	iv	i	iii	ii
(D)	ii	iii	i	iv

35. Match the following standard sub-divisions from DDC :

	List - I	**List - II**
a.	Philosophy & Theory	i. 07
b.	Serial Publications	ii. 05
c.	Collections	iii. 01
d.	Study and Teaching	iv. 08

Codes :	**(a)**	**(b)**	**(c)**	**(d)**
(A)	i	ii	iv	iii
(B)	iii	iv	ii	i
(C)	iii	ii	iv	i
(D)	ii	iv	i	iii

36. Arrange the following in chronological order of their establishment :
   (i) ARPANET
   (ii) DARPA
   (iii) SPUTNIK
   (iv) ICCB (Internet Configuration Control Board)

   Codes :
   (A) iv i iii ii (B) iii ii i iv
   (C) ii iii iv i (D) i ii iv i

37. Arrange the following according to their year of origin :
   (i) APA (ii) MLA
   (iii) Chicago (iv) Turbian

   Codes :
   (A) ii iii i iv (B) i iv ii iii
   (C) iii ii iv i (D) iv iii i ii

38. Arrange the following State Library Acts according to their year of establishment :

(i) Goa (ii) West Bengal

(iii) Orissa (iv) Karnataka

Codes :

(A) iv ii iii i (B) iv ii i iii

(C) ii i iii iv (D) iii ii i iv

39. Give the following in sequence according to the year of their first publication :

(i) Bibliographic Classification

(ii) Universal Decimal Classification

(iii) Library of Congress Classification

(iv) Colon Classification

Codes :

(A) ii iii i iv (B) iv ii iii i

(C) i iii ii iv (D) iii ii iv

40. **Assertion (A) :** All research require hypotheses to be proposed and tested.

Reason (R) : No research is complete without testing of hypotheses.

Codes :

(A) (A) is false but (R) is true.

(B) Both (A) and (R) are false.

(C) (A) is true but (R) is false.

(D) Both (A) and (R) are true.

41. **Assertion (A) :** Historical Research has been regarded to be truly scientific by many authorities.

Reason (R) : Historical evidences can be replicated.

Codes :

(A) Both (A) and (R) are true.

(B) (A) is false but (R) is true.

(C) Both (A) and (R) are false.

(D) (A) is partially true, but (R) is true.

42. **Assertion (A) :** There is a dismal scene relating to the development of public libraries especially rural libraries in India.

    Reason (R) : Majority of the states do not have library legislation.

    Codes :

    (A) Both (A) and (R) are true.

    (B) Both (A) and (R) are false.

    (C) (A) is true but (R) is false.

    (D) (A) is false but (R) is true.

43. **Assertion (A) :** It would be logical to replace catalogue with metadata.

    Reason (R) : Metadata is useful for organising and managing information resources.

    Codes :

    (A) (A) is false and (R) is true.

    (B) (A) and (R) are true.

    (C) (A) is true and (R) is false.

    (D) (A) and (R) are false.

44. **Assertion (A) :** The use of the symbol 'double colon' (: :) in UDC allows fixed order of component numbers in a compound subject.

    Reason (R) : The fixed order facilitates easy access in computer based information retrieval.

    Codes :

    (A) (A) is true and (R) is false.

    (B) (A) is false and (R) is true.

    (C) Both (A) and (R) are true.

    (D) Both (A) and (R) are false.

45. **Assertion (A) :** There is criticism by academicians

and scientists on the use of impact factor as a measure of importance.

Reason (R) : Impact factor is a journal metrics and can not be used to assess quality of individual research.

Codes :

(A) (A) is false but (R) is true.

(B) Both (A) and (R) are true.

(C) Both (A) and (R) are false.

(D) (A) is true but (R) is false.

Read the following passage and answer the questions 46-50:

Computing is in nature a problem-driven science and therefore PBL approaches have been applied to teach various subjects. Kay etal. (2000) describe PBL in foundation courses in computer science. The course is driven by specific problems related to programming skills and the instructors have set specific criteria to measure the success of their approach at the end of each problem. Having applied the approach for three years the authors of the study conclude that the PBL approach promoted the collaboration among students and their problem solving abilities. A problem-based approach is used in a software development project (O'Kelly and Gibson, 2006). The authors claim that, with this approach, students are provided with the freedom to think for themselves, activate their prior knowledge and acquire new knowledge in an explorative and creative way. Another study supports that lecture based approaches are not stimulating and the computer skills learnt are not transferable to other situations (Lai, 2005). The author applied PBL in teaching pre-school teachers popular computer applications such as Microsoft Office. Based on their evaluation of the activities, the author concludes that the course was motivational and also promotes higher order thinking skills. Ellis et al. (1998) refer to the fullproblem-based learning and the guided problem-based learning approaches. In full problem-based learning, the nature of the problem guides and drives the entire learning experience. There are no formal expositions of knowledge from the "expert", and the students develop resources based on requirements they determine. In guided problem-based learning, students have a problem to solve as a group.

46. What was the result of problem based learning approach ?
   (A) Improved peer coordination
   (B) Promoted collaboration among students
   (C) Applied to teach subjects
   (D) Applied to teach only computer science
47. What are the advantages of PBL application in teaching ?
   (A) Self study
   (B) Exploration of literature
   (C) Acquire soft skills
   (D) Freedom to think
48. What are the limitations of lecture based approach?
   (A) Stimulating
   (B) Not stimulating
   (C) Not repetitive
   (D) Transferable to others
49. Which types of approaches are described by Ellis ?
   (A) Group based
   (B) Expert based
   (C) Lecture based
   (D) Guided problem based

50. Which approach has no formal exposition of knowledge from experts ?
    (A) Full problem based
    (B) Guided problem based
    (C) Expert based
    (D) Both (A) and (B)

ANSWERS

1. C	2. D	3. B	4. D	5. B	6. D
7. A	8. C	9. A	10. C	11. D	12. C
13. D	14. A	15. A	16. C	17. D	18. D
19. C	20. A	21. B	22. D	23. A	24. D
25. B	26. C	27. B	28. A	29. C	30. B
31. D	32. C	33. A	34. B	35. C	36. B
37. C	38. B	39. D	40. B	41. C	42. C
43. A	44. A	45. B	46. B	47. D	48. B
49. D	50. D				

JUNE 2013 NET III RECONDUCTED
08/09/2013 DELHI & RANCHI

1. Which one of the following is not the feature of H-index ?
   (A) Mathematically simple index
   (B) Applied to any level of aggregation
   (C) Publication that are hardly ever cited don't influence it.
   (D) Sensitive to performance change.
2. An Application Program Interface (API) language is used for
   (A) Network Management
   (B) Graphical user Interface
   (C) Relational Interface in Data Base Management
   (D) Database Management System
3. The correlational coefficient is
   (A) A strength of relationship between two variables.
   (B) A typical relationship between two variables.
   (C) A linear relationship between two variables.
   (D) Non-linear relationship between two variables.
4. The following is a collaborative network of Reference Librarians
   (A) Worldcat (B) INDEST
   (C) Question point (D) Global scholar
5. Which of the following is not a synchronous virtual reference service ?
   (A) Chat (B) E-mail
   (C) Video-conferencing (D) Voice over IP
6. Which of the bibliometric law describes the frequency of publications by author ?

(A) Zipf's law (B) Bradford's law
(C) Lotka's law (D) None of the above

7. Indian patents on all areas are published in
(A) India : A reference annual
(B) Indian chemical patent index
(C) Gazette of India, Part-III
(D) None of the above

8. Which of the following does not protect intellectual property ?
(A) Encryption of data
(B) Digital watermark
(C) Uniquely encoded licences
(D) Plug-ins

9. "World directory of sources of Patents" is published by
(A) Bowker-Saur, U.S.A.
(B) WIPO
(C) Patent Information System, India
(D) Derwent, London

10. 'Web of Science' covers
(A) Sciences (B) Social Sciences
(C) Arts of Humanities (D) All the above

11. What does encrypting a file mean ?
(A) Set the read only property
(B) Hiding the file
(C) Set a password
(D) Scrambling the contents

12. Which of the following identifies user by a login permission to a licensed site.

(A) Authorization (B) Authentication
(C) Digital signature (D) All of the above

13. Papyras was used as a writing material by
(A) Summarians (B) Italians
(C) Egyptians (D) Assyrians

14. The intrinsic value of information lies in its
(A) Procurement
(B) Processing and Storage
(C) Communication and Retrieval
(D) Usage

15. Identification of an e-article and paying for full-text is known as
(A) Pay-per-view (B) Consortium
(C) Campus license (D) E-subscription

16. Which of the following web resource for LIS has been compiled by academic librarians of universities of California ?
(A) Infomine
(B) Internet Public Library
(C) Internet Library for Librarians
(D) Current Informed Librarian

17. Who said, "Public Library is the responsibility of Local and National Authorities. It must be supported by specific legislation and financed by National and Local Govnerments" ?
(A) S.R. Ranganathan (B) Gopala Rao Ekbote
(C) Sinha Committee (D) UNESCO Manifesto

18. The formula $K(S) + \Delta I = K(S + \Delta S)$ for summation of information is propounded by
(A) Claude Shannon (B) George Gerbner
(C) Charles Osgood (D) Mandy Broo

19. 'Library Technology Project (LTP) Reports' are published by ________.
    (A) ILA (B) ALA
    (C) CILIP (D) SLA
20. Which Education Commission observed "Nothing can be more damaging to a growing department than to neglect its library or give it a low priority" ?
    (A) Kothari Education Commission
    (B) Radhakrishnan Education Commission
    (C) Calcutta University Commission
    (D) Mudaliar Commission on Secondary Education
21. International Advisory Committee on Documentation, Libraries and Archives (UNESCO) was established in
    (A) 1966 (B) 1967
    (C) 1968 (D) 1969
22. Which law of Library Science states that information is basic input to human growth and development ?
    (A) Fourth Law (B) Third Law
    (C) Second Law (D) Fifth Law
23. "Pro Quest" is ________.
    (A) Traditional Commercial Publisher
    (B) Scholarly Society Publisher
    (C) Electronic Aggregator
    (D) Publisher of Higher Learning Institutions
24. Which of the following is/are part(s) of classified catalogue ?
    (A) An author-title file
    (B) Subject file arranged by library classification
    (C) An alphabetical index to the subject file
    (D) All of the above

25. The main components of an RFID system include
    (A) Handheld Reader, RFID label printer, server and External book return
    (B) RFID tags, readers or sensors, Antenna and server
    (C) RFID label printer, sensors, antenna and server
    (D) RFID tags, server, external book return, sensors

26. Which of the following is not the component of a search engine ?
    (A) Spider
    (B) Index
    (C) Search of retrieval mechanism
    (D) Natural language technique

27. 'Communities' is a component of following digital library software
    (A) GSDL (B) D space
    (C) Fedora (D) i-core

28. Which one of the following is not an operation involved in quality circles ?
    (A) Problem identification
    (B) Problem selection
    (C) Solution recommendation
    (D) Problem shifting

29. In a database table, the category of information is called _______.
    (A) Tuple (B) Field
    (C) Record (D) All the above

30. The web address that acts as permanent identifier is ______.
    (A) URL (B) DOI
    (C) PURL (D) U

31. Who developed the sense making approach for human information behaviour which is implemented in terms of four constituent elements?
    (A) T.D. Wilson (B) B. Dervin
    (C) D. Ellis (D) C.C. Kuhlthau

32. MARC records contain
    (i) Description of library materials
    (ii) Searchable headings
    (iii) Elements to organize collection
    (iv) List of index terms

    Codes :
    (A) (i), (ii), (iii) are correct.
    (B) (ii), (iii), (iv) are correct.
    (C) (iii), (iv), (i) are correct.
    (D) (iv), (i), (ii) are correct.

33. RDBMs are advantageous as they :
    (i) Manage and Maintain
    (ii) Represent data in the form of tables
    (iii) Facilitate handling of objects rather than records
    (iv) Are developed with mathematic theory of relations

    Codes :
    (A) (i), (iv) are correct.
    (B) (ii), (iii) are correct.
    (C) (ii), (iv) are correct.
    (D) (iii), (iv) are correct.

34. When a library is planning for a new building project, which of the following technique/(s) is/are applicable to the plan and control the complex, long-term project ?

(i) PERT (ii) TQM
(iii) CPM (iv) MBO

Codes :

(A) (i) and (iii) are correct.
(B) (ii) and (iii) are correct.
(C) (i) and (iv) are correct.
(D) (ii) is correct.

35. Which of the following leadership style(s) are suitable for change management with persuation and inclusiveness ?

(i) Authority
(ii) Systems of Management
(iii) Contingency
(iv) Management

Codes :

(A) (i), (ii) are correct.
(B) (ii), (iii) are correct.
(C) (ii), (iv) are correct.
(D) (ii) is correct.

36. Arrange in sequence, the steps in programming :

(i) Program code
(ii) Program Documentation
(iii) Program test
(iv) Program design

Codes :

(A) iii ii i iv (B) iv i iii ii
(C) iv iii ii i (D) ii iv i iii

37. Which of the following is/are the major activities/ services of a library and networks in India ?

(i) Consortium purchase
(ii) Indexing of Internet resources
(iii) Document delivery
(iv) Staff training

Codes :

(A) (i), (iii), (iv) are correct.
(B) (ii), (iii), (iv) are correct.
(C) (i), (ii), (iii) are correct.
(D) (i), (ii), (iii), (iv) are correct.

38. The normal curve in a distribution is

(i) Symmetrical, bell shaped continuously curve
(ii) Asymmetrical, bell shaped continuously curve
(iii) Symmetrical, bell shaped curve which does not touch the 'X' axis
(iv) Bell shaped curve

Codes :

(A) (i) and (iv) are correct.
(B) (i) and (iii) are correct.
(C) (ii) and (iv) are correct.
(D) (i) is correct.

39. Arrange the following MARC formats in order of year of their emergence :

(i) CAN MARC (ii) US MARC
(iii) LC MARC (iv) MARC 21

Codes :

(A) i ii iii iv (B) ii iii iv i
(C) iii i ii iv (D) iv ii iii i

40. Arrange in sequence the following committees in order of that year of commencement :

(i) Library Committee

(ii) Committee on national network system for university libraries

(iii) Review committee on Library Science

(iv) Curriculum Development Committee on Library and Information Science

Codes :

(A) i ii iii iv (B) iii iv ii i

(C) iii ii i iv (D) i iii ii

41. Match the following :

List - I	List - II
a. Every unit of population has equal chance of being selected	i. Systematic sampling
b. Every nthcase is selected from the list of population	ii. Cluster sampling
c. Units are randomly selected from the subgroups	iii. Random sampling
d. Geographic area based units	iv. Stratified sampling

Codes :	**(a)**	**(b)**	**(c)**	**(d)**
(A)	i	iv	iii	ii
(B)	iv	ii	i	iii
(C)	iii	i	iv	ii
(D)	ii	iii	iv	i

42. Match the following :

	List - I	List - II
a.	Approach of measuring two opposite sets of items	i. Semantic-differential scale
b.	Approach of measurement yielding a single score	ii. Cumulative scale
c.	Approach of measurement adopting bi-polar objective rating to study a social phenomenon	iii. Sociometric scale
d.	Approach to measure interaction pattern among close associates in a variety of groups	iv. Summated scale

Codes :	(a)	(b)	(c)	(d)
(A)	ii	iii	i	iv
(B)	iii	i	iv	ii
(C)	i	ii	iv	iii
(D)	iv	ii	i	ii

43. Match the following :

	List - I	List - II
a.	Σ111/110 – EF2	i. df(degree of freedom)
b.	"XN	ii. S.D. (Standard Deviation)
c.	(R – 1) (C – 1)	iii. Mean
d.	"X2N	iv. Chi-square

Codes :	**(a)**	**(b)**	**(c)**	**(d)**
(A)	iv	i	iii	ii
(B)	iv	iii	i	ii
(C)	iii	i	ii	iv
(D)	ii	i	iii	iv

44. Match the following :

List - I	**List - II**
a. Algorith	i. Instruction to the computer
b. Flow charts	ii. Debugging
c. Program code	iii. Pictorially represented direction lines
d. Program test	iv. Set of explicit and finite steps

Codes :	**(a)**	**(b)**	**(c)**	**(d)**
(A)	ii	iii	iv	i
(B)	iii	i	iv	ii
(C)	iv	iii	i	ii
(D)	i	ii	iv	iii

45. Match the following :

List - I	**List - II**
a. Cumulative Book Index	i. D.K. Publishers & Distributors
b. Publisher's weekly	ii. Whitaker
c. Publishing in India	iii. Wilson
d. Book seller	iv. R.R. Bowker

Codes :	**(a)**	**(b)**	**(c)**	**(d)**
(A)	ii	i	iv	iii
(B)	iii	iv	i	ii
(C)	i	iii	ii	iv
(D)	iv	ii	i	ii

46. Match the following :

	List - I		**List - II**
a.	INDEST-AICTE	i.	Centrally funded
b.	CSIR consortia	ii.	Open
c.	UGC Infonet	iii.	Shared Budget
d.	IIM consortia	iv.	Closed group

Codes :	**(a)**	**(b)**	**(c)**	**(d)**
(A)	ii	iv	i	iii
(B)	i	iii	ii	iv
(C)	iii	ii	iv	i
(D)	iv	iii	i	ii

47. Match the following :

List - I	**List - II**
a. Special library	i. Provides bibliographical services
b. Public library	ii. Conservation of knowledge
c. National library	iii. Popularisation of Govt. information
d. Academic library	iv. Critical compilation

Codes :	**(a)**	**(b)**	**(c)**	**(d)**
(A)	i	iii	iv	ii
(B)	ii	iv	i	iii
(C)	iii	iv	i	ii
(D)	iv	iii	i	ii

48. Match the following language and their function :

List - I	List - II
a. Procedural	i. Scan arbitrary files and extra information
b. Special purpose	ii. Manipulate data and change memory
c. Practical extraction report	iii. Create documents to view with web server
d. Hyper text mark up	iv. Data base queries

Codes :	**(a)**	**(b)**	**(c)**	**(d)**
(A)	ii	iv	i	iii
(B)	i	iii	ii	iv
(C)	iii	iv	i	ii
(D)	ii	iii	iv	i

49. Match the following :

List - I	List - II
a. Information over load	i. Indexing and abstracting
b. Variation in quality and reliability	ii. Translation
c. Multiplicity of language	iii. Reviews and digests
d. Information scatter	iv. Alert services

Codes :	**(a)**	**(b)**	**(c)**	**(d)**
(A)	i	ii	iii	iv
(B)	iv	iii	ii	i
(C)	ii	iv	iii	i
(D)	iii	i	ii	i

50. Match the following :

List - I	List - II
a. Coding	i. Received signal not the one transmitted
b. Noise	ii. Measure of closeness of relationship
c. Entropy	iii. Message to a signal
d. Equivocation	iv. Measure of uncertainty

Codes :	**(a)**	**(b)**	**(c)**	**(d)**
(A)	iv	ii	iii	i
(B)	ii	iii	iv	i
(C)	i	ii	iii	iv
(D)	iii	i	iv	ii

51. Match the following :

List - I	List - II
a. Information Theory	i. Ogden and Richards
b. Theory of Signs	ii. Locke
c. Triadic Relationships	iii. Shannon
d. Doctrine of Signs	iv. Morris

Codes :	**(a)**	**(b)**	**(c)**	**(d)**
(A)	ii	iii	iv	i
(B)	iii	iv	i	ii
(C)	i	iii	iv	ii
(D)	ii	i	iii	iv

52. Match the following :

List - I	List - II
a. Intra-Facet Relation	i. S : 5210t3
b. Intra-Array Phase Relation	ii. Q 20 m4
c. Intra-Facet Phase Relation	iii. SO b2
d. Inter-Subject Phase Relation	iv. X.440j56

Codes :	**(a)**	**(b)**	**(c)**	**(d)**
(A)	iv	i	ii	iii
(B)	iv	ii	iii	i
(C)	ii	iii	i	iv
(D)	i	iv	iii	i

53. Match the following :

List - I	**List - II**
a. Organisational chart	i. Identification of responsibility for specific tasks
b. Flow charts	ii. Examine specific detailed procedure
c. Activity charts	iii. Division of responsibility & functions
d. Decision table	iv. Diagrams composed of symbols and directional lines

Codes :	**(a)**	**(b)**	**(c)**	**(d)**
(A)	i	iv	ii	iii
(B)	ii	iii	iv	i
(C)	iii	iv	i	ii
(D)	iv	ii	iii	i

54. Match the following :

List - I	**List - II**
a. Information should be as accurate as possible	i. Broadus
b. Get the best title on any subject but add midiocres that are well read.	ii. Haines
c. Know the community's character and interest	iii. McColvin
d. Consider the duration as well as intensity of the demand	iv. Drury

Codes :	**(a)**	**(b)**	**(c)**	**(d)**
(A)	iii	iv	ii	i
(B)	ii	iii	i	iv
(C)	i	ii	iv	iii
(D)	iv	i	iii	ii

55. Match the functions performed by different layers of OSI model :

List - I	**List - II**
a. Delivery of Packets from source of destination	i. Application layer
b. Data transmission rate	ii. Data link layer
c. Access to network resources	iii. Network layer
d. Provide hop-to-pop delivery	iv. Physical layer

Codes :	**(a)**	**(b)**	**(c)**	**(d)**
(A)	i	iii	ii	iv
(B)	ii	iv	i	iii
(C)	iii	iv	i	ii
(D)	iii	i	iv	ii

56. Match the following :

List - I	**List - II**
a. Gender	i. Dependent variable
b. Information Technology	ii. Variable
c. Usership in libraries	iii. Binomial variable
d. Logical set of attributes	iv. Independent variable

Codes :	**(a)**	**(b)**	**(c)**	**(d)**
(A)	i	iv	ii	iii
(B)	iii	iv	i	ii
(C)	ii	i	iv	iii
(D)	iv	iii	ii	i

57. Match the following :

	List - I		List - II
a.	The assessment device that appears to measure the subject matter it purports to	i.	Content validity
b.	The assessment device in which individual's test score predicts the probable behaviour on a second variable	ii.	Construct validity
c.	The assessment device which adequately measures the major dimensions of the behaviour under consideration	iii.	Criterion-related validity
d.	The assessment device which appears to measure the general elements it purports to measure	iv.	Face validity

Codes :	**(a)**	**(b)**	**(c)**	**(d)**
(A)	i	ii	iv	iii
(B)	ii	i	iii	iv
(C)	iv	iii	i	ii
(D)	iii	i	ii	iv

58. Match the following :

	List - I		List - II
a.	Behaviour studies	i.	Extent of use of facilities/services
b.	Use studies	ii.	Pattern of Science communication

c. User studies	iii. Interaction of user with communication system
d. Information flow studies	iv. Use of communication medium

Codes :	(a)	(b)	(c)	(d)
(A)	i	iv	ii	iii
(B)	iii	iv	i	ii
(C)	ii	iii	i	iv
(D)	ii	iv	iii	i

59. Match the following :

List - I	List - II
a. National Library of the World	i. Wilfred Ashworth
b. Special Libraries	ii. L.J. Strauss
c. Scientific and Technical Libraries	iii. A. Esdaile
d. Handbook of Special Libraries	iv. C.M. Lewis

Codes :	(a)	(b)	(c)	(d)
(A)	i	iv	iii	ii
(B)	ii	iii	iv	i
(C)	iii	iv	ii	i
(D)	iv	ii	iii	i

60. Match the following :

List - I	List - II
a. Halftone	i. Translate instructions from original software to new platforms
b. Threshold	ii. Imaging with varying densities
c. Emulation	iii. Transfer of digital materials
d. Migration	iv. Minimum level to detect a signal

Codes :	**(a)**	**(b)**	**(c)**	**(d)**
(A)	i	iii	iv	ii
(B)	iii	ii	iv	i
(C)	ii	iv	i	iii
(D)	ii	i	iii	i

61. **Assertion (A) :** Colon classification is the most successful classification schemes in India.

Reason (R) : The most important factor behind the success of any classification scheme is the revision and publication of different editions at regular intervals.

Codes :

(A) Both (A) and (R) are true.
(B) (A) is true but (R) is false.
(C) (A) is false but (R) is true.
(D) Both (A) and (R) are false.

62. **Assertion (A) :** Proliferation of LIS schools in India produced mediocre professionals.

Reason (R) : Curriculum and teaching techniques have not been upgraded at university level.

Codes :

(A) Both (A) and (R) are partially true.
(B) Both (A) and (R) are false.
(C) (A) is true and (R) is false.
(D) (A) is false and (R) is true.

63. **Assertion (A) :** Several Library Science departments in India have shifted to integrated MLIS program.

Reason (R) : MLIS Program (integrated) is a right solution to knowledge explosion in the field.

Codes :

(A) Both (A) and (R) are false.

(B) (A) is true and (R) is false.

(C) Both (A) and (R) are true.

(D) (A) is false and (R) is true.

64. **Assertion (A) :** UGC is financially supporting all academic libraries.

Reason (R) : UGC is primarily responsible for the overall development of libraries of higher education in India.

Codes :

(A) (A) is false and (R) is true.

(B) (A) is true and (R) is false.

(C) Both (A) and (R) are true.

(D) Both (A) and (R) are false.

65. **Assertion (A) :** The entire scholarly publishing system is in danger of eroding due to increasing influence of predatory publishing.

Reason (R) : Many prey on Junior researchers and graduate students with personalised messages praising their earlier work and inviting them to submit a new manuscript.

Codes :

(A) (A) is true but (R) is false.

(B) (A) is false but (R) is true.

(C) Both (A) and (R) are false.

(D) Both (A) and (R) are true.

66. **Assertion (A) :** Metrics based evaluation is not suitable for assessing research performance of individual.

Reason (R) : Construction of citation profiles depend upon the databases used.

Codes :

(A) Both (A) and (R) are true.

(B) Both (A) and (R) are false.

(C) (A) is true, but (R) is false.

(D) (A) is false, but (R) is true.

67. **Assertion (A) :** Effective methods of communicating in H.R. Management of libraries still remains elusive.

Reason (R) : The management do not have the needed direction of approach, precision of thoughts and their expression and empathy.

Codes :

(A) (A) is true, (R) is false.

(B) Both (A) and (R) are false.

(C) (A) is true, (R) is partially true.

(D) (A) is false, (R) is true.

68. **Assertion (A) :** UDC is used in subject gateways for resource discovery with high recall.

Reason (R) : In online environment, a faceted scheme has a distinct advantage over an enumerative one.

Codes :

(A) (A) is true but (R) is false.

(B) (A) is true, (R) is partially true.

(C) (A) is false, (R) is true.

(D) (A) is partially true, (R) is true.

69. **Assertion (A) :** MARC should never be used outside the context of the cataloguing rules.

Reason (R) : MARC is simply a coding scheme for entering bibliographic information into computer records.

Codes :

(A) Both (A) and (R) are true.

(B) (A) is true but (R) is false.

(C) (A) is false but (R) is true.

(D) Both (A) and (R) are false.

70. **Assertion (A) :** Library Associations in India striving hard for the enactment of Library Acts.

Reason (R) : Library Acts help in systematic development of libraries.

Codes :

(A) Both (A) and (R) are true.

(B) Both (A) and (R) are false.

(C) (A) is true, (R) is false.

(D) (A) is false, (R) is true.

71. **Assertion (A) :** It is a time to separate the copyright issues for scholarly works from entertainment works.

Reason (R) : The scholarly works are public funded fact based, collaborative and intellectual heritage of the institution.

Codes :

(A) (A) is false and (R) is true.

(B) Both (A) and (R) are true but (R) is not the correct explanation of (A).

(C) Both (A) and (R) are false.

(D) (A) is true but (R) is false.

72. **Assertion (A) :** With quick and comprehensive availability of informative through internet resources, need for reference service with a human touch is decreasing.

Reason (R) : Internet resources can satisfy all types of information needs of information seekers.

Codes :

(A) (A) is true and (R) is false.

(B) Both (A) and (R) are false.

(C) (A) is false and (R) is true.

(D) (A) and (R) are true.

73. **Assertion (A) :** Scholar frequency to visit academic libraries has decreased tremendously over the period of last two decades.

Reason (R) : E-scholarly resources are easily accessible to everyone from anywhere anytime.

Codes :

(A) Both (A) and (R) are true.

(B) Both (A) and (R) are false.

(C) (A) is true, but (R) is false.

(D) (A) is false, but (R) is true.

74. **Assertion (A) :** H-index lacks sensitivity to performance changes.

Reason (R) : It can never decrease and is insensitive to number of citations received.

Codes :

(A) Both (A) and (R) are false.

(B) Both (A) and (R) are true.

(C) (A) is true but (R) is false.

(D) (A) is false, but (R) is true.

75. **Assertion (A) :** Z 39.50 standard protocol enables communication among networked computers through a single search interface.

Reason (R) : Z 39.50 application in library consortia environment can enhance resource sharing.

Codes :

(A) Both (A) and (R) are true.

(B) Both (A) and (R) are false.

(C) (A) is true and (R) is false.

(D) (A) is false and (R) is true.

ANSWERS

1. D	2. B	3. A	4. C	5. B	6. C
7. C	8. D	9. B	10. D	11. D	12. B
13. C	14. D	15. A	16. A	17. D	18. D
19. B	20. A	21. B	22. B	23. C	24. D
25. B	26. D	27. B	28. D	29. B	30. C
31. B	32. A	33. C	34. A	35. C	36. B
37. A	38. B	39. C	40. D	41. C	42. D
43. B	44. C	45. B	46. A	47. D	48. A
49. B	50. D	51. B	52. A	53. C	54. A
55. C	56. B	57. C	58. B	59. C	60. C
61. C	62. A	63. B	64. A	65. D	66. A
67. C	68. A	69. A	70. D	71. B	72. A
73. C	74. B	75. A			

DEC 2013 NET PAPER-III

1. A Boolean query using only AND and NOT is
   (A) Fuzzy query (B) Conjunctive query
   (C) Routing query (D) Probabilistic query
2. In which year Janet (U.K.) was established ?
   (A) 1957 (B) 1983
   (C) 1987 (D) 1989
3. Who developed Repertory Grid Technique for assessing how the users view the world from their own perspective ?
   (A) A. Delphi (B) Calvin Mooer
   (C) J. Belkin (D) George Kelley
4. A chart in which some figures are broken down into its constituent parts is
   (A) Bar chart (B) Column chart
   (C) Pie chart (D) Band chart
5. OAISTER is an example of digital libraries architecture based on
   (A) CORBA
   (B) Software Agents Architecture
   (C) Federated Database System
   (D) Metadata Harvesting
6. RSS feed is a tool of
   (A) Web 2.0 (B) Web 1.0
   (C) Web 3.0 (D) Graphic Design
7. The use of more words or symbols than are necessary to convey a meaning results in
   (A) Efficiency (B) Accuracy
   (C) Redundancy (D) Precision

8. A rubber stamp impressed on the verso of title page giving information concerning the records and processing of each individual book acquired is called

(A) Book stamp (B) Process stamp

(C) Date stamp (D) Accession stamp

9. Ontology is

(A) A Documentation service

(B) An Indexing method

(C) Classification of Internet based documents

(D) Cataloguing of Internet based documents

10. In colon classification, which mnemonic is displayed in the use of digit '4' as for pathology, disease, transport, hybrid etc. ?

(A) Seminal (B) Systematic

(C) Scheduled (D) Alphabetical

11. Name the similarity measure in which similarity of a document is adjusted such that the similarity of a document to itself is 1.

(A) Cosine measure

(B) Distance measure

(C) Swet's measure

(D) Normalised similarity measure

12. Which law states that "An information retrieval system will tend not to be used whenever it is more painful and troublesome for a customer to have information than for him not to have it" ?

(A) Bradford's Law (B) Mooer's Law

(C) Ziff's Law (D) Lotka's Law

13. Who is the compiler of Web-Bibliography of Rabindranath Tagore ?

(A) Bengal Library Association
(B) RRRLF
(C) National Library of India
(D) IASLIC

14. Who are the publishers of 'Year Book on Human Rights' ?
(A) United Nations
(B) Ministry of Law, Govt. of India
(C) Europa Publishers
(D) R.R. Bowker

15. ASTINFO stands for
(A) Asian Scientific and Technological Information Network
(B) Association of Scientific and Technological Information Scientists in Asia
(C) International Network for Exchange of Science and Technology Information
(D) Regional Network for the Exchange of Information and Experience in Science and Technology in Asia and the Pacific

16. IFLA's programme for capacity building of library associations is named as
(A) BSLA (B) ALP
(C) CLM (D) PAC

17. The measure of certainty or predictability is called as
(A) Entropy (B) Feedback
(C) Redundancy (D) Distortion

18. A characteristic in which information tends to leak and the more it leaks,the more we have, is

(A) Synergetic characteristics
(B) Diffusive characteristics
(C) Compressible characteristics
(D) Shareable characteristics

19. Which of the following organizations are associated with the concept of '1000 crore plan to link 9000 libraries in India'?
(i) National Library of India
(ii) National Mission on Libraries
(iii) INFLIBNET
(iv) RRRLF

Codes :
(A) (ii) and (iii) are correct.
(B) (iii) and (iv) are correct.
(C) (i) and (iv) are correct.
(D) (ii) and (iv) are correct.

20. Which of the following are the core content of ISI web of knowledge?
(i) Current Contents
(ii) ISI proceedings
(iii) Derwent Information Index
(iv) AGRICOLA

Codes :
(A) (i), (iv) and (iii) (B) (i), (ii) and (iii)
(C) (ii), (iii) and (iv) (D) (i), (ii) and (iv)

21. Which of the following are value added information services?
(i) Aggregator Service
(ii) Referral Service
(iii) Document Delivery Service
(iv) Research Reports/Market Survey Reports

Codes :

(A) (i) and (iii) are correct

(B) (ii) and (iv) are correct

(C) (ii) and (iii) are correct

(D) (i) and (iv) are correct

22. Identify the methods used for plagiarism detection:

(i) Term occurrence analysis

(ii) API Testing

(iii) Citation-based plagiarismdetection

(iv) Local similarity assessment

Codes :

(A) (i), (ii) and (iv) are correct.

(B) (i), (iii) and (iv) are correct.

(C) (ii), (iii) and (iv) are correct.

(D) (i), (ii) and (iii) are correct.

23. Which of the following are the main role operators of PRECIS ?

(i) Key System (ii) Action

(iii) Performer of action (iv) Form of Document

Codes :

(A) (i), (ii) and (iii) (B) (ii), (i) and (iv)

(C) (i), (iii) and (iv) (D) (ii), (iii) and (i)

24. Which of the following are the advantages of RFID technology in libraries ?

(i) Tags can be read inside a case.

(ii) Hundred of tags can be read ata time.

(iii) Cheaper than Barcode

(iv) More security and Privacy

Codes :

(A) (i) and (iii) are correct

(B) (i) and (ii) are correct

(C) (ii) and (iii) are correct

(D) (iii) and (iv) are correct

25. Which of the following are not Change Management Models ?

(i) Kurtlewin's Model (ii) Beer's Model

(iii) Lasswell's Model (iv) Epidemic Model

Codes :

(A) (i) & (iii) are correct.

(B) (ii) & (iii) are correct.

(C) (iii) & (iv) are correct.

(D) (ii) & (iv) are correct.

26. Which of the following are the International Cooperative Serials Control Program ?

(i) CONSER (ii) BIBCO

(iii) SERLINE (iv) CATLINE

Codes :

(A) (i) & (ii) are correct.

(B) (ii) & (iii) are correct.

(C) (i) & (iii) are correct.

(D) (ii) & (iv) are correct.

27. Which of the following are called 'path finders' to the literature ?

(i) Bibliography (ii) Catalogue

(iii) Shelf List (iv) Indices and Abstracts

Codes :

(A) (i) & (ii) are correct

(B) (i), (ii) & (iv) are correct

(C) (i) & (iv) are correct

(D) (ii) & (iii) are correct

28. Which of the following facilitate informal communication on the web ?

(i) Split Screens (ii) Chat

(iii) Wikis (iv) RSS feeds

Codes :

(A) (i) & (iii) are correct

(B) (ii) & (iii) are correct

(C) (iii) & (iv) are correct

(D) (i) & (ii) are correct

29. Which of the following associations have sponsored the Text Encoding Initiatives (TEI) ?

(i) ACL (ii) ACRL

(iii) ALLC (iv) ACH

Codes :

(A) (i), (ii) and (iii) are correct

(B) (ii), (iii) and (iv) are correct

(C) (i), (iv) and (ii) are correct

(D) (i), (iii) and (iv) are correct

30. Which of the following are limitations of digital libraries ?

(i) Full text searching

(ii) Operational costs

(iii) Rights management

(iv) Hyper text linking

Codes :

(A) (ii), (iii) and (iv) are correct

(B) (ii) and (iii) are correct

(C) (i), (ii) and (iv) are correct

(D) (i) and (iv) are correct

31. The sources of hypothesis, as enunciated by P.V. Young are

(i) Genealogy (ii) Culture

(iii) Experiment (iv) Analogy

Codes :

(A) (i), (ii) and (iii) are correct

(B) (i), (iii) and (iv) are correct

(C) (i), (ii) and (iv) are correct

(D) (ii), (iii) and (iv) are correct

32. "Women are more in library profession than men." Identify the variable in the statement.

(i) Men and women areindependent variables.

(ii) Men and women are dependentvariables.

(iii) Library profession is adependent variable.

(iv) Library profession is anindependent variable.

Codes :

(A) (i) and (iii) are correct

(B) (i) and (iv) are correct

(C) (ii) and (iii) are correct

(D) (ii) and (iv) are correct

33. Systematic sampling is

(i) A type of probability sampling.

(ii) A type of non-probabilitysampling.

(iii) In which first unit is selectedrandomly.

(iv) Selected on the basis ofspecified characteristics.

Codes :

(A) (i) and (iii) are correct

(B) (i) and (iv) are correct

(C) (iii) and (iv) are correct

(D) (ii) and (iv) are correct

34. Who are associated with the digitization of the collection of Rabindra Bhavan, Vishav Bharati ?
    (i) RRRLF
    (ii) C-DAC
    (iii) NIC
    (iv) National Library of India

    Codes :
    (A) (i) and (iii) are correct
    (B) (i) and (ii) are correct
    (C) (ii) and (iv) are correct
    (D) (iii) and (iv) are correct

35. Which of the following are the Pillars of SCONUL Seven Pillar Model ?
    (i) Recognising Information need
    (ii) Locating and accessing information
    (iii) Using information technology for assessing information need.
    (iv) Comparing and evaluating information.

    Codes :
    (A) (i), (ii) and (iii) are correct
    (B) (i), (ii) and (iv) are correct
    (C) (ii), (iii) and (iv) are correct
    (D) (i) and (iv) are correct

36. Resource Description Framework consists which of the following ?
    (i) Subject (ii) Thread
    (iii) Predicate (iv) Object

    Codes :
    (A) (i), (ii) and (iii) (B) (ii), (iii) and (iv)
    (C) (iii), (iv) and (i) (D) (iv), (i) and (ii)

37. Arrange the following factors of TQM in the order of their implementation :
    i. Development of Human Resource Management
    ii. Standardisation of Workprocess
    iii. Improvement in Internal Organisation Management
    iv. Quality Management Procedures

    Codes :

    (A) ii iii i iii (B) iii iv ii i
    (C) iv iii ii i (D) ii iv iii i

38. Arrange the following according to their year of emergence :
    i. ADINET ii. SIRNET
    iii. MANLIBNET iv. DELNET

    Codes :

    (A) i iv ii iii (B) iv ii iii i
    (C) iv iii ii i (D) iii i iv ii

39. Arrange the following according to their year of origin :
    i. Indian National Bibliography
    ii. British National Bibliography
    iii. Cumulative Book Index
    iv. Books in Print

    Codes :

    (A) i ii iv iii (B) iii iv ii i
    (C) ii iii iv i (D) iv i ii iii

40. Arrange the following according to their levels :
    i. Canons of Cataloguing
    ii. Laws of Library Science

iii. General Normative Principles

iv. Principles of Cataloguing

Codes :

(A) ii iv i iii (B) i iii ii iv

(C) iv i iii ii (D) iii ii i iv

41. Arrange the following according to their year of emergence :

i. LISA

ii. Dissertation Abstracts International

iii. Indian Science Abstracts

iv. Indian Library & Information Science Abstracts

Codes :

(A) iii iv ii i (B) iv iii i ii

(C) ii i iii iv (D) i ii iii iv

42. Arrange the following according to their year of emergence :

i. INIS ii. AGRIS

iii. NATIS iv. UNISIST

Codes :

(A) iii iv ii i (B) iv i iii ii

(C) ii iv i iii (D) i iii iv ii

43. Arrange in sequence the following Model Public Library Acts/Bills in India:

i. Model Public Library Bill by M.D. Sen Committee

ii. Model Public Library Act by S.R. Ranganathan

iii. Model Public Library Act of ILA

iv. Model Public Library Bill by working group of Planning Commission

Codes :

(A) i ii iii iv (B) ii i iv iii

(C) iii iv i ii (D) iv iii ii i

44. Arrange in sequence the medium used for 'Virtual Reference' in the order of their progress.

i. Web form ii. Ask a Service

iii. E-mail iv. Social Networking

Codes :

(A) i ii iii iv (B) ii iii iv i

(C) iii i ii iv (D) iv ii i iii

45. Arrange in order the process of stock rectification and stock verification as suggested by S.R. Ranganathan :

i. Checking with charged tray

ii. Shelf Rectification

iii. Shelf checking

iv. Deciding the Quota

Codes :

(A) iii i iv ii (B) iv i ii iii

(C) iv ii iii i (D) ii iv i iii

46. Match the following :

List - I	**List - II**
a. Outdated Information	i. Information Diffusion
b. Condensed Information	ii. Obsolete Information
c. Message	iii. Compressible Information
d. Vintage model	iv. Understanding

Codes :	**(a)**	**(b)**	**(c)**	**(d)**
(A)	iv	iii	ii	i
(B)	i	ii	iv	iii
(C)	iii	iv	ii	i
(D)	ii	iii	iv	i

47. Match the following :

	List - I		List - II
a.	Technique for identifying the theme of adocument	i.	Cataloguing
b.	Prussian Instruction	ii.	Standard for encoding dataon CD-ROM
c.	ISO-9960	iii.	Data Transmission Speed
d.	Baud	iv.	Bibliographic coupling

Codes :	**(a)**	**(b)**	**(c)**	**(d)**
(A)	iv	i	ii	iii
(B)	i	ii	iii	iv
(C)	ii	iii	iv	i
(D)	iii	ii	i	iv

48. Match the following :

	List - I		List - II
a.	Maurice B. Line	i.	Resource Management in Academic Libraries
b.	David Baker	ii.	Planning Academic and Research Library Buildings
c.	Peter Brophy	iii.	Academic Library Management
d.	K. D. Metcalf	iv.	The Academic Libraries

Codes :	**(a)**	**(b)**	**(c)**	**(d)**
(A)	iii	i	iv	ii
(B)	i	ii	iii	iv
(C)	iv	i	ii	iii
(D)	ii	iii	i	iv

49. Match the following :

List - I	List - II
a. Digital Library	i. Collections are stored in electronic media formats and accessible via computers
b. Hybrid Library	ii. Access to electronic information in avariety of remote locations through a local online catalogue or other gateway
c. VirtualLibrary	iii. Provides services ina mixed mode electronic and paper environment
d. Electronic Library	iv. Collection of electronic resources that provides direct/indirect access to a systematically organised collection of digital objects

Codes :	**(a)**	**(b)**	**(c)**	**(d)**
(A)	iv	iii	ii	i
(B)	i	iii	iv	ii
(C)	iii	i	ii	iv
(D)	ii	ii	i	iii

50. Match the following :

List - I	List - II
a. Survey ofrequirements	i. Design phase
b. Determining cost efficiency & effectiveness	ii. Installation phase
c. Review of the programs and their goals	iii. Analysis phase
d. Complete change over basics of system	iv. Evaluation phase

Codes :	(a)	(b)	(c)	(d)
(A)	i	ii	iii	iv
(B)	ii	iii	iv	i
(C)	iii	iv	i	ii
(D)	iv	i	ii	iii

51. Match the following :

List - I	List - II
a. Nadir to Ascending	i. Hypothesizing
b. Ascending to Zenith	ii. Verification
c. Zenith to Descending	iii. Deductive
d. Descending to Nadir	iv. Empirical

Codes :	(a)	(b)	(c)	(d)
(A)	i	iii	ii	iv
(B)	ii	iv	i	iii
(C)	iii	i	iv	ii
(D)	iv	i	iii	ii

52 Match the following characteristics of DBMS with respective activity :

List - I	List - II
a. Reduction of redundancy	i. Encryption
b. Data sharing	ii. Centralized control
c. Data integrity	iii. No. of application programs
d. Data security	iv. Accurate and consistent data

Codes :	(a)	(b)	(c)	(d)
(A)	ii	iii	iv	i
(B)	iv	iii	ii	i
(C)	iii	iv	i	ii
(D)	i	ii	iv	iii

53. Match the following :

List - I	List - II
a. XML	i. Joe Becker
b. METS	ii. Defence Organizations
c. UNICODE	iii. W3C
d. Cryptography	iv. Library of Congress

Codes :	**(a)**	**(b)**	**(c)**	**(d)**
(A)	i	ii	iii	iv
(B)	iii	iv	i	ii
(C)	ii	iii	iv	i
(D)	iv	i	ii	iii

54. Match the following :

List - I	List - II
a. Social Microscope	i. Cluster Technique
b. Fundamental Research	ii. No control over variance
c. Ex-post facto research	iii. Case study method
d. Multi stage random sampling	iv. Knowledge for knowledge sake

Codes :	**(a)**	**(b)**	**(c)**	**(d)**
(A)	i	ii	iii	iv
(B)	iii	iv	ii	i
(C)	ii	iii	i	iv
(D)	iv	i	ii	iv

55. Match the following :

List - I	List - II
a. Estimation of future expenditure on the basis of previous year expenditure	i. Programme

b. '15 per studentand' 200/-per teacher	ii. Comparison
c. 6.5%-10% of university budget for the development of library	iii. Per capita
d. Activities to be accomplished by the library	iv. Proportional

Codes :	**(a)**	**(b)**	**(c)**	**(d)**
(A)	ii	iii	iv	i
(B)	i	ii	iii	iv
(C)	iii	iv	i	ii
(D)	iv	i	ii	iii

56. Match the following :

List - I	**List - II**
a. Identification of user categories	i. Market positioning
b. Prioriting user groups and services	ii. Segmentation
c. Information seeking behaviour of users	iii. Marketing Mix
d. Product, price, place, promotion	iv. Consumer analysis

Codes :	**(a)**	**(b)**	**(c)**	**(d)**
(A)	i	ii	iii	iv
(B)	ii	i	iv	iii
(C)	iii	iv	i	ii
(D)	iv	iii	ii	i

57. Match the following :

	List - I		List - II
a.	FRBR	i.	Paul Otlet
b.	POPSI	ii.	IFLA
c.	UDC	iii.	G. Bhattacharya
d.	www	iv.	Tem Berners-Lee

Codes :	**(a)**	**(b)**	**(c)**	**(d)**
(A)	ii	i	iii	iv
(B)	ii	iii	i	iv
(C)	ii	iv	i	iii
(D)	iv	ii	iii	i

58. Match the following :

	List - I		List - II
a.	Index Translationum	i.	NISCAIR
b.	Translation Register Index (TR-I)	ii.	NTC, Chicago
c.	World Trans Index	iii.	UNESCO
d.	Common-wealth Index of Unpublished Transtations	iv.	ITC, Delft, Netherlands
		v.	ASLIB

Codes :	**(a)**	**(b)**	**(c)**	**(d)**
(A)	ii	iii	i	iv
(B)	iii	ii	iv	v
(C)	v	iii	i	ii
(D)	iv	ii	v	iii

59. Match the following evaluation criteria of print materials :

	List - I		List - II
a.	Authority	i.	Typography
b.	Scope	ii.	Stated purpose
c.	Format	iii.	Publisher's reputation
d.	Arrangement	iv.	Cross references

Codes :	**(a)**	**(b)**	**(c)**	**(d)**
(A)	ii	iii	i	iv
(B)	i	iv	ii	iii
(C)	iii	ii	i	iv
(D)	iii	iv	ii	i

60. Match the following :

	List - I		List - II
a.	Measure of similarity between two documents	i.	Proportion of coefficient association
b.	Similarity measure based on overlap interms between two documents	ii.	Rectangular distance coefficient
c.	Document similarity based solely on the occurrence of words	iii.	Coefficient of association
d.	Similarity measure which is based on the city block distance between two documents	iv.	Lexical similarity

Codes :	**(a)**	**(b)**	**(c)**	**(d)**
(A)	i	iii	ii	iv
(B)	iii	i	ii	iv
(C)	iii	i	iv	ii
(D)	ii	iii	iv	i

61. Match the following authors with their statements on information characteristics :

List - I	**List - II**
a. Peter Drucker	i. Human andshareable
b. Borlando Cleveland	ii. Quantity, Quality, Life
c. K.J. McGarry	iii. Natural and man-made physical resources
d. Williams	iv. Resources by analogy with classic resources of labour

Codes :	**(a)**	**(b)**	**(c)**	**(d)**
(A)	iii	i	iv	ii
(B)	iii	ii	i	iv
(C)	i	iii	iv	ii
(D)	i	iv	ii	iii

62. Match the following :

List - I	**List - II**
a. Saraswati Mahal Library, Tanjavur (1535)	i. Lord Curzon
b. Khuda Baksh Oriental Public Library, Patna (1876)	ii. Telugu Nayakas
c. Library of Asiatic Society of Bengal (1784)	iii. Maulana M.B. Khan
d. Imperial Library, Calcutta (1901)	iv. Sir G.William Jones

Codes :	**(a)**	**(b)**	**(c)**	**(d)**
(A)	iii	ii	iv	i
(B)	ii	iii	i	iv
(C)	ii	iii	iv	i
(D)	iii	ii	i	iv

63. **Assertion (A) :** With the introduction of Internet, need for reference librarians has been minimised to fulfil the users reference needs.

    Reason (R) : FAQ facility on internet is substituting the need for human interface in libraries.

    Codes :

    (A) Both (A) and (R) are partiallytrue.
    (B) Both (A) and (R) are true.
    (C) Both (A) and (R) are false.
    (D) (A) is true but (R) is false.

64. **Assertion (A) :** Approaches to Research is not dependent on Epistemologies.

    Reason (R) : Scientific research relies on the application of the scientific method.

    Codes :

    (A) Both (A) and (R) are true.
    (B) Both (A) and (R) are false.
    (C) (A) is true and (R) is false.
    (D) (R) is true and (A) is false.

65. **Assertion (A) :** According to the Third Law of Librarianship given by Michael Gorman, we need to use technology intelligently to enhance service.

    Reason (R) : Technology is used to solve problems and improve services and achieve costeffectiveness rather than adopted for its own sake.

Codes :

(A) (A) is true, but (R) is false.

(B) Both (A) and (R) are true, but (R) is not correct explanationof (A).

(C) Both (A) and (R) are false.

(D) Both (A) and (R) are true.

66. **Assertion (A) :** All reference sources provide uptodate information in their respective categories.

Reason (R) : As these are compiled from primary sources of information.

Codes :

(A) Both (A) and (R) are true.

(B) Both (A) and (R) are false.

(C) (A) is false but (R) is partiallytrue.

(D) (A) is true but (R) is false.

67. **Assertion (A) :** The hierarchy based classification schemes have a major role in the organization of the web.

Reason (R) : The 'hotlists' retrieved by robots based search engines use the technique of relevance of subject descriptors.

Codes :

(A) (A) is true, but (R) is false.

(B) (A) is false, but (R) is true.

(C) Both (A) and (R) are correct.

(D) Both (A) and (R) are wrong.

68. **Assertion (A) :** Performance Based Budgeting demands that the objectives and goals of agency be clear and performance measures and target to put inplace.

Reason (R) : The key to success firmly rely upon its

clear sense of mission and objectives which the funding agencies have proposed to reach them.

Codes :

(A) (A) is true, but (R) is false.

(B) (A) is false, but (R) is true.

(C) Both (A) and (R) are true.

(D) Both (A) and (R) are false.

69. **Assertion (A) :** Majority of University Libraries in India are not fully automated.

Reason (R) : University Libraries in India are meddling with automation of circulation activities.

Codes :

(A) (A) is true but (R) is false.

(B) (A) is false but (R) is true.

(C) Both (A) and (R) are true.

(D) Both (A) and (R) are false.

70. **Assertion (A) :** Mean, median and mode are the simple techniques to get exact averages for data analysis in research.

Reason (R) : These are the well accepted statistical techniques of research for data analysis of historical data.

Codes :

(A) (A) is false, but (R) is true.

(B) Both (A) and (R) are true.

(C) (A) is true but (R) is false.

(D) Both (A) and (R) are false.

71. **Assertion (A) :** Online Reference Service can be offered using IMs, SMs, VoIP, Video, Blogs, Websites and host of such other mechanisms.

Reason (R) : Majority of academic libraries in India are equipped with required infrastructure.

Codes :

(A) Both (A) and (R) are true.

(B) (A) is true, (R) is false.

(C) (A) is false, (R) is true.

(D) Both (A) and (R) are false.

72. **Assertion (A) :** Semantic web is an extension of www in which web contents cannot be expressed in natural language.

Reason (R) : Semantic web can be easily associated with spider web.

Codes :

(A) Both (A) and (R) are false.

(B) (A) is true, but (R) is false.

(C) Both (A) and (R) are true.

(D) (A) is false, but (R) is true.

73. **Assertion (A) :** BIOS is a set of programs that handles startup operations in a computer such as power on, self tested and low level control for hardware.

Reason (R) : The graphical display at the beginning of the program prolongs the life of monitor.

Codes :

(A) Both (A) and (R) are true.

(B) (A) is false, but (R) is true.

(C) Both (A) and (R) are false.

(D) (A) is true, but (R) is false.

74. **Assertion (A) :** For providing an effective reference service, best & up to date reference collection is not as important as is the competent reference librarian.

Reason (R) : An efficient reference librarian can

serve the users more effectively even in the absence of best reference collection.

Codes :

(A) (A) is true but (R) is false.

(B) Both (A) and (R) are true.

(C) (A) is false but (R) is true.

(D) Both (A) and (R) are false.

75. **Assertion (A) :** India's contribution to LIS literatures is decreasing.

Reason (R) : Authors find it more convenient to get their articles published in open access journals.

Codes :

(A) Both (A) and (R) are true.

(B) (A) is false, but (R) is true.

(C) Both (A) and (R) are false.

(D) (A) is true but (R) is false.

ANSWERS

1. B	2. B	3. D	4. C	5. D	6. A
7. C	8. D	9. C	10. A	11. D	12. B
13. B	14. A	15. D	16. A	17. C	18. B
19. D	20. B	21. D	22. B	23. A/D	24. B
25. C	26. C	27. C	28. D	29. D	30. B
31. C	32. A	33. A	34. B	35. B	36. C
37. D	38. B	39. B	40. D	41. C	42. D
43. B	44. C	45. B	46. D	47. A	48. A
49. A	50. C	51. D	52. A	53. B	54. B
55. A	56. B	57. B	58. B	59. C	60. C
61. A	62. C	63. A	64. A	65. D	66. C
67. A	68. C	69. C	70. C	71. B	72. A
73. D	74. B	75. B			

DEC. 2013 NET PAPER-II

1. Name the scientist who said that Information Science is cluster of many disciplines where in the central core is 'Information'.
   (A) B.C. Brooks (B) Fritz Machlup
   (C) Daniel Bell (D) N.J. Belkin
2. Which committee recommended that imperial library be designated as copyright library ?
   (A) Fayzee Committee, 1939
   (B) Richey Committee, 1926
   (C) Statham Committee, 1932
   (D) Sadler Committee, 1916
3. Who was the first Librarian of Imperial Library, Calcutta ?
   (A) John MacFarlane (B) Harinath De
   (C) B.S. Kesavan (D) S.R. Ranganathan
4. Who coined the phrase 'Information Retrieval' ?
   (A) Calvin Mooers (B) S.R. Ranganathan
   (C) J.D. Brown (D) H.P. Luhan
5. In colon classification which indicator has been used for indicating interpolation ?
   (A) Comma (B) Hyphen
   (C) Astericks (D) Ampersand
6. What is Denudation ?
   (A) Is dividing classes to decrease the extension.
   (B) Is dividing classes to increase the extension.
   (C) Is dividing classes to increase intension and decrease extension.
   (D) Is dividing classes to decrease intension.

7. The International Body that coordinates the assignment of unique domain names, protocol address is

   (A) IGF (B) IANA

   (C) ICANN (D) ISP

8. Name the Indian Librarian who was honoured with the title of "Khan Bahadur" in 1935 by the British Government.

   (A) S.R. Ranganathan (B) B.S. Kesavan

   (C) K.M. Asadullah (D) D.R. Kalia

9. Which approach of information is not given by Wersig and Neveling ?

   (A) Structural Approach

   (B) Knowledge Approach

   (C) Meaning Approach

   (D) Technique Approach

10. Which of the following citation style manuals are from the same publisher ?

    (i) A.P.A. (ii) Turabian

    (iii) Chicago (iv) M.L.A.

    Codes :

    (A) (i) and (ii) are correct.

    (B) (ii) and (iii) are correct.

    (C) (iii) and (iv) are correct.

    (D) (ii) and (iv) are correct

11. Pre co-ordinate Indexing system perceives :

    (i) Syntax (ii) Semantic

    (iii) Context (iv) Relation

Codes :

(A) (i) and (iv) are correct

(B) (i), (ii) and (iii) are correct

(C) (ii), (iii) and (iv) are correct

(D) (ii) and (iv) are correct

12. An indispensable function of Thesaurus is to

(i) Knowledge Classification

(ii) Grouping the words together according to similarity of meaning

(iii) Representation of Relationship between concepts

(iv) Knowledge Engineering

Codes :

(A) (i) and (ii) are correct.

(B) (ii) and (iii) are correct.

(C) (iii) and (iv) are correct.

(D) (i) and (iv) are correct.

13. Which of the following are the basic components of expert system ?

(i) User interface

(ii) Knowledge base

(iii) Inference Mechanism

(iv) Schema

Codes :

(A) (i), (ii) and (iii) (B) (ii), (iii) and (iv)

(C) (iii), (iv) and (i) (D) (iv), (iii) and (ii)

14. Which of the following are the types factors studies under ANOVA ?

(i) Fixed (ii) Frequency

(iii) Calculated (iv) Random

Codes :

(A) (ii) and (iii) are correct.

(B) (i) and (iv) are correct.

(C) (i) and (iii) are correct.

(D) (ii) and (iv) are correct.

15. Which of the following are the models of communication ?

(i) Economic Theory Model

(ii) Stock Adjustment Model

(iii) Shanon Weaver Model

(iv) Schramm Model

Codes :

(A) (iii) and (iv) are correct.

(B) (ii) and (iii) are correct.

(C) (i) and (ii) are correct.

(D) (ii) and (iv) are correct.

16. Which of the following are criteria for Web evaluation ?

(i) Revision (ii) Response time

(iii) Format (iv) Archiving facility

Codes :

(A) (i) and (ii) are correct.

(B) (ii) and (iv) are correct.

(C) (i) and (iii) are correct.

(D) (ii) and (iii) are correct.

17. Which of the following countries do not have a code of Ethics for library profession ?

(i) America (ii) Sri Lanka

(iii) India (iv) China

Codes :

(A) (i) and (ii) are correct.

(B) (i) and (iv) are correct.

(C) (iii) and (ii) are correct.

(D) (iii) and (iv) are correct.

18. Which of the following are the components of Search Engine ?

(i) Spider (ii) TCP/IP

(iii) Search Mechanism (iv) Index

Codes :

(A) (iv), (i) and (ii) (B) (iii), (ii) and (i)

(C) (i), (iii) and (iv) (D) (ii), (iv) and (iii)

19. When the permission of copyright owner is not needed ?

(i) Criticism or review (ii) Translation

(iii) Research purpose (iv) Photocopy for sale

Codes :

(A) (i) and (iii) are correct.

(B) (i) and (iv) are correct.

(C) (iii) and (iv) are correct.

(D) (ii) and (iii) are correct.

20. Which of the following are Library net works ?

(i) Internet (ii) Indonet

(iii) INFLIBNET (iv) OCLC

Codes :

(A) (i) and (ii) are correct.

(B) (ii) and (iv) are correct.

(C) (iii) and (iv) are correct.

(D) (i) and (iv) are correct.

21. Arrange the following University Libraries according to the year of their establishment :
    (i) Madras University Library
    (ii) Delhi University Library
    (iii) Calcutta University Library
    (iv) Bombay University Library

    Codes :
    (A) (iv) (ii) (iii) (i) (B) (ii) (i) (iv) (iii)
    (C) (i) (iii) (ii) (iv) (D) (iii) (iv) (i) (ii)

22. What is the correct sequence of the following sections of the main entry as per classified catalogue code(CCC) ?
    (i) Note Section (ii) Leading Section
    (iii) Heading Section (iv) Title Section

    Codes :
    (A) (i) (iv) (iii) (ii) (B) (ii) (iii) (iv) (i)
    (C) (iii) (iv) (ii) (i) (D) (iv) (i) (iii) (ii)

23. Arrange the following indexing sources according to the year of their first publication :
    (i) Biological Abstracts
    (ii) Chemical Abstracts
    (iii) Index Medicus
    (iv) Poole's Index to PeriodicalLiterature

    Codes :
    (A) (i) (ii) (iii) (iv) (B) (iv) (iii) (ii) (i)
    (C) (iv) (ii) (i) (iii) (D) (i) (iv) (iii) (ii)

24. Arrange the following library associations according to their year of emergence :
    (i) CILIP (ii) ALA
    (iii) SLA (iv) ASLIB

Codes :

(A) (iii) (iv) (i) (ii) (B) (iii) (iv) (ii) (i)

(C) (ii) (iii) (iv) (i) (D) (ii) (iv) (i) (iii)

25. Match the following :

List - I	List - II
i. 1962	a. Library Advisory Committee
ii. 1963	b. Review Committee
iii. 1957	c. DRTC
iv. 1961	d. Sarada Ranganathan Endowned

Codes :	(a)	(b)	(c)	(d)
(A)	iv	iii	ii	i
(B)	iii	iv	i	ii
(C)	ii	i	iii	iv
(D)	i	iv	iii	ii

26. Match the following :

List - I	List - II
a. Facts on File Directory	i. Periodical
b. World of Learning	ii. Index
c. Concordance Digest	iii. Newspaper
d. Willing's Press Guide	iv. Directory

Codes :	(a)	(b)	(c)	(d)
(A)	i	iii	iv	ii
(B)	ii	i	iii	iv
(C)	iii	iv	ii	i
(D)	iv	ii	i	iii

27. Match the following :

List - I	List - II
a. McGroger Theory X	i. Less External Control
b. McGroger Theory Y	ii. PERT
c. Unity of Command	iii. Workers' Participation in decision Making
d. Time andCost	iv. All Powers in One Person

Codes :	**(a)**	**(b)**	**(c)**	**(d)**
(A)	iii	i	iv	ii
(B)	iv	i	iii	ii
(C)	ii	iv	iii	i
(D)	i	iii	ii	iv

28. Match the following :

List - I	List - II
a. User Education	i. James I Wyer
b. Conservative, Liberal and Moderate Theory of Reference Service	ii. Patricia B.Knapp
c. Minimum, Middling and Maximum Theories of Reference Service	iii. Eugene P.Sheehy
d. Guide to Reference Book	iv. Samuel Rothstein

Codes :	**(a)**	**(b)**	**(c)**	**(d)**
(A)	ii	i	iv	iii
(B)	i	ii	iv	iii
(C)	iii	ii	iv	i
(D)	iv	iii	i	ii

29. Match the following :

List - I	**List - II**
a. W. Edward Deming	i. Quality Control Circles
b. Joseph M. Juran	ii. TQM
c. Armand V. Feigenbaum	iii. Planning, Control, Improvement
d. Kaoru Ishikava	iv. Plan, Do, Check, Act (PDCA)

Codes :	**(a)**	**(b)**	**(c)**	**(d)**
(A)	ii	iii	iv	i
(B)	iv	ii	i	iii
(C)	iii	iv	i	ii
(D)	iv	iii	ii	i

30. Match the following :

List - I	**List - II**
a. Encyclopaedia of Associations	i. Secondary sources
b. Whitaker's Almanac	ii. Primary sources
c. LISA	iii. Directories
d. Economic Times	iv. Yearbooks

Codes :	**(a)**	**(b)**	**(c)**	**(d)**
(A)	iii	iv	i	ii
(B)	iv	iii	i	ii
(C)	ii	i	iv	iii
(D)	i	iv	iii	ii

31. Match the following :

List - I	**List - II**
a. Books in Print	i. National Bibliography
b. Social Science : A Bibliography of Doctoral Dissertations	ii. Trade Bibliography

c. Asian Social Science Bibliography	iii. National & Trade Bibliography
d. Cumulative Book Index	iv. Subject Bibliography

Codes :	**(a)**	**(b)**	**(c)**	**(d)**
(A)	ii	i	iv	iii
(B)	i	iii	ii	iv
(C)	iv	i	ii	iii
(D)	iii	ii	i	iv

32. Match the following :

List - I	**List - II**
a. Dictionary	i. Foreign Language
b. Glossary	ii. Synonymous terms
c. Thesaurus	iii. Words, Synonyms
d. Lexicon	iv. Specific subjects

Codes :	**(a)**	**(b)**	**(c)**	**(d)**
(A)	iii	iv	ii	i
(B)	iv	iii	i	ii
(C)	i	ii	iv	iii
(D)	ii	iv	iii	i

33. Match the following :

List - I	**List - II**
a. Curriculum Development Committee (P. N. Kaula)	i. 2001
b. Curriculum Development Committee (C. R. Karrisidappa)	ii. 1992
c. Working Group on Libraries	iii. 1910
d. Library Movement in Baroda	iv. 1964

Codes :	**(a)**	**(b)**	**(c)**	**(d)**
(A)	ii	i	iv	iii
(B)	i	ii	iv	iii
(C)	iv	ii	iii	i
(D)	iii	iv	ii	i

34. Match the following :

List - I	**List - II**
a. Current Biography	i. Russia
b. Index Translationum	ii. University of Illinois
c. VINITI	iii. U.S.A.
d. Library Trends	iv. UNESCO

Codes :	**(a)**	**(b)**	**(c)**	**(d)**
(A)	iii	iv	i	ii
(B)	iv	i	ii	iii
(C)	i	ii	iii	iv
(D)	ii	iii	iv	i

35. Match the following :

List - I	**List - II**
a. Herbert Hicks	i. The Elements of Administration
b. F.W. Taylor	ii. The Management of Organisation
c. Henry Fayol	iii. Scientific Management
d. Colonel L.Urwick	iv. Administrative Management

Codes :	**(a)**	**(b)**	**(c)**	**(d)**
(A)	i	iv	ii	iii
(B)	iv	ii	iii	i
(C)	ii	iii	iv	i
(D)	iii	iv	i	ii

36. **Assertion (A) :** In the study of History, as an academic discipline, a primary source is an artefact, a document, a recording or other source of

information that was created during the event or immediately after the event.

Reason (R) : Primary sources are considered as original material or evidences about the topic and are fundamental to history.

Codes :

(A) (A) is true, but (R) is false.

(B) (A) is false, but (R) is true.

(C) Both (A) and (R) are true.

(D) Both (A) and (R) are false.

37. **Assertion (A)** : Indian National Bibliography is the most comprehensive source of Indian publications.

Reason (R) : National Library of Kolkata is entitled to receive one copy of each Indian publication under Delivery of Book Act.

Codes :

(A) (A) is true, but (R) is false.

(B) (A) is false, but (R) is true.

(C) Both (A) and (R) are true.

(D) Both (A) and (R) are false.

38. **Assertion (A)** : As per the generally accepted principles of construction of statistical tabulation, every table should have a clear, concise and adequate title so as to make the table intelligible without reference to the text and this titleshould always be placed just below the body of the table.

Reason (R) : A statistical table which reflects its title just above the table and supply information about several interrelated characteristics of data makes thetable unwield and inconvenient.

Codes :

(A) Both (A) and (R) are true.

(B) Both (A) and (R) are false.

(C) (A) is true, but (R) is false.

(D) (A) is false, but (R) is true.

39. **Assertion (A) :** Knowledge Management involves a number of assets and value added to .hem.

Reason (R) : Knowledge Management is the core activity of information transfer.

Codes :

(A) (A) is true, but (R) is false.

(B) (A) is true, but (R) is partiallytrue.

(C) Both (A) and (R) are true.

(D) (A) is partially true but (R) istrue.

40. **Assertion (A) :** According to Horton and Merchant, information is a commodity like other resources.

Reason (R) : Information is a tangible commodity.

Codes :

(A) (A) is true, but (R) is false.

(B) Both (A) and (R) are false.

(C) Both (A) and (R) are true.

(D) (A) is false, (R) is true.

41. **Assertion (A) :** Reference section in a Library became insignificant.

Reason (R) : The Web. 2.0 services replaces the reference desk services.

Codes :

(A) (A) is true, but (R) is false.

(B) Both (A) and (R) are true.

(C) Both (A) and (R) are false.

(D) (A) is false and (R) is true.

42. **Assertion (A) :** Newspaper Digests are the best sources of information to get current and authentic information like books.

Reason (R) : These sources are compiled by going through various newspapers.

Codes :

(A) Both (A) and (R) are true.

(B) (A) is partially true but (R) is true.

(C) Both (A) and (R) are false.

(D) (A) is true but (R) is partially true.

43. **Assertion (A) :** Encyclopaedias have been regarded as the substitute of all categories of reference sources as these provide all types of information.

Reason (R) : Encyclopaedias provide comprehensive information on all aspects which otherwise are scattered in different categories of reference sources.

Codes :

(A) (R) is true but (A) is false.

(B) Both (A) and (R) are true.

(C) (A) is true but (R) is false.

(D) Both (A) and (R) are false.

44. **Assertion (A) :** Chi-square is an important non-parametric test which does not require rigid assumptions in respect of the type of population being studied.

Reason (R) : Since ÷2 is a nonparametric test, it requires onlythe degrees of freedom (implicitly, the size of the population) for using the test.

Codes :

(A) (A) is true, but (R) is false.

(B) Both (A) and (R) are true.

(C) (A) is false but (R) is true.

(D) Both (A) and (R) are false.

45. **Assertion (A) :** Information is commodity.

Reason (R) : Commodity is a marketable item produced to satisfy human wants or needs.

Codes :

(A) (A) is false, and (R) is true.

(B) (R) is false and (A) is true.

(C) Both (A) and (R) are false.

(D) Both (A) and (R) are true.

Read the passage given below and answer the questions based on your understanding of the passage (Question Nos. 46-50) :

According to Wikipedia 'socialmedia' is media designed to be disseminated through social interaction, created using highly accessible and scalable publishing techniques. According to search engine partner, the term socialmedia describes media that is posed by theuser and can take many different forms. Some type of social media are forums, message boards, blogs, wikis and podcarts. Social media applications include Google, Facebook and You tube. In social media, communication takes place through messages, status updates, voice chats etc. or through photos/videos sharing, games, virtual goods etc. Antony Mayfield in hise-book titled 'What is Social Media'? has defined social media as online media, which encourages contributions and feedback from every one who is interested, is open to feedback and participation, is a two way conversation, allows communities to form quickly and communicate effectively to share common interests and thrive on their connectedness. The growth of social media is phenomenal. It is being used by allnetizens all over the world to a great extentin all areas including business, government, fashion etc. A research conducted by the Institute for Prospective Technological Studies (IPTS) indicates thathigh take up of social media application outside formal educational settings provides new opportunities for innovation and modernisation. With this growing trend, political leaders have also realized its importance as an effective tool to spread awareness and to reach out their voters. Democratic presidential candidate Barack Obama used it during the Presidential elections. Since then, social media is being highly used by a number of politicians all over the world. Myspace has more than 7400 discussion groups related to politics. According to a survey by manpower, 29% of the companies in America and 20% of companies worldwide have a social media policy. People even update themselves through micro-blogging on every aspect of human life including the natural and human diasters. In China, Twitter became the first media in the world to break the news of the Wenzhou earthquake. Social media is being used in fashion industry as well to generate interest in a brand through publicity across online communities andwebsites.

India is one of the most culturally, linguistically and genetically diverseregions having more than one billion people. It is ranked third in Asia in terms of the internet users and quite a number of them are using social media. In fact, approximately 60 millions to 65 millionsnetizens in India open most of their time on social media/ networking sites.

46. Who defined social media as 'online media' which encourages contributions and feedback from everyone who is interested ?

(A) Wikepedia
(B) Institute for Prospective Technological Studies (IPTS)
(C) Myspace
(D) Antony Myfield

47. Who used the social media for conversing during recent Presidential Election in U.S.A. ?
(A) Jimmy Carter (B) Barack Obama
(C) George Bush (D) John F. Kennedy

48. In China, which social media became the first media to break the news of earthquake ?
(A) Facebook (B) Youtube
(C) Twitter (D) Myzamana

49. In Asia, which country is ranked third in terms of using social media by the people ?
(A) China (B) Pakistan
(C) Japan (D) India

50. Which social website has more than 7400 discussion groups relate to politics ?
(A) Orkut (B) Myspace
(C) Facebook (D) Twitter

ANSWERS

1. B	2. B	3. A	4. A	5. C	6. C
7. C	8. C	9. D	10. B	11. C	12. B
13. A	14. B	15. A	16. B	17. C	18. C
19. A	20. C	21. D	22. B	23. B	24. C
25. B	26. C	27. A	28. A	29. D	30. A
31. A	32. A	33. A	34. A	35. C	36. C
37. B	38. B	39. B	40. A	41. D	42. B
43. C	44. B	45. D	46. D	47. B	48. C
49. D	50. B				

SEP. 2015 MH-SET PAPER-II

1. First state-aided Public Library inIndia was established by :
   (A) William Jones
   (B) W.A. Borden
   (C) Maharaja Sayajirao Gaekwad
   (D) Raja Ram Mohan Roy
2. In a virtual library :
   (A) There is no corresponding physical collection
   (B) Collection is available online aswell as offline
   (C) Collection is available online aswell as print form
   (D) Collection is available on CD aswell as print form
3. DOS, UNIX, LINUX, Windows are examples of :
   (A) Application software
   (B) System software
   (C) Computer language
   (D) Operating system
4. Lotka's law is related to :
   (A) Word frequency count
   (B) Scientific productivity
   (C) Distribution of papers in theperiodicals
   (D) Citation analysis
5. Which of the following cannotbe considered as probability sampling ?
   (A) Lottery method of sampling
   (B) Systematic sampling
   (C) Snowball sampling
   (D) Cluster sampling

6. Who provided the first explication of a theory of scales for the measurement of operational variables?
   (A) E.S. Pearson (B) S.S. Stevens
   (C) F.W. Lancaster (D) Steve Leach
7. The standard deviation of a population is :
   (A) Mean of the squared deviations
   (B) Mean deviation
   (C) Simply the variance
   (D) Simply the square root of theVariance
8. Abstracts in LISA (Library and Information Science Abstracts) are arranged according to :
   (A) DDC
   (B) Colon classification
   (C) A special scheme ofclassification
   (D) UDC
9. According to Dr. S.R. Ranganathan the proportion of expenditure of University Library budget on books and other reading materials should be :
   (A) 60% (B) 50%
   (C) 40% (D) 30%
10. A Standard TQM tool would be :
   (A) Questionnaire (B) Interview
   (C) Diary (D) Flow chart
11. Which management school regards management as a Universal process ?
   (A) The Human Relations School
   (B) The Classical School
   (C) The System School
   (D) The Social Systems School

12. In 1990 4P's were translated into 4C's of marketing. Here 'Promotion' (P) represents :
    (A) Cost to users
    (B) Customer needs and wants
    (C) Communication
    (D) Convenience
13. Systems study involves :
    (A) Analysis only
    (B) Analysis, evaluation and design
    (C) Analysis and design only
    (D) Analysis and evaluation only
14. Likert's name is associated with :
    (A) Theory of Motivation
    (B) Evolving organizational structure
    (C) Style of leadership
    (D) Decision-making theory
15. Management of the Library by Library Committee is an example of ....
    (A) MBO
    (B) Participative Management
    (C) Decentralisation
    (D) Consultative Management
16. Delegation of authority involves :
    (A) Responsibility only
    (B) Authority and Accountability only
    (C) Accountability and Responsibility only
    (D) Responsibility, Authority and Accountability
17. Index Translationum is a world bibliography of translations of :

(A) Periodical articles
(B) Books
(C) Books and periodical articles
(D) Patents

18. With whom would you relate 'Dissertation Abstracts International'?
(A) Pro-quest (B) Springer
(C) Emerald (D) OUP

19. INSPEC database records ....
(A) Full text
(B) Index and Abstract
(C) Numerical
(D) Abstract and Full text

20. Which of the following journals is available only in electronic form ?
(A) D-Lib Magazine
(B) Journal of Documentation
(C) Library Quarterly
(D) Library Trends

21. The best strategy for a high recall for a user who has one concrete reference with him would be :
(A) Building block
(B) Successive fractions
(C) Citation Pearl Growing
(D) Boolean search

22. Name the author of 'Grammar of Classification' :
(A) S.R. Ranganathan (B) H.E. Bliss
(C) W.C.B. Sayers (D) J. Mills

23. 'OCLC' was founded in the year :

(A) 2001 (B) 2000

(C) 1967 (D) 1978

24. Who is responsible for registration of Indian Publishers ?

(A) INFLIBNET (B) DELNET

(C) RRRLF (D) R.R. BOWKER

25. Which of the following evaluation techniques is used in forecasting ?

(A) Market research

(B) Performance evaluation

(C) Cost-benefit analysis

(D) Delphi technique

26. The basic components of network analysis in PERT/ CPM are :

(A) Event and performance

(B) Event and activity

(C) Activity and conditions

(D) Conditions and dummy activity

27. National Library (Kolkata) receives books on deposit under :

(A) Registration of Books Act, 1867

(B) The Delivery of Books Act, 1956

(C) The Copyright Act, 1985

(D) Right to Information Act, 2003

28. Who was the first Librarian of Imperial Library ?

(A) John Macfarlane

(B) J.A. Chapman

(C) Khan Bahadur MA Asadullah

(D) B.S. Kesavan

29. In the context of extension services mark the odd one :

(A) Public lectures and talks byeminent persons
(B) Celebration of festivals
(C) Arranging the music show etc.
(D) Providing information pin pointedly

30. Bodleian Library is in the University of :
(A) Cambridge (B) Oxford
(C) Harvard (D) Stanford

31. When was Encyclopedia Britannica first published?
(A) 1758 (B) 1768
(C) 1865 (D) 1875

32. Who wrote the book titled "An Introduction to Library Classification" ?
(A) J.D. Brown
(B) S.R. Ranganathan
(C) W.C. Berwick Sayers
(D) Howard Phillips

33. The concept of systematic indexing was devised by:
(A) E.J. Coates (B) J.E.L. Farradane
(C) H.P. Luhn (D) J. Keiser

34. SQL stands for :
(A) Structured Query Language
(B) Standard Query Language
(C) Systematic Query Language
(D) Soft Query Language

35. Which one of the following reference source attempts to explain the literary terms and works ?
(A) Oxford Dictionary of Quotations
(B) Who's Who of Indian Writers
(C) Information please Almanac
(D) Benet's Reader's Encyclopedia

36. 'Shodhagangotri' Project is concerned with :
    (A) Theses (B) Synopsis of Theses
    (C) Books (D) E-Journals
37. The formula for the Chi-square testis :
    (A) a2 (B) b2
    (C) _2 (D) c2
38. Who is the author of the book"Organization of Knowledge in Libraries" ?
    (A) S.R. Ranganathan (B) W.C.B. Sayers
    (C) J. Mills (D) H.E. Bliss
39. Name the two states of India, in which the Public Libraries Act was passed in 1989 ?
    (A) Kerala and Haryana
    (B) Haryana and Goa
    (C) Manipur and Mizoram
    (D) Kerala and Goa
40. The first Library Association formedin India is :
    (A) Andhra Pradesh Library Association
    (B) Bengal Library Association
    (C) Indian Library Association
    (D) Madras Library Association
41. Who has introduced Advancement of Librarianship Programme ?
    (A) IFLA (B) UNESCO
    (C) FID (D) ICSU
42. The significant characteristic of an analogue signal is :
    (A) it is discrete (B) it is continuous
    (C) it transmits fast (D) it has less noise

43. Identify the Dublin Coremeta data element that is not related to the resource as intellectual property :

(A) Creator (B) Publisher

(C) Title (D) Contributor

44. Prof. D.P. Chattopadhyaya was Chairman of the committee related to :

(A) National Policy on Library and Information System

(B) Development of Libraries and their Organization

(C) Curriculum Development in Library and Information Science

(D) Public Libraries in India

45. Zero Based Budgeting means :

(A) A budgeting without funds

(B) Budgeting afresh

(C) Budgeting based on previous year's expenses

(D) Performance budget

46. Which indexing system uses a single term and an accession number of the document as an indicator of reference ?

(A) POPSI (B) KWIC

(C) Index of DDC (D) Relative Index

47. Identify the entity that belongs to first group of entities in FRBR :

(A) Object (B) Event

(C) Concept (D) Expression

48. In CCF, the equivalent of leader in MARC 21, is called:

(A) Directory (B) Record Label

(C) Record Separator (D) Data Fields

49. Which of the following is not a canon for characteristics ?
    (A) Canon of Differentiation
    (B) Canon of Exclusiveness
    (C) Canon of Ascertainability
    (D) Canon of Permanence
50. Which of the following is an example of equivalence relationship ?
    (A) Nervous system—Centralnervous system
    (B) Freedom—Liberty
    (C) Hunting—Hunters
    (D) Weaving—Cloth

ANSWERS

1. C	2. A	3. D	4. B	5. C	6. B
7. D	8. C	9. C	10. D	11. B	12. C
13. B	14. C	15. B	16. D	17. B	18. A
19. B	20. A	21. C	22. C	23. C	24. C
25. D	26. B	27. B	28. A	29. D	30. B
31. B	32. C	33. D	34. A	35. D	36. B
37. C	38. D	39. A	40. A	41. A	42. B
43. C	44. A	45. B	46. B	47. D	48. B
49. B	50. B				

SEP 2015 MH-SET PAPER-III

1. Lotka's law of scientific productivity is expressed by the equation :

   Y = C/Xn Here Y represents :

   (A) Frequency of authors making X contribution
   (B) The number of articles
   (C) Frequency of authors writing only one paper
   (D) The year of publication

2. Identify the factor that may cause in consistency in indexing :

   (A) When number of concepts represented are less
   (B) When the indexer is a very experienced person
   (C) When number of concepts represented are more
   (D) When a thesaurus is used to control the vocabulary

3. Arrange the following catalogue codes in the chronological sequence of their publication and choose the correct answer by using the codes given below :

   (i) Classified cataloguing code
   (ii) AACR-2
   (iii) ALA Code
   (iv) British Museum Code

   Codes :

   (A) (iii), (i), (ii), (iv) (B) (iii), (iv), (ii), (i)
   (C) (iv), (iii), (i), (ii) (D) (ii), (i), (iii), (iv)

4. Which of the following is a primary document ?

   (A) Science
   (B) Indian Science Abstracts
   (C) Science Citation Index
   (D) Chemical Abstracts Service

5. Match the following List I and List II and choose the correct answer by using the codes given below:

	List-I		List-II
(i)	RTI	(a)	1972
(ii)	Delivery of Book	(b)	2005 Act
(iii)	Press and	(c)	1867 Registration of Book Act
(iv)	RRRLF	(d)	1954

Codes :	**(i)**	**(ii)**	**(iii)**	**(iv)**
(A)	(b)	(d)	(c)	(a)
(B)	(d)	(b)	(a)	(c)
(C)	(a)	(d)	(b)	(c)
(D)	(c)	(a)	(d)	(b)

6. Match the following List-I and List-II and choose the correct answer by using the codes given below:

	List-I		List-II
(i)	DOAJ	(a)	Science Direct
(ii)	Thomson Reuters	(b)	Web of Science
(iii)	Elsevier	(c)	Open Access Journals
(iv)	ASLIB Proceedings	(d)	Emerald

Codes :	**(i)**	**(ii)**	**(iii)**	**(iv)**
(A)	(b)	(d)	(c)	(a)
(B)	(a)	(c)	(d)	(b)
(C)	(c)	(b)	(a)	(d)
(D)	(d)	(c)	(a)	(b)

7. The main entry heading according to AACR2 (Revised Edition) for a sound recording of the book by Lewis Carroll titled 'Alice's Adventures in Wonder land; read and sung by Cyril Ritchard; the music composed by Alec Wilder and played by the New York Woodwind Quintet would be :

(A) Carroll, Lewis

(B) Ritchard, Cyril

(C) Wilder, Alec

(D) New York, Woodwind Quintet

8. LANs are distinguished from other types of networks by three characteristics ?

(i) Speed

(ii) Size

(iii) Topology

(iv) Transmission technology

Select the correct answer :

Codes :

(A) (ii) (iii) (iv) are correct

(B) (ii) (iii) (i) are correct

(C) (iii) (iv) (i) are correct

(D) (i) (ii) (iv) are correct

9. While formulating a budget for a library, the following factors have to be considered :

(a) Type of Organisation

(b) Size of the Organisation

(c) Type of Users

(d) Number of books issued to a users

Select the correct answer :

Codes :

(A) (a), (b) and (c) are correct

(B) (b), (c) and (d) are correct

(C) (c), (d) and (a) are correct

(D) (a), (b) and (d) are correct

10. Match the following List-I and List-II and choose the correct answer by using the codes given below:

List-I	List-II
(i) In AACR-II connecting symbol for size of the document	(a) Colon
(ii) Connecting symbol for statement of responsibility	(b) Plus
(iii) Connecting symbol between place and name of the publisher	(c) Semicolon
(iv) Connecting symbol for accompanying material	(d) Diagonal Slash

Codes :	**(i)**	**(ii)**	**(iii)**	**(iv)**
(A)	(d)	(c)	(b)	(a)
(B)	(c)	(d)	(a)	(b)
(C)	(c)	(a)	(b)	(d)
(D)	(d)	(c)	(b)	(a)

11. Match List-I and List-II and choose the correct answer by using the codes given below :

List-I	List-II
(i) Books in Print	(a) Guardian
(ii) Newspaper	(b) Information Please
(iii) News Digest	(c) R.R. Bowker
(iv) Almanac	(d) Asian Recorder

Codes :	**(i)**	**(ii)**	**(iii)**	**(iv)**
(A)	(c)	(d)	(a)	(b)
(B)	(c)	(d)	(b)	(a)
(C)	(a)	(c)	(d)	(b)
(D)	(c)	(a)	(d)	(b)

12. Match List-I and List-II and choose the correct answer by using the code given below :

List-I	**List-II**
(i) Papyrus	(a) Skin of Calf
(ii) Parchment	(b) Skin of Sheep
(iii) Vellum	(c) Ancient Paper
(iv) Birch	(d) Bark of a Tree

Codes :	**(i)**	**(ii)**	**(iii)**	**(iv)**
(A)	(c)	(b)	(a)	(d)
(B)	(b)	(c)	(d)	(a)
(C)	(d)	(a)	(b)	(c)
(D)	(a)	(d)	(b)	(c)

13. If selected plays of Vijay Tendulkar have been translated by Yogesh Sharma and compiled with an introduction by S.M. Chari, the main Entry in AACR II Revised Edition would be made under :
    (A) Tendulkar, Vijay
    (B) Sharma, Yogesh
    (C) Chari, S.M.
    (D) Selected Plays of Vijay Tendulkar
14. **Statement (a) :** LISA is an abstracting database which has independent thesaurus for searching abstract.
    Statement (b) : LISA abstracting database is available in electronics and print form select the correct answer :
    (A) Statement (a) is wrong but (b) is correct
    (B) Both statements (a) and (b) are false
    (C) Both statements (a) and (b) are correct
    (D) Statement (b) is wrong but (a) is correct
15. Arrange the following Associations as per their establishment year :

(a) ALA (b) LA

(c) IFLA (d) SLA

Select the correct answer :

Codes :

(A) (a) (b) (d) (c) (B) (b) (a) (c) (d)

(C) (d) (a) (b) (c) (D) (c) (a) (b) (d)

16. Match List-I and List-II and choose the correct answer by using the codes given below :

List-I	List-II
(i) Baroda Library Association	(a) 1927
(ii) Uttar Pradesh Library Association	(b) 1914
(iii) Madras Library Association	(c) 1910
(iv) Andhra Pradesh Library Association	(d) 1956

Codes :	**(i)**	**(ii)**	**(iii)**	**(iv)**
(A)	(d)	(c)	(b)	(a)
(B)	(c)	(d)	(a)	(b)
(C)	(c)	(d)	(b)	(a)
(D)	(a)	(b)	(d)	(c)

17. **Assertion (A) :** Cataloguing in Publication (CIP) is initiated by IFLA.

Reason (R) : It helps individual libraries in copying down the data.

Select the correct answer from the codes given below :

Codes :

(A) (A) is false but (R) is true

(B) (A) is true but (R) is false

(C) Both (A) and (R) are false

(D) Both (A) and (R) are true

18. Match List-I and List-II and choose the correct answer by using the codes given below :

	List-I	**List-II**
(i)	Radhakrishnan Commission	(a) 1979
(ii)	Mudaliar Commission	(b) 1964
(iii)	Kothari Commission	(c) 1952
(iv)	Karnataka State University Review Committee	(d) 1948

Codes :	**(i)**	**(ii)**	**(iii)**	**(iv)**
(A)	(d)	(c)	(b)	(a)
(B)	(a)	(c)	(d)	(b)
(C)	(b)	(a)	(c)	(d)
(D)	(d)	(c)	(a)	(b)

19. A router :
    (A) Receives a signal and retransmits it at a higher level
    (B) Helps you interface with another network
    (C) Essentially translates protocols
    (D) Forwards data packets between tale communications networks

20. ISO-2709 exchange format specifies which of the following :
    (A) The tag to be used
    (B) Structure for MARC
    (C) Size of RFID tag
    (D) Specification for ICT Components

21. Which of the following can be identified with Ranganathan's fifth law of Library Science ?
    (A) Providing SDI Service
    (B) Providing Open Access
    (C) Providing analytical entries
    (D) Opening Branch Libraries

22. The term 'Canon' was introduced by :
    (A) S.R. Ranganathan (B) H.E. Bliss
    (C) W.C.B. Sayers (D) E.C. Richardson
23. According to CCC which one of the following entry does not give Class Number ?
    (A) BIE (B) CIE
    (C) Main Entry (D) CRIE
24. The term 'Exponential Growth' is referred to :
    (A) Linear Growth
    (B) Geometrical Progression
    (C) Arithmetical Progression
    (D) Normal Frequency Distribution
25. Data mining is :
    (A) A technique for searching large scale databases
    (B) A database used for reporting
    (C) A repository of an organisation's stored data
    (D) The process of designing, building and maintaining and organisation's database
26. Match List-I and List-II and choose the correct answer by using the codes given below :

List-I	List-II
(i) E spirit-de-corps	(a) Herzberg
(ii) Theory X and theory Y	(b) Maslow
(iii) Hierarchy of human needs	(c) Douglas McGregor
(iv) Hygiene-motivation theory	(d) Henry Fayol

Codes :	(i)	(ii)	(iii)	(iv)
(A)	(a)	(b)	(c)	(d)
(B)	(b)	(c)	(d)	(a)
(C)	(c)	(d)	(a)	(b)
(D)	(d)	(c)	(b)	(a)

27. Identify the statement that is not true about ISDN :
    (A) ISDN is not limited to transmission of voice only
    (B) ISDN is simply a point-to-point solution like a leased line
    (C) ISDN is purely digital communication
    (D) ISDN can provide simultaneous voice, video and text transmission
28. 'Half Life' relates to :
    (A) Rate of Growth (B) Rate of Obsolescence
    (C) Degree of Scatter (D) Life of a Journal
29. In experimental research method treatment is administered to members of the :
    (A) Control Group
    (B) Both Experimental and Control Group
    (C) Experimental Group
    (D) To neither of the two groups
30. Which is not applicable to the Digital Library ?
    (A) Digital library is a logical extension of the traditional library
    (B) Digital library is a system that provides community of users with coherent access to a large repository of knowledge
    (C) Digital library is an organisation that does not require the specialised staff
    (D) Digital library is used by manyat the same time
31. When the value of the correlation coefficient r is near –1 (i.e., minus one), it indicates ?
    (A) A perfect inverse relationship
    (B) A perfect direct relationship
    (C) A strong inverse relationship
    (D) No correlation

32. **Statement (1) :** RRRLF which is an agency that supports public library services and systems is not an autonomous organization.

    Statement (2) : RRRLF is fully financed by the Ministry of Culture, Government of India.

    In the above statement :

    (A) Both (1) and (2) are true

    (B) (1) is true but (2) is false

    (C) (1) is false but (2) is true

    (D) Both (1) and (2) are false

33. **Statement (1) :** The British library is very young as it was set up under the British Library Act that was passed in 1972.

    Statement (2) : The Library of the British Museum which was set up in 1753 is part of the British Library today.

    In the above statements :

    (A) Both (1) and (2) are true

    (B) (1) is true but (2) is false

    (C) (1) is false but (2) is true

    (D) Both (1) and (2) are false

34. The concept of 'Bibliographic Coupling' was given by :

    (A) Small and Griffith (B) M.M. Kessler

    (C) Allan Pritchard (D) Melvin Weinstock

35. Match List-I and List-II and choose the correct answer by using the codes given below :

List-I	List-II
(i) John Macfarlane	(a) Library of Congress
(ii) B.S. Kesavan	(b) British Museum Library
(iii) John J. Beckley	(c) Imperial Library
(iv) Anthony Panizzi	(d) National Library of India

Codes :	**(i)**	**(ii)**	**(iii)**	**(iv)**
(A)	(d)	(c)	(a)	(b)
(B)	(c)	(d)	(a)	(b)
(C)	(d)	(c)	(a)	(b)
(D)	(a)	(c)	(b)	(d)

36. The new name of Standing Conference of National and University Libraries (SCONUL) is :
    (A) Standing college, National and University Libraries
    (B) Society of college, National and University Libraries
    (C) Standing Council on National and University Libraries
    (D) Standing Committee on National and University Libraries

37. In the hypothesis, "shelf height is a major determining factor of book use", shelf height is :
    (A) The dependent variable
    (B) Independent variable
    (C) It is not a variable
    (D) It is a sample

38. Match List-I and List-II and choose the correct answer by using the codes given below :

List-I	**List-II**
(i) American Library Association	(a) 1946
(ii) Canadian Library Association	(b) 1932
(iii) Special Library Association	(c) 1909
(iv) The Association of Research Libraries	(d) 1876

Codes :	**(i)**	**(ii)**	**(iii)**	**(iv)**
(A)	(a)	(c)	(d)	(b)
(B)	(c)	(a)	(b)	(d)
(C)	(d)	(a)	(b)	(c)
(D)	(d)	(a)	(c)	(b)

39. Canon of Sought Heading takes care of :
    (A) Permanence of headings
    (B) Approaches of users
    (C) Arrangement of entries
    (D) Consistency in preparation of entries
40. Canon of Prepotence :
    (A) Decides the position of an entry among the various entries in a catalogue
    (B) Prescribes that the information on the title page of a document and its overflow pages should determine the choice and rendering of headings
    (C) Says that headings of a catalogue entry should be individualised
    (D) Prescribes that rules of a catalogue should be revised from time to time
41. 'World of Learning' is published from :
    (A) Oxford (B) London
    (C) Cambridge (D) Yorkshire
42. Double Colons (: :) are used in :
    (A) Library of Congress Classification Scheme
    (B) Colon Classification 7th Edition
    (C) Universal Decimal Classification
    (D) Bibliographic Classification
43. Match List-I and List-II and choose the correct answer by using the codes given below :

List-I	List-II
(i) National Medical Library	(a) Mumbai
(ii) Saraswati Mahal Library	(b) Tanjore
(iii) Bhandarkar Oriental Research Institute's Library	(c) Delhi
(iv) Asiatic Society's Library	(d) Pune

Codes :	**(i)**	**(ii)**	**(iii)**	**(iv)**
(A)	(c)	(b)	(d)	(a)
(B)	(a)	(b)	(c)	(d)
(C)	(b)	(c)	(a)	(d)
(D)	(d)	(a)	(b)	(c)

44. **Statement (1)** : The copyright laws prevent unauthorised production of any literary and artistic work.

Statement (2) : The copyright is enfringed even if the copy is made or supplied by or on behalf of a librarian.

In the above statements :

(A) Both (1) and (2) are true

(B) Both (1) and (2) are false

(C) (1) is true but (2) is false

(D) (1) is false but (2) is true

45. General Information Programme was launched by:

(A) UNESCO (B) IFLA

(C) FID (D) ISO

46. Which of the following canons of cataloguing prescribes that the information found on title and its overflow pages should be used for preparing main entry ?

(A) Canon of context

(B) Canon of prepotence

(C) Canon of Ascertain ability

(D) Canon of Sought Heading

47. Match List-I and List-II and choose the correct answer by using the codes given below :

List-I	**List-II**
(i) NISCAIR	(a) Union Catalogue of Social Science Periodicals and Serials in India
(ii) INFLIBNET	(b) Technology focus
(iii) NASSDOC	(c) TKDL
(iv) DESIDOC	(d) CALIBER

Codes :	**(i)**	**(ii)**	**(iii)**	**(iv)**
(A)	(d)	(a)	(c)	(b)
(B)	(c)	(d)	(a)	(b)
(C)	(c)	(a)	(b)	(d)
(D)	(b)	(c)	(d)	(a)

48. Which of the following is a strategy for Knowledge Management ?

(A) Indexing (B) Annotation

(C) Personalisation (D) Abstracting

49. Which of the following is an example of Associative relationship ?

(A) Vertebrates—Mammals

(B) Photocopies—Xeroxes

(C) Polling—Public Opinion

(D) Polyvinyl Chloride/PVC

50. In an Empirical study on impact of internet on reading, 'reading' would be :

(A) An independent variable

(B) The dependent variable

(C) An intervening variable

(D) The continuous variable

51. Match List-I and List-II and choose the correct answer by using the codes given below :

List-I	List-II
(i) Fusion	(a) Metaphysics
(ii) Fission	(b) Humanities
(iii) Cluster	(c) Indology
(iv) Agglomeration	(d) Astrophysics

Codes :	(i)	(ii)	(iii)	(iv)
(A)	(b)	(d)	(a)	(c)
(B)	(a)	(b)	(c)	(d)
(C)	(d)	(c)	(b)	(a)
(D)	(d)	(a)	(c)	(b)

52. Invisible colleges are :
(A) Network of individuals interested in a subject field
(B) Group of scientific meetings
(C) Both (A) and (B)
(D) Neither (A) nor (B)

53. Match List-I and List-II and choose the correct answer by using the codes given below :

List-I	List-II
(i) CeRA	(a) Education
(ii) FORSA	(b) Agriculture
(iii) INDEST	(c) Astrophysics
(iv) ERIC	(d) Engineering

Codes :	(i)	(ii)	(iii)	(iv)
(A)	(a)	(d)	(c)	(b)
(B)	(d)	(a)	(b)	(c)
(C)	(c)	(b)	(d)	(a)
(D)	(b)	(c)	(d)	(a)

54. In Building Block Search Strategy adding an extra facet would result in :
    (A) Higher recall
    (B) Higher precision
    (C) Increase in recall as well as precision
    (D) Lower precision

55. Which is not applicable to extensible Mark up Language ?
    (A) It is compatible with SGML
    (B) It is usable over Internet
    (C) XML documents are easy to create
    (D) It has to do with semantics to Data

56. **Statement (1)** : Cross-reference entry of the classification catalogue code is a number entry.

    Statement (2) : It is entered under the dominant class of the document.

    In the above statements :
    (A) Both (1) and (2) are true
    (B) (1) is true but (2) is false
    (C) (1) is false but (2) is true
    (D) Both (1) and (2) are false

57. Arrange the following Public Library Acts according to their year of enactment.
    (i) Mizoram Public Libraries Act
    (ii) Tamil Nadu Public Libraries Act
    (iii) Haryana Public Libraries Act
    (iv) Orissa Public Libraries Act

    Codes :

    (A) (iv) (iii) (i) (ii) (B) (ii) (iii) (i) (iv)
    (C) (ii) (i) (iv) (iii) (D) (iii) (ii) (i) (iv)

58. ....Search gives more information output :

(A) Boolean 'And' (B) Boolean 'Or'

(C) Boolean 'Not' (D) Phrase Search

59. **Assertion (A) :** Loose Assemblage is the process of linking together different classes.

Reason (R) : The number of subjects are restricted.

In the above statements :

(A) (A) is true but (R) is false

(B) (A) is false but (R) is true

(C) Both (A) and (R) are true

(D) Both (A) and (R) are false

60. Identify the MARC tag that is used for variable fields containing data related to subject access to the document :

(A) 7 XX (B) 6 XX

(C) 5 XX (D) 2 XX

61. Which of the following is not the characteristics of the information society ?

(A) Information used as an economic source

(B) People use information intensively in their activities

(C) Information sector within the economy is developed

(D) Dependence on traditional Knowledge

62. How to write the size of book having height 21.5 cm and width 30 cm ina catalogue entry according toAACR II ?

(A) 21 cm (B) 22 cm

(C) 21 × 30 cm (D) 22 × 30 cm

63. According to ISBD format the GMDis recorded :

(A) After the statement of responsibility
(B) After the title proper
(C) After the subtitle
(D) After the series statement

64. Match List-I and List-II and choose the correct answer by using the codes given below :

List-I	List-II
(i) Maslow	(a) Hygienic factors
(ii) McGregor	(b) Immaturity /Maturity
(iii) Argyris	(c) Theory Y
(iv) Herzberg	(d) Hierarchy of needs

Codes :	**(i)**	**(ii)**	**(iii)**	**(iv)**
(A)	(a)	(b)	(c)	(d)
(B)	(d)	(a)	(b)	(c)
(C)	(d)	(c)	(b)	(a)
(D)	(d)	(c)	(a)	(b)

65. Which one of the following is the function of a library committee ?
(A) To produce useful reading material
(B) To lay down general library policy
(C) To render adequate reference service
(D) To arrange for resource sharing and interlibrary loan

66. Match List-I and List-II and choose the correct answer by using the codes given below :

List-I	List-II
(i) Primary document	(a) LISA
(ii) Geographical source	(b) Library Herald
(iii) Abstracting service	(c) Bibliography of Bibliographies
(iv) Tertiary document	(d) Fodor's India

Codes :	**(i)**	**(ii)**	**(iii)**	**(iv)**
(A)	(b)	(d)	(a)	(c)
(B)	(a)	(d)	(b)	(c)
(C)	(d)	(b)	(c)	(a)
(D)	(b)	(d)	(c)	(a)

67. Arrange the following classification schemes in their chronological order of origin :
    (i) Bibliographic Classification
    (ii) Colon Classification
    (iii) Universal Decimal Classification
    (iv) Dewey Decimal Classification
    (A) (i) (ii) (iii) (iv) (B) (iii) (iv) (ii) (i)
    (C) (iv) (iii) (ii) (i) (D) (i) (iv) (iii) (ii)
68. Which of the following is an indicator of dispersion for a set of observations ?
    (A) Central tendency
    (B) Correlation coefficient
    (C) Regression line
    (D) Standard Deviation
69. **Statement (1) :** Unity of Direction implies one manager and one plan for all the operations which have the same objective in view.
    Statement (2) : This principle is useful for creating departments and sub departments for designing and functioning of the organization structure.
    In the above statements.
    (A) Both (1) and (2) are true
    (B) (1) is true but (2) is false
    (C) (1) is false but (2) is true
    (D) Both (1) and (2) are false

70. Which of the following sequences is correct about Maslow's hierarchy of needs ?
    (A) Physiological, social, security, esteem and self actualization
    (B) Security, physiological, social, self-actualization and esteem
    (C) Physiological, security, social, self-actualization and esteem
    (D) Physiological, security, social, esteem and self actualization

71. Match List-I and List-II and choose the correct answer by using the codes given below :

List-I	List-II
(i) Hawthorne studies	(a) Maslow
(ii) Theory X and Theory Y	(b) George Elton Mayo
(iii) Hierarchy of Needs	(c) R. Likert
(iv) Leadership Styles	(d) Douglas McGregor

Codes :	**(i)**	**(ii)**	**(iii)**	**(iv)**
(A)	(a)	(c)	(d)	(b)
(B)	(b)	(d)	(a)	(c)
(C)	(a)	(b)	(d)	(c)
(D)	(b)	(c)	(d)	(a)

72. Arrange the following in chronological sequence of their year of establishment :
    (i) IASLIC (ii) IATLIS
    (iii) SIS (iv) ILA
    (A) (iv) (i) (ii) (iii) (B) (i) (ii) (iv) (iii)
    (C) (ii) (i) (iv) (iii) (D) (i) (iii) (iv) (ii)

73. The Intellectual property that does not come under copyright is :

(A) Paintings
(B) Databases
(C) Computer Programmes
(D) Industrial Designs

74. Methods of experimental enquiry were advocated by :
(A) Charles Darwin (B) Copernicus
(C) J.S. Mill (D) Plato

75. What is not true about spamming ?
(A) The most widely recognized form of spam is e-mail spam.
(B) It is the abuse of electronic messaging systems
(C) Spamming is expensive to advertisers
(D) Spamming costs huge in terms of loss of productivity

ANSWERS

1. A	2. C	3. C	4. A	5. A	6. C
7. A	8. A	9. A	10. B	11. D	12. A
13. A	14. C	15. A	16. B	17. D	18. A
19. D	20. A	21. D	22. C	23. D	24. C
25. A	26. D	27. B	28. B	29. C	30. C
31. C	32. C	33. A	34. B	35. B	36. B
37. B	38. D	39. B	40. A	41. B	42. C
43. A	44. C	45. A	46. C	47. B	48. A
49. C	50. B	51. D	52. C	53. D	54. B
55. D	56. B	57. B	58. B	59. A	60. B
61. D	62. D	63. B	64. C	65. B	66. A
67. C	68. D	69. A	70. D	71. B	72. A
73. D	74. C	75. C			